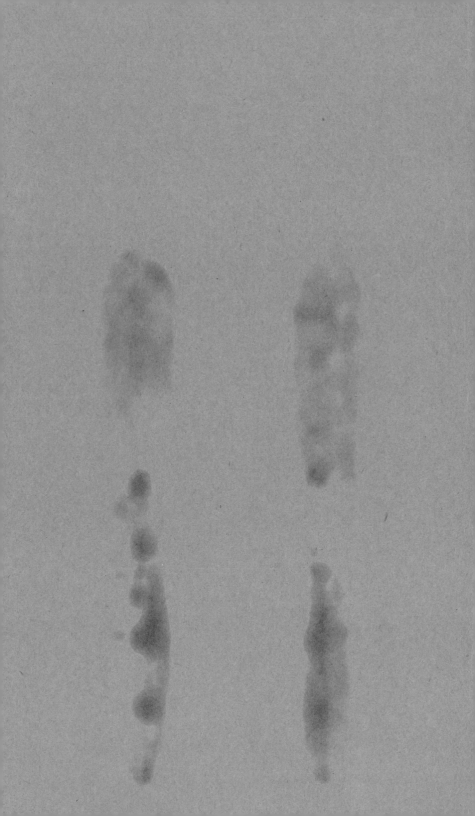

Life, Literature, and Learning in America

# Observations

### *by Henri Peyre*

## on

# Life, Literature, and Learning

# in America

*Southern Illinois University Presss · Carbondale*

# ACKNOWLEDGMENTS

The essays in this volume were originally published in the following books and periodicals:

The Émigré Scholar in America—as "The Study of Literature" in *Cultural Migration* (Philadelphia: University of Pennsylvania Press, 1953). Reprinted with the permission of Pennsylvania Press.

French and American Education—*The American Society Legion of Honor Magazine*, vol. 20, no. 4 (winter 1949).

American Literature Through French Eyes—*The Virginia Quarterly Review*, vol. 23, no. 3 (summer 1947). Reprinted with the permission of the *Virginia Quarterly Review*.

Humanistic Scholarship and National Prestige—*The ACLS Newsletter*, vol. 4, no. 2 (spring 1953).

The Need for Language Study in America Today—published as a pamphlet in 1954 by the Cultural Division of the French Embassy in the United States.

American Scholarship in the Field of Foreign Literatures—*PMLA*, vol. 64, supplement, part 2 (March 1949).

Comparative Literature in America—as "A Glance at Comparative Literature in America," *The Yearbook of Comparative and General Literature*, no. 1 (1952).

A Backward and a Forward Glance—as "Seventy-Five Years of Comparative Literature: A Backward and a Forward Glance," *The Yearbook of Comparative and General Literature*, no. 8 (1960).

Humanities and Social Studies—in *Both Human and Humane* (Philadelphia: University of Pennsylvania Press, 1960).

*Acknowledgments*

Reprinted with the permission of the University of Pennsylvania Press.

Facing the New Decade—*PMLA*, vol. 75 (March 1961).

Higher Education in the United States—was delivered as an address at a Fulbright Terminal Conference at Brown University and reproduced in *Purposes and Patterns of Higher Education in the United States* (Providence, R. I.: Brown University, 1960).

A Bid for Contemplation—*The Yale Undergraduate*, vol. 1, no. 1 (autumn 1954).

From Knowledge to Wisdom—*The ACLS Newsletter*, vol. 6, no. 2 (summer 1955).

# CONTENTS

Life, Literature, and Learning in America

# An Apology for Offering Advice to Americans

I N  THE  EIGHTEENTH  CENTURY the Jesuit relations, the
idealization of the Indians, the popularity of Franklin,
the admiration of the "corrupt French" for the Quakers and
for the frugal and moral farmers of the young republic had
helped create an "American myth" in France. Then, for
more than a hundred years, in spite of Chateaubriand's
glowing and mendacious descriptions of the American
scenery from Niagara to the land of the Natchez, appre-
hension and condescension prevailed in many of the allusions to the materialism of the New World scattered in
the writings of Stendhal, Balzac, Baudelaire, Flaubert,
Renan. Youthful readers of Fenimore Cooper, Mayne Reid,
and later of Jack London lavished their fervor on Indians
or animals rather than on the pioneers pushing the frontier
westward; their sympathies went to the Negroes rather than
to the plantation owners or to the first industrial barons.

Up to 1917, when the author of the following essays happened to hear the United States mentioned at school,
apropos of a few anecdotes on Washington, of a revolution
which the subsequent French one was supposed to have
broadened and universalized, of the "War of Secession,"
his imagination was hardly touched. The French have always been more partial to their own past, glamorous and

turbulent as it is, to world history, and their philosophy of history has traditionally been content with explaining the greatness and decline of the ancient world and the French march to classical or Napoleonic greatness; Voltaire alone, mischievously seeking to belittle the claims of Christianity, undertook to give prominence to non-Mediterranean lands in his remarkable account of the growth of civilization. A few sketches from Washington Irving, a few moral precepts culled from Emerson, occasionally some very didactic novel recommended by the pastor's wife to French Protestant families, and of course the rapturous discovery of "The Raven," "Ulalume" or "Annabel Lee" and of samples of Whitman's strangely elongated lines which French teachers quoted as having dealt the first deadly blows to classical French versification and to have given heart to the Symbolist rebels: such was about all the literary baggage from the New World with which a boy of seventeen left his "lycée."

Woodrow Wilson and 1918 changed all that. In 1925, this writer was one of many who sailed from Europe to export French culture to the country which had captured the imagination of French youth and won the gratitude of a whole nation. Few of these had ever taken the trouble to read Tocqueville, whose return to the pinnacle of French political thinkers and of cheerless but lucid prophets of the mass age only occurred in the late nineteen thirties and in the forties, when the world in dismay looked for conservative ancestors. But far too many of these travelers, lecturers, and teachers thought they could not do less than dash off a volume on America, her women, her speakeasies, her factories, her slums, her marble palaces in California and Florida, her campuses teeming with athletes, squirrels, friendly teachers and experimenters of the companionate marriage. Amid such a plethora of travel diaries or of analyses and psychoanalyses of the American soul, the best of which were easily those by André Siegfried and by Jean Prévost in *Usonie*, an ignorant and timid professor vowed to observe and to serve, but not to add another volume to that most exasperating and most ephemeral province of

European letters: impressions on and lavish advice to the United States. The sweetest sermons are probably those which remain unheard melodies and at any rate unwritten ones. Years of acquaintance with a country, as with a person, wear off the excitement and destroy the innocence required to maintain a sense of wonder or the eager registering of details. Dissections of the American national temper had better been left to social anthropologists. The most profound interpretation of America, as of Soviet Russia, will some day be proposed by novelists or dramatists, in Europe or in the United States, who will do for this country what Tolstoy, Balzac or Dickens did for theirs.

It remains for a teacher and a scholar who prefers having the world too much with him to haughty indifference to his surroundings, to express himself when urged to do so on the education, the culture and the literature, hence almost inevitably also on the politics of the country which he has adopted as his second home. His vantage ground is solid. He seeks no publicity, no financial increment from such writings, and, while not necessarily equating the duty of educating with that of being tedious, he does not have to strive for entertainment or for striking anecdotes. He does not have to be obsequious or flattering, and tact and common sense forbid him condescension. He may avoid that banality which turns everything to insipid silliness and eschew also the search for originality, for "L'Amérique insolite," which obscures the essentials and aims at childish novelty. Frenchmen have produced the smallest group of immigrants to the United States of any large European country and have probably, as a nation, remained coolest to the myth of America and the slowest to melt in the famous caldron. They have seldom forsaken the prerogative of criticizing the land of promise and bounty which they admired and envied, and even of barking at the hand which fed them. They could securely rely on the capital of good will accumulated by Lafayette and Rochambeau, Tocqueville and Pasteur, by Mont Saint Michel, Verdun and the Folies-Bergère. The Statue of Liberty, after which every American schoolboy molds his ideal of womanhood and his reassuring acceptation of the surrounding matriarchate, came after all from the land of small, dapper, vocal Frenchmen. A stern Gallic professor may be forgiven if he prefaces a motley volume of essays, elicited from him at some time or other by kindly requests from colleagues and friends, with a few remarks aimed only at serving his adopted country.

Let him state baldly at the outset that he has not stayed and worked in this country for thirty odd years for the sake only of half belonging and not belonging, and thus venting his gall in turn on each of the two countries which he considered as his. He hopes to have thus far been that creature of exception: the Frenchman who never listened to the protests of his liver and whose bile never yet had to be kept under control by Vichy water. He did undergo passing moments of disappointment at American policy; he suffered, and not in panicky silence, while a demagogic Senator frightened all but a few courageous intellectuals and caricatured the true face of America to foreign observers. His inside knowledge of the country's youth maintained his faith in American common sense and idealism, even in 1939 and in 1950. He did not have to endure World War II in Europe and was thus kept from the illusions of a starved and besieged continent which pictured Roosevelt's compatriots as messiahs and saviors. He was likewise spared the revulsion from such a messianic mood which subsequently led Europeans to rejoice in pointing to flaws in the American colossus and to all-too-human frailties in its spiritual armor. Behind much anti-Americanism, in the early fifties, there lurked the disillusionment of frustrated romantic love and the growing but annoying conviction that America pictured the condition which was, in its worst but not always in its best features, to be that of Western Europe within a very few years: digests, television, milk bars, tabloid newspapers, delinquent youth, fascination with "circuses" increasing just as people ate less bread but drank more whiskey, cult of foreign princesses in the process of marrying, etc. Self-hatred in disguise paraded behind the scorn for allegedly soulless Yankees and between the letters of the "Americans go home" slogans.

It would be pointless to yield to the common weakness of teachers, their obsession with the past; to condemn the mistakes of the last thirty years with jaundiced hindsight and to heap sanctimonious blame on those who, since Yalta and Potsdam or even earlier, missed some of the most golden opportunities ever tendered to rulers by fickle destiny. This writer's unambiguous conviction is stated in the following pages: that the balance sheet of American policy since 1941 is heavily favorable and no other country can match the achievement in education, in political leadership, in civic generosity and foreign assistance, which has, for fifteen years at least, been that of the United States. Cantankerous recrimination against a number of mistakes would be as unjustified as it would be discouraging.

Whether they themselves and the rest of the Western world like it or not, Americans have to continue, presumably for fifty years at least, which is about as far as can ever be envisaged in human affairs, bearing the brunt of guiding our civilization. They might, in thus doing, disregard all adverse criticism and trust their own instinct as the France of Louis XIV, the Great Britain of Queen Victoria, the Germany of Bismarck once did. Because they are modest, even overly diffident of their own ability to blaze the path for others, and since persuading one's fellow beings has, even more than in Pericles' time, become a prerequisite for effecting their good, contemporary Americans lend a receptive ear to advice offered by foreigners in their midst. Thirty-five years of teaching have assured this provider of gratuitous counsel, for one, that young Americans, and even those who are gracefully growing old, seldom resent strictures which are meant to be constructive. From the heritage of Puritanism, they have salvaged an earnest desire for self-improvement.

What are the goals which this French-American teacher would, when he formulates his testament of good will, like to see young Americans pursue more energetically? What benefits may he rashly hope that the publication of these sundry essays could provide? What, as a European attempting to contribute in his own modest measure to American education and to American attitudes, does he hope to have achieved? First, some broadening of the American curiosity. A decade or so after the Peace of Versailles and the ensuing disillusion with all foreigners who were pictured as preying on the gullible innocence of Americans, those new Adams who had ventured beyond the gates of their Garden of Eden to rub shoulders with the evil men of Sodom and Gomorrah, a trend set in which favored isolation, America first, and social sciences as the only path to salvation. That traumatic break with Old-World culture which had too long looked upon America as its mere appendage was necessary and in some respects beneficent. European art critics, commentators on American literature, visitors to American campuses, lecturers to ladies' groups, analysts of the American psyche from London, Paris or Vienna, all had treated the culture of the country much too patronizingly. (The French record in that respect was, however, not the worst one. Already in the late eighteenth century, French—or Swiss French—writers had been the first to encourage the rest of Europe to shake off the yoke of French imitation and to draw from their reading of French authors a lesson of independence and even of nationalist audacity. In the years following 1930, while Britain was still reluctant to grant recognition to "the American imagination" and to found chairs of American history and literature, the rebels of the Lost Generation were admired and followed in France, and professors lectured, from Lille to Algiers, on Melville, Henry James, O'Neill, Faulkner and Charlie Chaplin.) Still, a concentration in this country on the American scene, on the social and economic problems of the United States, on a reinterpretation of American history, and a consequent disregard for the ancient and the foreign languages appeared to be the inevitable accompaniment of America's impetuous coming of age.

The historians, the social thinkers, and even more the educators of the years 1925–40 failed, however, to realize

that the international responsibilities devolving upon their
country were going to be heavier than ever before—the
heaviest yet incurred by any great nation. They neglected
advocating the acquisition of foreign languages, not only
as a tool, but as a key to the understanding of other countries which, at the very moment of her preponderance,
America had to win, to persuade, even to court. Courtship,
as the playwright Giraudoux once remarked, must be well
nigh impossible to the deaf and mute; the art of prepara-
tions, which roués regard as (next to the skill in breaking
off) the most demanding in love, and the art of making
friends in foreign trade and relations, all need words ex-
pertly placed and preferably words spoken in the partner's
own language. Too many American scientists, educators,
men of affairs, army officers called upon to administer and
train oftener than to fight, politicians and diplomats, businessmen and officials of international organizations behave
like mute and inglorious cripples when attending meetings
where a language other than their own is spoken. Even
when simultaneous translation is provided, they lie at the
mercy of interpreters; and while multilingual foreigners do
part of their work in the lobbies, at the bars where truth in
wine is revealed, in conversation with wives at which masks
might be lifted and playful hints dropped and picked up,
monolingual Americans feel out-talked and outwitted.

A determined campaign initiated by the Modern Language Association of America, equally strenuous and fervent endeavors by Ambassador James Conant and other
statesmen, the active interest of several foundations and at
last the Government and Congress, impelled by the need
to meet Russian competition, have finally reversed the trend
which had banished foreign languages from many a school
and not a few colleges. Arguments for such study, perhaps
more necessary today than the strengthening of our scientific education, are developed in some of the essays collected in this volume. Obstacles in the way of intensified,
and especially of improved, language study are, on the
other hand, real: the lack of qualified teachers is the worst.
Second and not far behind is the tendency of many grown-

ups to blame, not themselves and their lack of obstinacy in pursuing a study barely sketched at school, but their teachers or the methods followed for their inadequate mastery of a foreign language. Few would similarly cast all the blame on their teachers of geometry, of spelling, of ethics or of marriage problems for their failure, as adults, in those disciplines or in applying them. In truth, the country as a whole has not yet had its imagination fired by the need to forsake its complacency and a trend to parochialism. It reads few foreign weeklies or monthlies; it is still afflicted by an inferiority complex when called upon to overcome frustrations and hesitations and formulate sentences in another tongue.

A teacher of languages does not deal only or primarily in words and sentences, declensions and conjugations, childish stories about a strange nation and the pursuit of all that may be queerly exotic in a Spaniard or a Russian. His role is also to make the student flexible enough so that he may borrow someone else's mental habits and ways of feeling, and thus enrich his own microcosm. A person can prove to be the most valuable of psychologists if he thus develops insight into the motives of men raised in a different environment. At least as much as the study of history, the intelligent study of a language provides lessons in perspective. It also should foster disbelief and the growth of critical spirit through the examination of how words look in another tongue, of how they denote and connote very different things in languages in which they had seemed to be alike, through the close literary commentary of difficult foreign texts. Contrary to a common prejudice, a critical spirit can and should coexist with enthusiasm; it strengthens rather than destroys faith in what stands the test of a severe scrutiny and deserves to be believed. There is perhaps no intellectual quality which a professor can be prouder of having imparted to his students.

Critical spirit need not mean reducing truth to consistency alone and worshipping logic to the point of hunting out all value judgments and all affective or irrational impulses. There may well be validity in C. M. Jung's asser-

tion that disagreement with himself is the surest mark of
the civilized man. There are other ways of reconciling two
contradictory statements than the summary elimination
of one of them or the silencing of impulses springing from
that obdurate organ which we call the heart. Where would
art and much literature be if creators did not start from a
chaos of inner contradictions and seek to live with them, to
bring some of them to a clarifying sunlight, or to instil the
more insidious ones and unsolvable dilemmas into their ac-
complices, the readers? The exercise of intelligence does
not entail the reduction to rational terms of what pertains to
other realms. Sophistry is a more harmful foe to intelligence
than sentiment.

But critical spirit is a prerequisite in our approach to
most disciplines and to every science and should be practiced at least provisionally, like Montaigne's and Descartes'
methodical doubt, before it is laid aside or transcended. It
is all the more necessary today as the modern mass media
all converge on its obliteration. Publicity dins its slogans
into our ears; the six or ten reasons why we should purchase
a product which we do not really want are loudly enumerated on the radio; salesmen and advertisers do not abide
our question; they assert, they repeat, they dull our capacity to resist, they rush the metamorphosis of an image into
another image before the prospective convert, or victim,
can develop the image into a reflection. It should not be un-
patriotic or anti-American to hint that the hypertrophy of
publicity in our midst constitutes the one grave flaw of
American culture, and perhaps of American capitalism
which relies too heavily upon it.

When applied to public affairs, to the press, to states-
manship, the evil is even graver. Such fatuous Madison-
Avenue slogans as "A Bigger Bang for a Buck" and "People to People" are accepted as considered and realistic
policies by—alas!—the very people who proclaim them. A
perennial surprise to any one who probes public opinion in
the most lavishly informed of countries is to notice how
little, and poorly, informed we are. The national neurosis
which swept the country during the McCarthy era would

not have occurred if the people had been more critically informed, hence less surprised by a few cases in which they read betrayal and spying. The shocked astonishment which followed the forced withdrawal of an aged Korean president, the quick overthrowing of a long tolerated Cuban dictator, the condemnation of a Dominican one by the United States which had long accepted, if not supported, him should never have occurred with a public critically informed by its press. The year 1960 brought a number of even ruder jolts to American confidence, or naïveté: in Africa, in Turkey, in the shooting down of a plane which had to be (or too generously was) acknowledged as spying, in the cooling off of Western Europe toward American leadership. A President who had entered the White House, hemmed in with worshipful solemnity, eight years earlier had to retort publicly to those who doubted it, that his country had not lost the first place among great powers; but the question, which would have been inconceivable in 1950, could be asked in 1960 by honest and disquieted Americans.

A good many countries in the Western Hemisphere have recently charged America with imperialism. Americans, candidly and generously devoted to the score of countries in their hemisphere which they had helped develop, proud of their record in the Philippines and Puerto Rico, could well feel outraged by such ingratitude. Did any statesman, did any one in the press, clearly explain that owning public utilities and factories in Cuba, investing heavily in Canadian industries and mines in need of capital, developing Bolivian tin and Venezuelan iron ore with their funds and their know-how, was indeed, in other people's eyes, a form of imperialism not so very remote from the abhorred colonialism attributed to greedy European countries? Even worse, has American business ever attempted to explain abroad that without similar European investments in the United States during the nineteenth century half of our population might still be scratching a comparatively mean existence from the soil?

Other nations have often been afflicted with a venal press,

swayed at will by government funds. This country's journalism is rightfully proud of warding off government interference in its reporting. It holds facts as sacred and presents
them, in its bulky newspapers, in such abundant confusion
that only those critically trained to sift and interpret could
possibly make head or tail even of the most reliable newspapers in New York, Washington or St. Louis. The obsession with news, that is with the happenings of a few hours
ago, obfuscates the perspective in which these happenings
should be viewed in order to be properly weighed. Thus, in
the fall of 1960, some of our best newspapers featured
developments in the Congo on their front pages rather
than in the theatrical or comic sections where they properly belonged. Editorials seeking to be impartial often succeed only in sounding sanctimonious and timid, and some
truths are practically never printed.

Perhaps this situation arises from the growing standardization of the American press. Cities that formerly had
three or four daily newspapers now have only one or two,
and even these rely heavily upon nationally-syndicated
columnists. There are no longer many opportunities in
American journalism for a William Allen White. The
mass-circulation magazines, fearful of offending advertisers and anxious to attract as many readers as possible,
seldom print anything but the most jejune intellectual pap.
Steady readers of some of our digest magazines, to use
in another context the words of an educator quoted elsewhere in this volume, inevitably learn less and less about
more and more until they finally know nothing about
everything. The nonspecialized quarterlies "slanted" for
the intelligent general reader have become a habit with pitifully few, and even fewer read British periodicals, to say
nothing of those published in Western Europe or Latin
America. A country gets the press that it wants but not
necessarily that it deserves. Those who train the intelligent
youth of America should teach it to want what it needs
and in truth deserves.

Some of the grievous events which marred the Korean
War, revealed in that disturbing book by Eugene Kink-

head, *In Every War But One* (1959), which pointed to a sad lack of intellectual lucidity and of moral resistance in American soldiers, might well have been prevented with a little more criticism, and a little more faith in their cause, in childishly uncritical men. There were a number of high school and even of college graduates among the hundred or so who absorbed enemy propaganda or allowed themselves to perish in Chinese prisons during that war; they, their teachers, or the methods used in educating them must have been glaringly deficient.

Continental Europeans have lately been called in substantial numbers to American universities, laboratories or journalism, or been driven there by the intolerance and folly of some European governments through the years 1917–45. There were few farmers or industrial workers among them, but many men versed in political thinking, psychology, art, literature and business. One of the essays which follows was written at the request of a university press anxious to appraise this curious intellectual migration to the New World, such as history had never known. The migration was so intellectual as to have colored with its cast of thought and with its language, often more Germanic than English, much of American writing since 1938 or so. Americans appear to have received patiently supercilious admonitions about their immature fear of thought, their cult of conformity, and their reluctance to grant honors or generous financial rewards to "intellectuals" in their midst.

The word smacks of continental foreignness in English, and even such a one as Bertrand Russell pretends to be insulted when referred to as an "intellectual," which implies that the person thus dubbed claims more intellect than he has. But the term is being naturalized in the United States. Those of us born and educated abroad who believe that they have learned from America—from their very students in many cases—as much as they taught, have tempered their haughty and vain conviction that ideas rule the world and that they are the depositors or the sowers of those ideas. For a Frenchman in particular, ever prone to regard-

ing himself as the heir to Montesquieu, Voltaire, Diderot
and Rousseau, hence as the potential architect of a revolution, an American experience is a sobering one. It brings
him to respect pragmatism and to plumb the depths of the
abyss which separates abstract thinking from action.
Goethe was not afraid to have his Faust end up prosaically
as an engineer and he repeatedly warned his readers that
"the law of life in the end always reduces itself to checking
thought with action and action with thought." The pride
of all brain trusts, of theoretical economists and political
thinkers, would be humbled if they realized how little of
their ambitious systems is actually ever put into use by
statesmen and men of affairs. Roosevelt, Churchill, De
Gaulle, Mussolini, Lenin himself, the most bookish of them
all, and certainly all of Lenin's successors picked an idea
here and there in the books that they read, mutilated a
coherent system to borrow from it only what suited them, or
suited the demands of the time which pressed on them,
discarded the rest, and sooner or later dismissed their
doctrinaire advisers. Ideas do act in history, but only
through men who deform and transform them in applying
them and according to a process of degradation which few
historians have yet cared to study.

Intellectual arrogance has little place in the United
States; and when all is considered, it never was justified in
Europe, where the record of men of letters, of artists, of not
a few professors and political theorists, under Hitler, Stalin, Mussolini, even under Pétain, did not prove to be one
of uncommon discernment. Let the European intellectual
who has placed himself at the service of America beware of
importing his passion for ideas divorced from reality into
a culture which rightly cherishes instinct and empiricism.
Nevertheless, he should point out that expediency, which
seems to have dictated too many decisions of late, usually
turns out to have been a shortsighted tactic, even in politics.
Realism and pragmatism are needed in the process of devising the means to an end, but, to be dynamic and "poetical," the end must first have been defined idealistically.
The quality of poetry, broadly conceived, is probably the

most sorely needed one today in the domestic and foreign policies of the great nations. Generosity, fraternity, even rashness or at least boldness, are elements of that poetical view of life which capitalism often practices but fails to express with warmth.

With all the mass media buzzing around us, it is far from certain that the goals of our foreign policy are clearly understood. Every one of the candidates, to the highest office and to many lower ones, is content with advocating more spending on armaments as if there lay a panacea. We are only now beginning to doubt that Asiatic allies, bought with weapons and forced out of their neutrality, would have heart for a fight if not immediately threatened.

Meanwhile we pour out millions to assist other nations, but tend to think that we have thus discharged our duty and that emergent nations in other continents can truly profit from such generosity, when in fact they have no administration to handle the funds, no competent civil service, very little know-how, and allow the equipment given for their armies, roads, harbors, and agriculture to rust and to rot for lack of upkeep and repair parts and because they do not truly want to receive bounty in that way. From Laos to Iraq and soon from north to south in Africa and in the Americas, we have taken it for granted that we had to spread our way of life and raise backward nations to a condition in which they could profit from our technology and our hygiene. But poor countries have only watched the poor among them grow poorer, and a few rich grow richer, from our foreign aid.

Our type of civilization demands not only a rate of investment which underprivileged countries cannot afford, a technological culture which can be acquired only gradually, but also a rapid depletion of water resources, mineral wealth, forests, nonrenewable fuels. After lavishly, short-sightedly, and greedily, exploiting our own resources, we may well have no moral right to counsel young nations or old nations in the process of rejuvenation, now embarking on a course which need not be the same as ours. The whole issue of foreign aid, or of aid to the emergent nations all over the world, connected with the other equally pressing issue of the stabilization of the price of raw materials, must be thought over constructively by the most imaginative brains in the country. It implies no disbelief whatever in the American way of life or in Western technology to suggest that we must not necessarily propose to all the new nations of the world an economy of unlimited growth, a philosophy of quick expansion, a lavish exploitation of their natural resources, and even encourage their nationalism, when such goals may well lead the Eastern or the African world to upheavals, discontentment and spiritual uprooting.

In several other regions of our planet, the policy makers of the Western nations, led today by the United States, similarly fail to think critically, lucidly, constructively. If our press dares not proclaim it, if our leaders choose to lull us to lethargy with rosy slogans, a few intellectuals, blending idealism in their broad principles with realism in their clamor for workable solutions, have the duty to raise their voices. How can countries which fought a bitter war against a fanatical persecutor of the Jews admit that the Suez Canal can be for years and years closed to ships bound for Israeli harbors? Is a perfunctory and mild denunciation sufficient to soothe our consciences? Can we long withhold recognition of the frontiers of Poland, or hope that the two Germanies can ever be reunited without a cataclysm, or expect the allegiance of our NATO allies in Europe after turning against them in their African difficulties or when they rashly undertake a Suez expedition? Finally, what will we do if Khrushchev ever becomes as overconfident as Stalin in 1950 and Hitler in 1939 and imposes an effective blockade on Berlin?

At home, equally momentous problems should challenge young Americans and draw the boldest of them away from the security of careers in advertising, finance, engineering and toward the one realm in which, ultimately, the critical decisions are prepared and made: politics. The excess production of wheat, cotton, meat and other agricultural goods is a chronic issue and can no longer be eluded. Statesmen will only face it if impelled by an enlightened public opinion. Labor relations are no less thorny, and it is easy to blame corrupt unions and not unjustified to do so; but we regularly wait for another steel or railroad strike to deplore the lack of an adequate system of arbitration, instead of preparing for, hence against, the eventuality. Our city planning and traffic in our congested streets are said to cause more mental worry to Americans than any other trouble, even more than sex, and yet imaginative solutions are hardly ever envisaged. We all know from historical precedents that armament races have regularly led to wars and that a war today would spell ruin to all of us; but who bravely and squarely faces the alternative, which is: can we afford to disarm? Can we avoid depressions without, as in 1940 and 1950, embarking upon an economy which must in all frankness be termed one of war? A first rate "intellectual" among us has done so: Gerard Piel, in the *Bulletin of Atomic Scientists* of April 1960. What echoes has he aroused in the thinking of businessmen, military and political leaders? Is it defeatist to maintain that, unless we discover ways in which mankind can survive in prosperity while producing fewer armaments, unless our imaginations can be fired for poetical and dynamic goals other than fighting, we shall have deserved to perish?

These questions and others are not rhetorical. To be sure, it is easier to ask them than to provide the answers. But it is essential that they be asked. The conviction of the author of these essays is firm: Americans have, today, to lead the rest of the world to constructive, even to grandiose, solutions. They must be aroused from a certain apathy and pursue important goals. They must recapture faith in better tomorrows and in progress. The framing of a renovated, less naïve, less materialistic philosophy of progress than prevailed in the eighteenth and nineteenth centuries is today an urgent necessity, disregarded by most of our thinkers. Challenges, we are told, are required for audacious men to rise up to them. There is an abundance of them for the American reaching manhood in 1960, but they are too seldom presented challengingly. May the intellectuals among their educators convince the youth that never was it more necessary to cultivate intelligence, strengthened by critical spirit, broadened by curiosity about the rest of the world, and multiplied by imagination.

Moral superiority does not lie on the side of the Old World. It was in the New World, with the assistance given to rehabilitate war-ridden nations, then with the Marshall Plan, that the principle of solidarity was first understood as extending to other nations and the sharing of national wealth with underprivileged peoples was first proclaimed as a duty. Today, however, inertia and passivity gravely threaten America's moral position. Behind some cynicism, and a liberation from puritanism and from all taboos on sex which has gone very far, behind even the revolt of the young today and the aberrations which lead some of them to delinquency, there lies a gnawing moral hunger. Young people do not want to find preachers in their teachers or parents, but they are only superficially amused when they discover cynics in them, or elders emulating the very young in their behavior with the advantage of a fatter pocketbook.

Our conviction is firm: American youth today lacks the awareness of a dynamic goal which it could be persuaded to strive for. Even though the survivors of the generation that made the Revolution voice the same complaint about Soviet youth, therein—and therein alone—America's only possible inferiority to Russia, perhaps even to Western Europe which, having sunk low during her years of occupation and abjection, has since been fired by eagerness to rehabilitate herself. It is up to men of an older generation, perhaps more particularly those who are familiar with history and with other cultures and wish the United States to shun mistakes committed earlier and elsewhere, to propose these goals after first brushing aside cobwebs of empty formulas. The most objective of scholars, even he whose vocation it is to interpret modern novels or plays where morality seldom triumphs and where restraint even more seldom prevails, cannot, without abdicating his role as teacher, avoid being, discreetly, a moralist.

# The Émigré Scholar in America

IT WOULD BE SHEER HYPOCRISY to deny or to ignore the implications of the title of this essay: one is forced to talk about oneself and to generalize from a personal and inevitably limited experience. For one's experience in a new country, one's adaptation to it, and one's influence on it are bound to depend largely upon a personal equation, which had better be stated frankly, if humorously and gracefully, so as to eschew the naïve egotism of those who are accustomed to having the youth take notes at their feet on each of their dicta. Yet, and in spite of our mild resentment whenever we are considered by others as typical of our native country and therefore as less unique than we should like to be, only those of our reactions which may be taken to have been shared by a number of others in similar circumstances should be stressed as embodying a valid body of reflections on American culture by a half-naturalized European. The lecturer's assumption that he is for a few hours "the Frenchman" vying with Fernandel's expressive mimicry must thus be forgiven. So must the broad claim that his specific title, "The Émigré Scholar in America," seems to put forward. Let it be recalled once and for all that America, because of its geographic immensity, its varied ethnic background, the utter lack of standardization which prevails in the field of education as contrasted

with European countries, offers a number of exceptions to
any general assertion which one may venture.

Another word of warning should be in order. The two
obvious pitfalls open before anyone who writes on America
are fulsome praise of everything American and systematic disparagement of all that is not sufficiently European
(hence cultured, refined, mature, spiritual) on this continent. Those same pitfalls have always been laid before anyone who wrote on any country, young or old, and the most
common of all complexes in nations is doubtless the in-
feriority-superiority complex. If touchiness is a feminine
prerogative (but women are too generous to have kept it to
themselves), from ancient Greece to Russia, from Iran to
France and Argentina, all nations have always been feminine, as the gender for the word nation in most languages
well indicates. Plutarch relates somewhere the fate of a
philosopher, not too remote from a sophist, by the name of
Callisthenes. He was asked to deliver an oration in praise
of the Macedonians and did it with such a flow of eloquence
that all who heard rose from their seats to applaud. Alexander, however, remarked, quoting Euripides:

> *I wonder not that you have spoke so well.*
> *'Tis easy on good subjects to excel.*

And he ordered him to display the true force of his eloquence by telling his Macedonians their faults, "that, by
hearing their shortcomings, they may become better in the
future." So did Callisthenes, who was later thrown into
prison by the King and put to death.

America has withstood an inordinate mass of criticism,
much of it acrimonious and derogatory, for she had served
as the subject of some of the best books ever written by foreign observers (Tocqueville, Bryce, Siegfried, Jean Prévost) and of many of the silliest travel books. Her own
literature is today more relentlessly self-critical than any
other. Her consciousness of her power is now keen and
sobering enough to make her lenient toward those critics
who may be envious of her or disappointed in too lofty expectations. She is now an old country, or at least a mature
lady who has received enough tributes to be inured to vain

flattery. The very idea for this series of lectures [published as *The Cultural Migration*], which was a timely and an original one, offered a challenge to scholars from whom devotion to truth, sense of proportion, fairness as well as gratitude to their adopted country, and a desire to serve it further through constructive criticism are naturally expected.

The question about which five representatives of varied fields of science or scholarship have been asked to do some soul-searching and a public confession is one on which they, like other men in the same predicament, had been led to reflect occasionally. The adoption of a new language, of novel sets of reference, the abrupt assumption in middle age of a new background, new traditions, a new relationship with a very different public could have been a traumatic experience. That it has been so in only an infinitesimal number of cases is a tribute to American hospitality and to a profession whose chief advantage is closeness with an ever-renewed youth. Any university bulletin, any table of contents of a learned journal, any list of recipients of fellowships, grants, and honors by foundations includes a substantial number of foreign-born scholars and scientists and bears eloquent testimony to the continued fertility and adaptability of men and women who came to these shores from Europe. Although the peak of that influx has long been passed, many of those newcomers are still in their full productive stage. Their children constitute in many cases a group of "hyphenated" young Americans whose gifts are above the average and who hold the cultural traditions of their families in high respect. They have trained many disciples over here. The extraordinary development of American universities and American science and culture in the last half-century—an even more remarkable phenomenon than the growth of American power or the industrial and business progress within the same span of years—is due primarily to Americans. Yet, at a time when mass emigration had stopped, since 1925, the contribution of émigrés who were welcomed here added materially to native achievements and often stimulated them.

Economic, military and political leadership has now been thrust upon this country. The burden was not sought for and is not altogether welcome. Complacency, intellectual security, reliance on one's self alone, isolation in relation to "old countries" and very old continents aroused by revolutionary impulses can no longer be practiced. No evasion is possible. The United States must assume the legacy of the Western World and carry that legacy still further: for nothing is safely preserved that is not assimilated and expanded. In doing so, this country will rely upon the continued assistance of foreign-born intellectuals who may have not higher, but other, gifts of imagination and of spirit, and know which of those gifts can be used to advantage by an eager and dynamic country anxious to save the world as well as herself. History will leave it to the credit of the United States, Canada and Mexico that, better than other nations of the New World, they knew how to attract, retain, utilize and develop energetic and gifted émigrés from a war-ridden continent.

The intellectual migration to America during the years 1925–50 or so may well rank one day as one of the very important migrations of history—not in terms of numbers, of course, but for the debt contracted by a few to many and for the invaluable contribution made by those few to the collective being of which they soon became part. It would be a boon to posterity if more of those émigrés (poets, painters, musicians, thinkers, teachers, political refugees, etc.) would write their memoirs, as Albert Guérard and Vladimir Nabokov have done, and would record their experience in their adopted land. Thomas Mann, Albert Einstein, Darius Milhaud, Marc Chadourne, Giovanni Borgese, Salvador Dali, Jorge Guillén, W. H. Auden, Igor Stravinsky, Henri de Kérillis, Heinrich Bruening, a score of other eminent persons, and a hundred or more distinguished academic scholars could for once compete on a similar theme and leave precious documents to the social historian. On similar migrations in the past we have ample and yet inadequate information.

Without going back to the Greek intellectuals who civilized "uncouth Latium" and made Lucretius, Terentius, Horace and Virgil possible, or to the handful of scholars who may have left Constantinople after the Turks seized the city in 1453, we may throw a quick backward glance on the first great intellectual migration of the modern world: that of the French Huguenots during the seventeenth century and especially after the Revocation of the Edict of Nantes in 1685. William Penn was one of the first to realize how valuable the Huguenots would prove to his colony, especially as weavers and growers of vines. He was also aware of the high cultural level which had been attained in France by those Huguenots, who belonged almost entirely to the middle classes and had displayed marked intellectual curiosity as well as independence of views. The role of the Huguenots in Prussia, in Holland, in Great Britain, and in America has been explored in several of its facets (the volumes on Huguenot emigration to America by Charles Baird and Gilbert Chinard are well known) but never yet surveyed in a comprehensive treatment: to them the modern world owes its first good dictionaries, grammars, and translations, a sturdy blossoming of periodicals, the dawn of a new literary cosmopolitanism, and a powerful impetus to the nascent spirit of the Enlightenment.

The second great cultural migration also started from France and during its course many members of the nobility fled to all parts of Europe and to America after the great upheaval of 1789. It is much better known, thanks to the research of Fernand Baldensperger. It gave teachers of languages, of fine arts, of good manners to Europe; more particularly journalists, essayists, and novelists to Germany (Rivarol, Chamisso, Charles de Villers); and sent a few gastronomes, speculators, and enthusiasts for primitive culture to America. But it altered France even more profoundly than it did the countries which provided hospitality to those émigrés fleeing the consequences of the French Revolution. For the exiles from the French nobility and the upper class, frightened by the Parisian mob in turmoil, had to substitute solitude for society life, regret of the past for their former Epicurean enjoyment of the present. Melancholy filled their souls, and an unquiet sensibility, prone to seeking comfort in religion, replaced the former mode of life which had stressed the senses and the intellect. They became receptive to a new literature which had not submitted to analysis and to classical rules or standards but celebrated passion, death, search for all that was vague and infinite. The majority of those émigrés returned to France, having learned little politically, but as one of them, Chateaubriand, well said in his Memoirs and as the remarkable study of Baldensperger was to confirm, having changed inwardly so much that they made the Romantic movement in France possible and provided a public for the writers of the new era.

The nineteenth century witnessed tremendous demographic upheavals: colonial expansion to Asia and Africa, the winning of huge segments of non-European population to Christianity, the settlement of an ever-growing number of Europeans in North and South America. Few of those migrations, however, may be said to have been predominantly intellectual or cultural, with the possible exception of the German liberal migration following the failure of the Revolution of 1848. The mass migration to America between 1880 and 1924 brought agricultural and industrial workers, pioneers and adventurers, members of oppressed ethnic minorities from Russia, Austria-Hungary, and Ireland, but relatively few intellectuals as such. The present century, however, was to be, as Nietzsche had prophesied, an era of revolutions, and those revolutions were to be the most relentless of all—ideological revolutions. Such civil wars as the religious conflicts of the sixteenth and seventeenth centuries, the Spanish struggle of 1936–39, even the American Civil War, are fought without mercy until unconditional surrender is obtained. For passions of the spirit are the fiercest of all. World War II merely superposed a war against Nazi Germany over a civil war between Right and Left in every country and a war of colored people in Asia and Africa against white colonial rule. Dictatorial and revolutionary régimes similarly single out spiritual and ideological dissent as their primary foe; anything which is not rendered unto Caesar is in their eyes to be eradicated as the most noxious of all weeds, that of heresy.

The era of revolutions which was heralded by that of Lenin in 1917 is therefore marked by the persecution of intellectuals and the exile of many of them. From the Russian emigrations which followed 1917, France and America have profited most, France particularly since Russian thinkers like Berdyaev and writers like Irene Nemirovski, Henri Troyat, and Zoë Oldenbourg seem to have become most easily acclimatized there, as had earlier Polish men of letters and Lithuanian poets like Milosz, one of the finest in French recently. But as years drew on and Fascism, then Nazism, appeared as a mortal threat to free culture in Europe, America became the haven for intellectuals. The incalculable consequences of the migration to the United States between 1933 and 1950 cannot yet be described.

Germans and Austrians, especially those who were early in danger in their native land because of their Jewish origins, naturally predominated in this influx. They constitute one of the most vigorous elements in present-day American intellectual life, around periodicals like the *Partisan Review* and *Commentary;* they have brought their methods, their concern for intellectual values, their capacity for productive work to many departments of German, Romance Philology, Political Science, Art, and Economics of American universities. In many respects and in spite of some mishandling of the English language (which in American economics, political thought, and criticism has alas! lost all kinship with the elegant prose of Adam Smith or John M. Keynes, of Richard Hooker and Walter Bagehot, of Hazlitt and Virginia Woolf), those exiles from Germanic lands have enabled American speculation in many fields to leap forward with unheard-of boldness. American pragmatism and fondness for factual empiricism were strengthened by the Germans' patience for the collection of data and their "Sachlichkeit." At the same time the other facet of the German mind, by which it suddenly challenges the respect for minute data and embarks upon systematic speculations, is mirrored in American culture. Philosophy has invaded many academic curricula; psychological or sociological generalizations fascinate college youth. Tocqueville had wisely remarked that "the Americans are much more addicted to the use of general ideas than the English." In several respects, American intellectual life is today closer to the German than to the British. (Many university press editors, thinking of the average scholar's use of footnotes, will immediately sigh and agree with another aspect of this statement.)

Next to the immense contribution of the German exiles, but surprisingly far behind it, considering the community of language and of tradition, has been that of the British. Obviously no compelling force has urged scientists, scholars and writers from Great Britain to emigrate to the United States. Very few professors from England seem to be called to the English departments of American universities, but some writers decided to establish residence in the New World: Alfred North Whitehead and I. A. Richards have exercised a lasting influence here. The gain in the literary output or to the continued growth of Aldous Huxley or W. H. Auden is more doubtful. Fascism drove but a very small number of Italian intellectuals over here: Enrico Fermi and Giuseppe Borgese are outstanding examples. Many distinguished Spaniards emigrated after the advent of Franco, almost all of them men of letters who have continued writing in their own language, teaching their literature, and living their own culture, with the admirable racy quality which is the privilege of Spaniards. They have not easily been integrated into the broad current of American culture, and their fundamental distrust of efficiency and productivity, of the subordination of the individual to the community and of the family to a broader civic group, hardly prepared them to merge themselves in this country. They have continued developing as Spaniards and as representatives of *Hispanidad*, which is a tribute to the hospitality they received in the United States.

A few features common to these exiles from Western Europe who hailed America as a land of promise may be enumerated: they arrived here fully trained abroad and brought with them set habits of work, fully perfected methods, and pride in their culture and their past achievement. They were uprooted in the sense that they were suddenly severed from their countrymen and had no reason to seek close association with foreign-language groups in America or with immigrants of their own nationality who had established themselves earlier in Chicago, Brooklyn, or Cambridge. Many of them were liberals and champions of democracy, but they had little in common with Calabrian peasants, German metallurgical workers, Polish miners, Irish policemen, or French-speaking textile workers from Canada. They were keenly conscious of a cultural past which they missed and which did not make assimilation as easy as it may have been for those who gained immediate advantages from a higher standard of living and a more equal distribution of the comforts of life. Many of them, being artists and writers or intellectuals in general, were by nature dissatisfied and reacted against any environment and any way of life which appeared to them as a leveling down and as unconcerned with their hyperdeveloped egos. The least adaptable of all seem to have been the artists, and among those the painters and sculptors more than the musicians. There are exceptions, and the names of foreign artists who left Germany after the closing of the Bauhaus school at Dessau come to one's mind: Archipenko, Gabo, Pevsner have settled here from Russia; Duchamp and Ozenfant from France; De Kooning from Holland; Feininger, Grosz, Moholy-Nagy from Germany. But few of those artists have been attracted to the portrayal of the American scene, not even through the transposition into abstract forms which is today their indirect means of representation. Chagall, Fernand Léger, Masson and Lipchitz chose to return to France after World War II. Since then not many newcomers of distinction among sculptors and painters have apparently been drawn to find a permanent abode and a creative stimulus here. Matta Echaurren, Dali, and Ernst had arrived here before 1941.

Frenchmen were once great pioneers, and their epic adventures as fur traders, missionaries, soldiers and sailors, even as administrators and friends of native populations hold no mean place in the history of North America, of India and the Near East, and of the South Pacific. Although their country was for centuries the most populous in Europe and had twice, if not thrice, as many inhabitants as their rival Great Britain, they seldom settled in large numbers in their colonies or in the territories which they explored. Their cultural influence abroad was immense; but they could wait for other countries to study their language, manners and art, and send their own citizens to Paris in search of the refinement, the *joie de vivre*, and the pleasant touch of immorality which is supposed to be an ingredient of culture. The defeat of France in 1940 and the Vichy régime drove a limited number of French or naturalized French intellectuals to America. Many of them returned to France after 1944. Complaints against economic and political conditions at home are often heard on the lips of French youth today, and a desire to emigrate to America is frequently expressed. It often remains a mere desire, and the low immigration quota of the French is in fact hardly filled. Many of the young men who had been tempted to teach in the United States at the close of World War II have flocked back to France. Not a little of the prestige enjoyed by French people in this country is probably due to their relative scarcity, and the few Frenchmen who are met by the average American belong to the so-called artistic professions: actors, dressmakers, barbers, professors of literature, cooks.

The French have proved more stubborn than most other Europeans in withstanding assimilation. Their resistance to the English language and to the Anglo-Saxon cuisine (as they mistakenly call it, lumping American cooking with that of England) is proverbial. Both in French Canada and Louisiana—to a much lesser extent in New York, Hollywood and San Francisco—the French have kept to themselves and to their own cultural traditions. The chief motive which impels French people to live or remain abroad seems indeed to be the delight afforded by the daily criticism of the strange eating, loving, drinking, and reading habits of the foreigners among whom they have transplanted their irony and their national passion for conversation. There is a strange mutual fascination between the two peoples, American and French. The shrewdest analysis of the United States has repeatedly been that made by French observers, and the appeal of France and of French literature and art is still unequaled in this country. But the intellectual migration from France remains but a trickle, and the first American question before a Frenchman's candidacy to a position over here is: Will he like our ways? Will he be adaptable?

The impediments to a true marriage of minds between the two nations are many: First, some cultural patriotism or even nationalism, deeply ingrained in the French, and persistent inclination on their part to view America as the land of Fenimore Cooper and Jack London and to find Americans most genuine when they act (at least in their novels) as primitives greedy for violence. Then the inveterate French habit of critically observing the wines and the women of foreign lands, and their stubborn conviction that if a man washes dishes in his home and works too hard at his office he has been turned into a slave of a perfidious matriarchate and is reduced to a tool pouring gold and his man's brain and tender male heart into a crucible to pamper woman's caprice. Some profound semantic misunderstandings separate the two civilizations: The word "leisure," for instance, and even the word "loitering" (*flâner*) are sacred to the French and to the Latin peoples generally, while even the most arduous workers among them refuse to proclaim the gospel of work and to present each of their activities as a service to the community. At the bottom of their hearts they protest against the condemnation of their first ancestors by a wrathful God who doomed them to eat bread in the sweat of their brows. To admit that a country which has no outdoor cafés can be civilized requires from them a painful stretch of the imagination. Americans, on their own side, will not easily concede that French is not necessarily synonymous with Gallic, hence charmingly but deeply immoral. For many years, in the nineteenth century, a prejudice opposed anything French as smacking of Catholicism and popery. The suspicion against Catholicism has not altogether died out even though France has supposedly become the country of free thought and existentialist atheism; ironically enough and for this very reason, suspicion of the French is now most prevalent among all but the most intellectual circles of American Catholicism. Only the name "Huguenot" has continued to be regarded as a fetish, and to give oneself out as a descendant of the French Huguenots (who, by that criterion, must have been more prolific than polygamous patriarchs) is a claim to nobility, to morality, higher than to be descended from one of William the Conqueror's knights.

French Protestants, who are such an infinitesimal portion of the French nation today (probably one-fiftieth or so), have always been more attracted to Anglo-Saxon culture than their compatriots. Some of their Sunday school stories and many of the novels which are allowed them in their teens are translations from the English and presumably safer than French books for their faith and morality. Their curiosity is thus drawn toward "the big mysterious island," as Proust called England. A significant proportion of the professors who subsequently seek or accept positions in American colleges are therefore French Protestants. Such were Albert Guérard, Fernand Baldensperger, André Morize, Louis Cons among those who recently taught here and are now dead. Such are several of the present holders of academic positions in French in this country.

The author of this chapter himself grew up in the Protestant faith, was attracted to the study of English and comparative literature after an earlier specialization in the classics, and first came to America in 1925 to teach in a renowned women's college. No compelling exterior reason, then or since—racial, political, or ideological—drove him to America. He had not even robbed a bank, killed a man in a duel or eloped with the wife of his employer, as used to be the case, or the legend, with the black sheep in French families who occasionally disappeared to tempt fortune in the New World or in one of the African or Oceanic colonies. He had not even nurtured an American myth, as many a French adolescent has or still does, whom an inordinate passion for movies, jazz, E. A. Poe, William Faulkner, or Henry Miller has lured to this country in the last three decades. He would in all honesty be at a loss to state the reasons for his first American experiment, and they are immaterial.

But once in this country and plunged first into an ocean of women, then into a very masculine academic community, he tried to understand it from the inside. While most Europeans seldom attempt to penetrate beyond their three poles in New York (Harlem, Chinatown, and Rockefeller Center), beyond the burlesque shows in Philadelphia and Boston, Poe's grave in Baltimore, the Chicago stockyards and, of course, Sunset Boulevard, it was his good fortune to work in America, to be immediately impressed by the qualities of his students and the kindness and intelligence of his colleagues. He read the essays in which apprentices treated the French grammar with a refreshing lack of deference but expressed a vigorous personality. He promised himself he would never write a book on his American experience, so that he did not have to stress the differences unduly and could thus meditate on the many points of similarity between Americans and Europeans. To be sure he kept shy of milk and mint sauce, vitamins and mayonnaise, and fruits on his salad, but rejoiced that others could like such delicacies while he could be spared them by alleging a mysterious allergy. He looked bewildered whenever sport metaphors were used by staid old gentlemen, and to this day remains puzzled by homers and first base and gridiron imagery almost as much as by that other invincible barrier separating Americans from continental Europeans: parliamentary procedure and the phraseology of committees. He did not speculate profusely, like his compatriots, on the alleged tyranny, dryheartedness, pride, and demoniacal greed for culture of the American women. He merely observed, accepted, and liked.

After an American experience of seven years, he returned to his own country where he had intended to make

his career. He taught there and in several other parts of
the world, compared, and in 1938, again with no compelling motive and not even sensing the ominous catastrophes which were to befall Europe, partly because he was
attracted by material advantages and partly because he had
retained excellent memories of American youth, he accepted a flattering offer to come back to this country. He
has been here ever since, and his adoption of the United
States may at least be said to have been a free one, based
upon comparative experience elsewhere and a cool estimate
of pros and cons. The decision to teach, to speak and write
and otherwise to pursue his career in this country has never
been regretted. In no country that he visited has the writer
of these lines found more good will in audiences and among
students, more alertness, more seriousness and, to use the
one word so dear to the French, more intelligence. Native
gifts may have been cultivated more sedulously elsewhere
and strengthened by more critical training, but nowhere
are they in fact more plentiful or more promising.

The personal equation thus stated may now be forgotten,
and the more general factors, both material and spiritual,
which brought or detained foreign scholars and educators
over here in the last few decades may be analyzed with
some objectivity. Adverse factors in their experience will
not be omitted, but favorable ones clearly prevailed and will
be stressed as in all justice they should be.

Scholars are less prone than other groups of newcomers
to America to wax rapturous over mechanical devices and
some of the advantages of comfortable living which may
also prove to be the foes of their one real need: silence and
some capacity for solitude. The material facilities enjoyed
by a literary scholar in particular do not rank with those
which may fill with delight an atomic physicist, an electri-
cal engineer, a voracious consumer of diagrams, curves,
guinea pigs, and Rohrschach tests. The advantages found
in this country by the historian, the philosopher, and the
literary scholar are nonetheless real ones, and they contrast,
for the newcomer especially, with conditions in shabby and
impoverished Europe.

The excellence of American libraries need not be praised once more. They are spacious, relatively dustless, well lighted, and they are run not for jealous and forbidding librarians but for readers. Books are brought to the reader with dispatch and courtesy. New volumes are bought at his request. Photographs, microfilms are readily provided. Catalogues actually include all the books stored and do justice even to the last letters of the alphabet which in other countries seem to strain the endurance of cataloguing departments. Librarians are competent, zealous, and smile intelligently to the awkward or absent-minded scholar. Libraries are indeed so excellent that the average American does not buy books and often cannot even conceive that books might also be read outside libraries, in his very home.

Research is also appreciably facilitated by assistants and secretaries. Data are compiled, bibliographical information is collected or verified for the scholar; trained secretaries type his manuscipts, point out grammatical or stylistic slips, gently persuade him that consistency should be his primary virtue and that contradictions are not merely, as Emerson called them, the hobgoblin of little minds but the foe, pitilessly hunted out, of those most logical of beings, women. The printing and editing standards of American presses are considerably higher than in several cities of Europe, and an author cannot but be flattered by the respect thus paid his prose.

Even more valuable to the émigré scholar teaching in America is the freedom which accrues to him from his new surroundings. The freedom to move from one university to another is greater than in Europe; offers are readily made, with increased bids, by rival institutions; invitations to lecture are lavishly extended. More important is a certain freedom from solemnity and hierarchy. One is relieved from pronouncing elaborate formulas of address to an Excellency, a *Hofrat*, or *Illustrissimo Direttore*. The custom of calling his new colleagues, after a few weeks, by their first names or even by their nicknames or some mysterious abbreviation of their first names does not make for clarity in social contacts; it is nevertheless, if not overdone, a mark of cordial simplicity. The foreigner is even more pleased to discover that a chairman does not dictate orders, indeed that he listens to others, accepts contradiction from committees that he has appointed, and refrains from placing himself above the law or above parliamentary procedure. Some loss of dignity in academic life may be entailed. Professors do not necessarily wear dark garb and solemn hats and decorations. Students do not bow to them on the stairs but treat them with cordiality and frankness. They put to them their naïve queries and expect them to listen to their confessions and solve their problems. An outward rejuvenation is often observed among European *chers maîtres* adopted by America. They soon discard the ponderous gravity of one who used to profess rather than teach, and display those flamboyant ties by which American men flaunt the denial of their Puritan heritage and proclaim their joy in living.

The first enthusiasm of the foreign-born scholar for the freedom and informality of American academic life soon wears off. Some disappointment often ensues before deeper values are appreciated. The intellectual in Continental Europe was surrounded with a more refulgent halo, and his vanity was flattered. He had only a modest share in the goods of this earth, since they should rightfully go as a solace to those who cannot enjoy the pleasures of the spirit. But in a stratified society he held an enviable rank. He was the heir to the medieval cleric or the Renaissance humanist. He received invitations from high officials or ambassadors, was consulted by fine ladies on what to read or what to think of what they should pretend having read. Articles by men of letters and professors were printed on the first page of newspapers and carried weight with the public. Several European countries had been governed by professors whom the Spanish or French intellectual had known at the University, and he could hope some day to emulate Herriot, Daladier, or Bidault, who had passed from a scholar's chair to the Premier's seat. Students hardly dared disturb him, and office hours were almost unheard of in Europe. Colleges existed for the sake of the professors there, and students were but an adjunct which had to be put up with, unlike America, where professors were expected to serve the pupils and respect in them the potential alumni.

No such reverence for intellectuals prevailed in the New World. Workmen, shopkeepers, insurance agents would bluntly ask the professor how much money he made, and fail to conceal their pitiful contempt at the answer. His pride could not easily take refuge in other standards, since financial values were the prevailing ones around him. Unconsciously, the American intellectual (the artist and the writer suffer far more acutely than the professor from this condition) is driven to emulate the businessman, who sets the standards and represents the norm of the successful person. He dresses and talks like him, answers letters dutifully like him, spends long hours at his office surrounded by three telephones and two dictaphones, aims at efficiency, haste and productivity.

The American attitude toward culture is healthier than that of the Renaissance, which idolized mediocre humanists, or than that of the French, who pry into the private life of Gide, Cocteau, or Sartre and deem a pronouncement by those men more momentous than a declaration by Stalin. Still it betrays a fundamental distrust of culture as integrated with life at a time when cultural values are essential in a war of ideas. When in 1952 the Russian press asserted vociferously that Leonardo da Vinci and Victor Hugo had been precursors of Communism, it paid culture the renowned compliment which vice, said La Rochefoucauld, bestows upon virtue and which goes by the name of hypocrisy. Specialists of propaganda have apparently overlooked the use to which names such as E. A. Poe could be put abroad. Railroad directors might well call one of their trains leaving daily a university town "The Professors" as against five or six termed "The Bankers," "The Merchants," or "The Legislator." Among several thousands of fancy names given to Pullman cars all over the country, why does not one find that of some literary heroine or hero, Daisy Miller, Roderick Hudson, Billy Budd,

The Great Gatsby, or Temple Drake? Among streets mo-
notonously called Market, Chapel, Church, Commerce,
Meadow, would it be excessive to dedicate some to Tho-
reau, Walt Whitman, Mark Twain, Eakins, Winslow
Homer, and to christen some college halls not only after
their donors but occasionally after the scholars who educated the donors and the donors' sons?

No jealousy is felt toward the man of affairs who is the
hero of American life (though hardly of American fiction).
Like the French bourgeois under Louis-Philippe, he con-
sents to be ridiculed by caricaturists, poets, and social reformers so as to enjoy undisturbed the one pursuit that is
truly dear to him: that of power, or perhaps that of perpetual work. In other lands the poet or the artist used to
be portrayed as the cursed one, trampled upon by society
and ruining his health and his normality to offer himself
up as the expiatory victim for the *profanum vulgus* whose
unacknowledged legislator he was. In America, the man of
affairs is the architect of the managerial revolution, the
scapegoat for society, the visionary of the future. One of
them, at a conference where American businessmen tried to
invite their European colleagues to play their parts as
martyrs, was reported by the London *Economist* of December 15, 1951, to have gravely stated: "The American
manager . . . has more ulcers and more heart involve-
ment per capita than any other class of the American people and he is considered by insurance companies a questionable risk. This may be pretty hard on him, but the
results have been very satisfactory for the nation as a
whole."

But the intellectual in the modern world stands in need
of one commodity above all others: leisure. The very name
of leisure meant "school" among the Greeks and has given
the word "scholarship." A most learned and painstaking
German writer, Friedrich Schlegel, in an enraptured prose
idyl praised idleness as the finest attribute of the gods.
Productivity is a very dubious ideal to be proposed to men
of thought and to educators. It encourages quantity at the
expense of quality and depth. It has lately sacrificed the

slow maturing of young men to the temporary need of industry for engineers and salesmen. The amount of learning and skill to be acquired by young men is incomparably vaster than ever before; sciences interlock on all sides and pose highly complex problems to bewildered individuals; any political or economic move may entail consequences for three continents instead of the three or four countries which alone counted two centuries ago. Higher education should reasonably be spread over one-tenth at least of adult life, and life expectancy has grown considerably. Four years in college are no longer adequate. Yet a misplaced standard of efficiency has led hurried educators to sacrifice the quality of the nation's training to speed.

Many of the mistakes of our time have been committed by men of good will and of blind devotion to their work who, carried away by the comforting delusion that hard work can take the place of other achievements, lived in a state of nervous tension under which they collapsed. The sad end of such devoted public servants as a former ambassador to London, a Secretary of Defense, a score of statesmen and envoys, is a gloomy reflection on a way of life which produces goods but consumes men. The duty of intellectuals and educators is to maintain the validity of their own standards against the drive of a surrounding society which tends to assimilate them to producers of merchandise. By stepping aside occasionally, thinking their problems anew, keeping their nerves relaxed, and bearing in mind the sad statement of Ruskin (who should have known) that "no great man ever stops working until he has reached his point of failure," intellectuals can best serve their country and suggest new ideas and imaginative solutions to our fagged brains dulled by the narcotic of unceasing toil.

While these are real drawbacks, they are not sufficient to offset the spiritual advantages which the refugee scholar gains in America. For while the material benefits mentioned above (higher salaries, better or more spacious buildings, ampler research and library facilities) are very real, they are not in most cases the factors which have lured or detained here the foreign scholars who were not driven out of their native land by force. During a stay of several years in Europe after he had become accustomed to the greater comfort and brighter promotion prospects of an American career, this author for one must acknowledge that he hardly missed the material advantages afforded by America. Indeed he had rather a lurking fear of the perils of intellectual comfort and of the excessive kindness of American audiences which uniformly greet a foreign lecturer with disarming stock phrases such as "It was most stimulating" or "It was a wonderful challenge" or "You have given us an inspiration." The role of excitement, of stimulant, or of challenge might well after all be reserved to drugs, cocktails, or to one's husband. There may occur moments of discouragement in the career of a middle-aged scholar who keeps in mind the need to renew himself and his stock of ideas periodically. He misses the pitiless criticism of his European countrymen, who will harshly take him to task for any slipping from his or their standards and publicly call him a fool, an idiot, or a doting cretin. Over here such gentle formulas of obloquy are replaced by a polite nod of the head on the part of the dissenting person and a courteous phrase such as "You may have got a point there." Agreeing to disagree is a virtue in political life, but it cuts short the discussion of ideas rather abruptly and sometimes stifles altogether the ideas that one might have developed.

But Europe in the years 1930–40 could no longer serenely afford the intellectual arguments and the intoxicating delight of the give-and-take of sparkling conversation. After the analytical works of the 1920–30 decade, the elaborate and anguished Hamletism of Proust, Gide, Kafka, and Pirandello, the complacent egotism of the generation which had escaped the slaughter of World War I, a new spirit appeared around 1929–33. Poets and novelists then realized that they could no longer enjoy the benefits of a stable political régime and polish their sentences undisturbed in a society threatened by war and misery. Educators and students of the past were confronted by the eventuality of a collapse such as the world had not known since the collapse of ancient civilization. Europe was torn by internecine feuds and a lurking civil or social war inside every country. Apathy could no longer be a refuge. Many a European scholar then looked upon America as upon the land where European culture, already robustly grafted and naturalized, could continue to flourish if some cataclysm were to spread ruins over France, Germany, Italy. A similar anguish fills those scholars today. The New World is no longer immune from the threats of atomic warfare; yet it seems reasonable to hope that the legacy of ancient and modern culture can best be preserved here. In any case, the foreign-born professor in this country is often haunted by the thought that the future and the very existence of the world as he knows it will be decided within the next ten or fifteen years; they will hinge upon the youth of this country primarily, or upon the collaboration of that youth and the generations then in their forties and fifties which he may have taught in college. The duty of an educator of American youth thus appears as one of formidable significance: to enable his students to understand the world around them, to prepare for it imaginatively, and to develop their capacity for leadership.

Everything around him tends to remind the foreign-born educator of his sense of urgency. In other countries and in different times, culture could be pursued for its own sake, and leisurely. It did not have to serve, and the criterion of usefulness was indeed scorned. Students were relatively few in numbers and came from a favored social background; they were seldom tempted to ask what advantage they would derive from a study of Plato or Virgil. Such is no longer the case. Even the young men and women who choose to acquire a liberal education are practical minded. They want culture to help them live and to have some immediate relevance to life. They flock to the social sciences because those appear to them more practical and factual, and claim to be concerned only with the immediate past and with the immediate future which they attempt to predict. The challenge is a beneficent one for the professor of literature. He must learn how to reexamine the legacy of the past which he had accepted blindfolded in Europe, boasting of a long line of ancestors whose heir he claimed to be. He takes to heart Faust's celebrated advice, when he meditates aloud after the departure of his famulus:

> *Was du ererbt von deinen Vätern hast,*
> *Erwirb es, um es zu besitzen!*
> *Was man nicht nützt ist eine schwere Last.*

The study of literature is probably the domain in which the accession of foreign-born scholars has been least marked in the last two or three decades. For, of all the fields of study, it is the one where style is of the greatest importance, and where nothing can replace the perception of the formal esthetic values which is naturally keener with the compatriots of the author than with foreigners. History of thought and of culture, even history of art, has benefited from a larger influx of European scholars than history and criticism of English and American literature: for the medium of the language is less essential in them. Departments of English in American universities have thus remained the least cosmopolitan of all, and the émigré scholars have, as was natural, been most fruitfully utilized by departments of foreign languages and literatures. Their contribution to Spanish and Germanic studies, to French and to medieval and comparative studies has been significant, at a time when the number of eminent native scholars in those domains was small. It is not certain, however, that the foreign professors thus welcomed in the United States have set themselves with the desirable zeal and promptitude to training Americans who would soon be in a position to succeed them. They may have suffered in several cases from the comforting prejudice that foreign literatures are best taught by natives, and thus have strengthened the American inferiority complex in the matter of foreign languages. Too many of them have complacently taken it for granted that students born and taught in New York or Chicago could never rival the native Parisians, the Spaniards who had imbibed Hispanidad in their infancy along with Spanish wine, olive oil, and a taste for bullfights, or the Germans who had sat at the feet of some revered master in Bonn or Freiburg and had Hegel, Dilthey, and Stefan George, as the phrase goes, in their veins.

Such occasional provincialism in the émigré scholars in America is regrettable and has, in our opinion, proved harmful to their field of study in the evaluation of many Americans. The study of foreign countries and of their literatures as an adequate path to the interpretation of the foreign countries, had become of singular urgency in the United States which suddenly was invested with the heavy responsibilities for world leadership. It should be practiced today with more energy than ever by gifted Americans. Those should be free from the national prejudices which have long been the privilege, and the bane, of European scholars, each tending to magnify the cultural uniqueness of his own country, be it Norway or Greece, France or Poland. The dicta of Parisian critics, of Spanish or German literary historians, on their own literature should be duly weighed but also firmly and respectfully set aside by apprentices of the study of literature in the United States. After all the Germans have long boasted of a brilliant school of Romance or of Shakespearean scholars, the French of equally brilliant groups of Germanic or English scholars who owed part of their originality to the fact that their methods and their backgrounds were foreign, and who made no effort to ape or echo the native criticism of those literatures. A sad gap in American leadership was revealed during World War II when this country had to resort liberally to German-born and German-trained specialists when it had to organize military government, economic assistance, and cultural propaganda in Germany. The devotion of those anti-Nazi German specialists to their adopted country in the New World was beyond question. But American prestige would have been far better served by an able group of specialists on Germany (and other countries of Europe or Asia) who would have been Americans looking at foreign problems with a keener awareness of the American scene and American moods and needs.

Once again the position adopted by the foreign-born specialist of literature in an American university should avoid the obvious and opposite extremes of carping and ungrateful criticism or of fulsome praise. There have been a few, a very few Europeans who, filled with rancorous spite at the treatment which had been meted out to them in their native land, eager to please those who had welcomed them over here and keenly conscious of the demands implied in the magic American formula "to fit in," decided to find everything wonderful in their adopted country and to look henceforth with condescension at shabby and unstable Europe. But American cordiality is not necessarily naïveté, and few intelligent Americans who ritually ask the question "How do you like America?" expect or appreciate excessive and probably insincere praise. Derogatory remarks about one's adopted country are obviously out of place if they reflect a negative attitude of narrow-mindedness and the inability of newcomers to enter into a way of life which is only superficially different from their own. They have seldom been uttered by scholars who have worked in this country and therefore learned to appreciate America from the inside, eschewing the hasty silliness of journalists who wish to entertain or to please their own public and sacrifice the delicate shades of truth to picturesqueness and sensationalism.

The position most truly worthy of a European scholar transplanted over here is, in our eyes, that which respects the difference between the two continents, seeks the originality of each contribution to civilization (that of America, that of Western Europe, not to mention South America and Asia or rather Asias in the plural, and of Russia), and conceives his own role as that of intermediary between the country of his birth and that which he has subsequently adopted. It would be foolish of a European, even one who has suffered in his native land, to repudiate the culture which molded him and to misjudge the intellectual and spiritual forces which still make Europe the most creative continent. At a time when America is expending money, machinery, men, and her confidence in Western Europe to preserve it not only as a fortress or as a bridgehead but as a bastion of civilization, it is fitting for an Americanized European to bear in mind the eloquent statement with which aging Michelet prefaced his volume *Du Dix-huit Brumaire à Waterloo:*

Europe, they say, is very old. But there is more youth in her apparent old age than anywhere else on the globe. Her living electricity, which makes her highly mobile, enables her daily to renovate herself through the spirit, and the spirit in turn endows will-power with unbelievable strength. Let a great idea appear, will-power weaves and creates a world with it.

Some of the differences between cultural conditions in the United States and in Europe are valuable ones and should be preserved; others can be eliminated through the mutual acquisition by each of what is best, and assimilable, in the other.

The first feature which impresses the literary scholars, like other scholars or scientists transplanted here, has often been described and praised. But it must be briefly recalled in any survey of the subject, for its importance is primary. The American academic atmosphere is relatively free from the pettiness that often prevails elsewhere and from the fear of risk and novelty which grants a premium to routine. There is relatively little envy, and the welcome which has gladly made room for the émigré scholars and has pushed them to top positions would be inconceivable in any other land. A scholar is encouraged to formulate new plans, to propose reforms, and, provided he does so in a co-operative and constructive spirit, is often greeted with the most beautiful of all American formulas: "Go ahead!" Money is seldom a problem, and it is eventually found. The more gigantic the undertaking, the more extensive the survey, and occasionally the bigger the words used by sociologists, psychiatrists, and even by humanists, the readier the financial response. At the same time, there prevails a spirit of co-operation which is conspicuously lacking in Europe, where not only scholarship but science depends mainly upon the individual. Collective undertakings can be carried through far more easily in America than in Europe. Nationalistic bias, social or political divergences do not interfere with the determination to accomplish a task in common. A cantankerous spirit is relatively rare. "Keep smiling" is an advice that arouses a smile on our lips, but it is taken seriously by many. Small colleges have several times been portrayed as poisoned "groves of Academe" and as surrendering to conventionality and cant; but the cordial breadth of mind encountered in most large American universities is undeniably superior to the mutual suspicion which prevails in countries where competition is keener and envy rife.

A ransom is to be paid for such good-humored cordiality and spontaneous trust in human nature. Irony is perhaps deficient or is frowned upon as destructive and malignant; for in irony there is iron and the sharpness of a blade, as a great master of language who was an imaginative etymologist, Victor Hugo, once said. Some of the solemn conventions of American oriental orders, some alumni gatherings in which staid if not sober alumni don fanciful garb, some gatherings of learned societies in which strings of abstruse papers are gravely and meekly listened to, amuse the foreign observer, who assumes that all this smacks of the child in man that should be outgrown when one has reached the age of reason. Humor is preferred to irony, and has indeed more charm, because it blends irony with sympathy, a pitiful heart with a keen and amused intellect; perhaps also because it is a means of eluding the tragedy of life, and of smiling in order to conceal or repress the emotion.

But the critical spirit, which unlike irony is an almost unadulterated virtue if practised with moderation, is not overdeveloped in American students. The first reaction of the newly arrived scholar from abroad is one of relief. In several countries of Europe, and in France in particular, education seems to have been primarily designed to train critics and to teach disbelief. Most of the thinkers proposed to the admiration of the youth were advocates of healthy, methodical doubt: Montaigne, Descartes, Voltaire, Renan,

Claude Bernard. The quality of the critical articles in periodicals is strikingly high: the very best minds seem concerned with examining, doubting, weighing, distrusting prejudice and appearances. Audiences at a lecture, concert or play seldom yield to rapturous enthusiasm. One word punctuates their comments: the little conjunction "but." "It could have been a good play, but . . ." or "It was an interesting lecture, but . . ." The marvel of it all is that such relentless criticism has not hampered creation, that, indeed, it seems to stimulate the writing of books and music, and that neither lecturers nor actors whose every intonation, every interpretation is scanned by pitiless observers appear to have been discouraged by those Parisians who will not accept on trust a new book or a much advertised film any more than they do a bottle of wine or a fiancée.

Americans are, in contrast, more readily addicted to enthusiasm or perhaps to polite praise of any foreigner who has come from abroad to play his music, expound his ideas, and vituperate against the shortcomings of American civilization. There may be some masochism in them when they meekly buy a ticket for a lecture in which a foreigner will assail their soullessness or their capitalist greed or their philistinism in art, or perhaps merely a fine sporting instinct which makes them shake hands with the vituperative lecturer and declare, "It is good for us to hear such things." But if the visitor from abroad settles here, he soon discovers that, behind the shallow and uncritical reception which is often given him, there is mostly reserve and shyness. If the young American is encouraged to form an opinion of his own and oppose it to others convincingly and with sincerity, he is eminently capable of having such an opinion and expressing it with wisdom and brilliance. It has been the frequent experience of many foreign teachers in this country to receive from the better undergraduates papers successfully rivaling the very best written by students at Oxford, the Sorbonne or Heidelberg. The quality of many Ph.D. theses in literature is now easily comparable to the best products from Europe. And if American periodicals do not as yet publish enough critical articles of outstanding merit, it is usually because their editors wrongly believe their readers prefer any fourth-rate short story to a first-rate critical study. The young men gifted enough to write such critical articles are here, in the universities, and could easily be drawn upon and encouraged.

The French professor of literature is also heard to deplore the lack of training and of skill in writing in American students, and consequently or similarly in American writers. Here again allowance must be made for a different background and a different set of values. America is now becoming a haven for rhetoricians; Kenneth Burke and some of the once "new" critics are unparalleled at the present time in the Old World. But less stress is placed at school on the subtleties of composition, and less effort is made to order one's thoughts in a manner which will both surprise and persuade. Transitions, on which Flaubert and many other Frenchmen have laboriously pondered, often leave the American writer beautifully unconcerned.

A young essayist will readily declare at the beginning of a paper, "I enjoyed reading this play of Racine" or "I hate that morbid writer Proust," which in Europe would afflict his professor with an apoplectic stroke or with a sudden baldness. Every third sentence in written and even in spoken French seems to be a litotes. The word is almost unknown in America, and innuendoes, even understatements, fail to play the same role of tempering every assertion. "Il n'y a de vérité que dans les nuances": this little maxim of Benjamin Constant is a favorite one with every French teacher of literature, and "nuance" is one of his key words.

Much has been lost with the disappearance of such a refined and allusive way of writing. The genteel and polished essay, such as was long written by English historians, critics, and urbane and humorous moralists, is perhaps the most original and, with due credit to Montaigne, autochthonous form in English letters. Virginia Woolf, G. M. Trevelyan, and Americans who had been profoundly anglicized, Logan Pearsall Smith, T. S. Eliot, have given admirable examples of it in the last few decades. As an art form that essay is unfortunately on its way out. Our magazines find it too leisurely, too long and rambling, too nonchalant, too subtle. They are swayed by the triumph of a journalistic technique, which affects a more abrupt and more crudely outspoken style and rates "punch," speed, effectiveness above the more traditional qualities of style. We can but mourn the loss. But the shock values which are at present favored by our magazines are responsible in part for the very trend which they deplore in American letters: the premium granted to violence and brutality, and the fear of the intellect in our creative writers, as if they might endanger their precious primitive and "grass roots" virtue if they once started having ideas or analyzing themselves.

The American has been defined by a Spanish thinker as "a civilized man with no traditions." The definition is of course deceptive; the taste for ancestors' portraits, a passion for genealogy, the hunting of antiques, the restoration of old houses, the naïve appeal of inns where Washington once slept or of houses which Jefferson once visited, the cult of legal precedents, are also American traits. It is probably more accurate to say that the sense of history is less deep and less all-pervading here than it is in Western Europe. The European is often crushed by the weight of his past. Unable to accept and assimilate the whole mass of it, he elects one period or one trend in that past as worthy of his cult and fights against the rest, and against his compatriots advocating the opposite trend or selecting another century as their utopia. Thus could Hilaire Belloc, an Englishman in whose veins ran some French blood, say that "civil war is a constant function of Gallic energy."

Americans are divided, and their own Civil War was more ruthless than any European revolution. It has left them with a secret but deep complex, a lurking fear of disunity which periodically flares up and is discernible today in their emotional wrath against Communism in their own midst. Their attempt at integrating the millions of foreign born among them has been inspired in part by that fear,

and pushed intelligently and, on the surface at least, successfully. The study of American history has recently been
strengthened in many schools and praised as a store house
of the best traditions which have made the American an
individualist, a pioneer, a tolerant and God-fearing democrat. Nevertheless the foreign teacher or lecturer in this
country is struck by the frailty of the knowledge of, and
of the sense for, history. While most Europeans remain
to this day sons of nineteenth-century historicism and tend
to explain any phenomenon by its genesis and any movement through its origins and slow growth, the revolt against
history is never very far from the American mind. It has
been the experience, rarely but occasionally, of a French
lecturer in this country to be imprudent enough to invite
questions from the floor, and to be startled by the realization that the king who had been described as introducing
the Renaissance from Italy into France had been surmised
by one as being Charlemagne, by another as being Louis
XIV. A naïve but eager traveler he once spoke to on a
train seized the opportunity of meeting a Frenchman to
clear up a point which had long puzzled him: whether Bonaparte and Napoleon had been two different rulers, or one
and the same man. Among better informed and more sophisticated persons, and notably among the adepts of the
social sciences, hostility to history has become a set policy.
An effort is made to break with the past altogether and to
concentrate on what has been observed, classified, and
translated into charts and diagrams only since censuses,
polls, and elaborately indiscreet questionnaires came into
being. Going back more than ten or twenty years in studying social behavior or international relations is frowned
upon, unless one jumps determinedly over the previous
thirty centuries and explores the artifacts of primitive men
and the sexual mores of remote oceanic tribes.

Some freshness is gained thereby. The European has
more than once been hampered by his obsession with history and has failed to envisage new situations as fundamentally new and failed therefore to propose imaginatively
new solutions for new problems. History with him has all

too often served to foster nationalistic suspicions, boastful claims, jealousies of other nations. European philosophers of history have often been obsessed with cyclical conceptions of man's evolution and have predicted tragic collapses for our culture on the strength of doubtful past parallels arbitrarily interpreted. Insofar as it has been a genetic study of hypothetical sources and has mistaken the previous occurrence of an idea or of a stylistic device as a cause and has thus helped produce the subsequent reemergence of the device or of the idea, scholarship has fallen into blind alleys. Michelet, in 1855, prefacing his volume on the Renaissance, looked back with gloom on the harm which the reign of history was causing his own country:

History, which is nothing less than understanding of life, was to vivify us; it has, on the contrary, weakened us, making us believe that time is everything, and will power nothing. We have conjured up history, and now it is everywhere around us; we are besieged, stifled, overwhelmed by it. . . . The past is killing the future. . . . In name of history itself, in the name of life, we must protest. History has nothing to do with such a heap of stones. History is history of the soul, of original thought, of fecund imagination, of heroism: the heroism of action and that of creation.

Nietzsche, in one of his *Unzeitgemässe Betrachtungen*, echoed such a protest when he, trained in philology and history, revolted against the historical intoxication of his age and wanted to substitute *memento vivere* as a motto for the *memento mori* of those who use history as a convenient way to avoid life and action. The blurred or vague historical sense of many Americans deprives them of much pleasure; for the intellectual joy of knowing the past and the poetical halo which transfigures even dull details as they appear in the perspective of the past are a source of enjoyment to the historian. But a certain freshness is also gained. Teaching unsophisticated young Americans can be a rejuvenating experience for a European. Chaucer, Racine, Bossuet, Dürer, Monteverdi suddenly spring alive to his American students, who treat them as if they were contemporaries. Some lovely coeds discover with raptures Plautus or Chrétien de Troyes or some other writer of old who to many a young European had appeared merely as an instrument for his mental torture in some required course. In some respects, the freshness of the happiest of all peoples, the Greeks, who had no ancient or foreign language or literature to study, few previous systems of philosophy, no catechism or dogmas, no chemistry or biology, and could concentrate on poetry, eloquence, art, dancing, gymnastics, and leisure, has been inherited by young American undergraduates. It is, however, fast disappearing.

"Freedom" is another word which recurs on the lips of those who have come over from Europe and praise the hospitable intellectual climate which they have found in the United States. It is, along with "charity" and "solidarity," the most beautiful of substantives, and those who had suffered from the eclipse of political and intellectual liberty in Europe are most eloquent in singing its praise. The noble word "freedom" may have lost some of its glamour when, in the first decades of our century, Western men, in their secure enjoyment of freedom, had become too sensitive to some of the vulgarizing or leveling effects of democratic rule. But Europe suddenly awoke to discover Fascism, Communism, Hitlerism, and to realize that the disappearance of freedom would be tantamount to the extinction of life. From Pericles and Cicero to Montesquieu, from Locke to John Stuart Mill and Croce, from Shelley to Eluard, passages should be culled which should be proposed as sacred texts for the study of the young in the one world that we like to envision. The present writer may be the least qualified of the authors in this volume to expound the advantages of freedom in America, for he had not suffered from any restrictions to freedom of thought in his native country. He may, however, bear witness to the utmost latitude which has always been granted him in private universities in this country, to think, write, and say anything that appeared to him as true. And he has not refrained, and never has been asked to refrain, from trespassing into the domains of religion, politics, economics, and international relations.

A word of warning may, however, well be in order.

Because there is more freedom in this country and because universities are free from federal supervision, because neither academies nor state-subsidized theatres exist, because (in a sense, at least) the American press is or calls itself free, some Americans are fond of assuming that thought, science, and literature are necessarily freer in the United States than elsewhere, and intellectual progress more assured. We smile, rightly no doubt but complacently, at Hitlerian anthropology and science under the Nazis, at the Stalinist rebukes to geneticists, semanticists, and musicians who fail to obey the Marxist line. No one wishes to suggest that Nazi or Communist restraints upon science are laudable or beneficent, or that restrictions and more Federal control be established in free America.

But it would be rash to fancy that no good science and no good literature flourished in the past under tyrannical régimes. French science was perhaps, in mathematics and physics, never greater than under the totalitarian rule of Richelieu and of Louis XIV, and the glory of French letters and philosophy then has hardly been excelled. Chemistry, biology, and physics with Carnot, Ampère and Fresnel shone brightly under the iron rule of the Terror and of Napoleon the First. The achievements of German chemists and engineers under Hitler, those of the Russian scientists today, must not be complacently underestimated. In literature, Goethe, Schiller, Hegel, and a dozen stars of German romanticism illumined the very years when Germany was cringing under Napoleon's scepter. Goethe bowed to every petty nobleman whom he encountered in the streets of Weimar, to Beethoven's disgust, and deemed it an exalted favor to receive the Napoleonic Legion of Honor and to be granted an interview with the Emperor then occupying his country, while Hegel contemplated him, riding on horseback in Jena, as the supreme embodiment of the historical process. Many a neutral observer of Italy when the country was occupied by Mussolini or by the Allies, or of Berlin under quadripartite rule, and of some neighboring free countries in Europe has remarked that "political freedom and freedom of the spirit do not necessarily go hand in hand" (Igor Markevitch, in *Made in Italy*, 1949). Free Switzerland and free and prosperous Holland or Denmark have not necessarily thought, composed music, or elaborated political and social systems with the greatest freedom.

Free discussion is everywhere allowed and encouraged in American colleges. Debating teams ritually, if sophistically, argue the pro and con of every question. Newspapers are fond of printing contradictory reports on many events, and radio time is carefully parceled out to the opposing sides in every important issue. Any professor may theoretically say anything he likes at a faculty meeting, and anyone from the floor may nominate any slate of officers and proclaim his disagreement with the majority or with the administration. But courtesy and respect for majority rule seem to be so ingrained in this happy land that dissent has become a rare occurrence, at least among academic people. Reverence surrounds any colleague who happens to have been nominated to any committee. Unanimous votes are the rule in those new Edens, college campuses. Student newspapers seldom criticize or even call into question the fundamentals of the education which has been organized for them by their elders. Since the pro and the con can be freely argued by the newspapers and the radio commentators, one listens nonchalantly and ritually skips the editorials. Shoulders are shrugged when a paradox is uttered, even if paradoxes often prove to be the truth of tomorrow or the unperceived truth of today. Theoretical freedom of thought becomes too little conducive to boldness of thought. Facts are presented liberally to newspaper readers, and means of knowledge are abundantly placed at the disposal of university students. But their passive resistance to thinking about the facts is underestimated. A certain lack of adventure in initiating new ideas, in making startling new discoveries, in predicting the apparently unpredictable has been noticed, by Americans themselves, as constituting the Achilles' heel of their culture. Knowing facts is doubtless important; but it is of little avail unless, as Shelley says toward the end of *Defence of Poetry*, "we imagine that which we know."

The greatest tribute that is paid America by the foreign scholar who has made America his home and who looks back with some pride at what he has been inspired to achieve in this country and gives thanks for it, is that he has been able to develop both as a teacher and as a scholar. For, just as his allegiance is to Europe, which trained him and which he carries with him to his adopted *patrie*, his function is both to train others and to contribute to knowledge himself, to pursue his research and publications. This twofold requirement is an exacting one, and it is becoming increasingly hard to meet owing to conditions around us. Contrary to the fond assumption of those who visit our Gothic towers and verdant lawns, and imagine that in an American university all is *luxe, calme et volupté* (the last, of course, spiritual), we are condemned to wage an unceasing fight to retain the time and the energy necessary for discharging one of our essential obligations: the accumulation and interpretation of knowledge.

In the domain of education a professor who has, impelled by circumstances or of his own free choice, made his career in the United States may well be proud of having played his part, however humble, in the most impressive educational development of the century. Legitimate disappointment, it is true, may be voiced regarding the schools of this country. Some, in the large cities and elsewhere, are excellent. Many are mediocre. Dissatisfaction with the secondary education that he received is a chronic cause of complaint with the thoughtful American of either sex. Far too little has yet been attempted to remedy glaring faults. The raw material of America, as we brutally call it, the children, are at least as gifted as in any other country. The best of them manage to achieve, in spite of the handicaps of a schooling of questionable quality, amazing results. Several signs, however, point at present to a slowing down in the rate of intellectual progress in this country. Only a thorough reform of the schools could again enable Americans to forge ahead and to rise up to the expectations that the world places in them: and these are none other than leadership of the world, technical, intellectual, and spiritual. America's chance is here and now. Tomorrow may favor other sections of our planet, for as the French historian Lavisse used to say, "La faculté de conduire l'histoire n'est point une faculté perpétuelle."

The fallacies from which our educational system suffers are the utilitarian one and a mistaken conception of democracy. Thoughtful visitors from abroad and scholars and scientists established here are unanimous in condemning them; and they do so out of earnest devotion to this country and not in an acrimonious spirit of disparaging all that differs from the traditions which Europe has inherited from the Renaissance. The utilitarian obsession has blinded many Americans, too many normal colleges and departments of education, too many taxpayers wanting to get "their money's worth" in the form of measurable and immediate returns and in fact encouraging routine and mediocrity. Young men and women must obviously acquire certain skills which they may need in different walks of life. But they would easily acquire those on the job itself, and fairly promptly. The fact is that, in America especially, one seldom stays in the career one had chosen at sixteen or twenty. The chances of travel, military service, of marriage, of friendly or family connections, plunge most young men into work for which they were not particularly prepared.

Consequently some general culture, the ability to exercise common sense or to display sound judgment, the discernment of men which is developed by the study of man in history, literature, and the humanities in general, some personal charm often more marked in a man with a broad cultural training and able to see his subject as part of a larger whole—these are more valuable assets in life than a narrow specialized training. The men who reach the top in their profession, in diplomacy, administration, banking, commerce, are in most cases those who had been shrewd enough not to stress the utilitarian aspect of their training and who, when studying, reading, and listening, had not been obsessed by the naïve question of some crude adolescents (echoed, alas! by some of their educators): "What use will this subject be to me?"

Democracy has been too often interpreted as leveling down; if envious masses cannot raise themselves to the level of their more fortunate neighbors, they will at least undertake to bring their neighbors down to their own none too exalted standards. Traditional subjects which now pass for aristocratic (the classics, even foreign languages, the arts, a certain variety of vocabulary and polish of style) are being expelled from many schools and even from colleges which train the teachers for the schools. It is claimed that the men of the future need primarily to be adjusted (to a none too perfect society, to be sure) and attuned to the mass and machine age in which they are to live. The educators who have been steeped in a European tradition cannot but think that most of the great scientists, engineers, biologists, in the past were brought up in a humanistic discipline and were not thus hampered from making startling discoveries. They are bound to confess, and many native American scientists have first proclaimed it, that even today many of the most original discoveries in science are made abroad and subsequently perfected here, and that the essential gifts of imagination and of original thinking flourish best in men whose training has not been narrowly circumscribed by one field of specialization. Pasteur was not specialized in medicine, and Claude Bernard began by writing a tragedy. Jefferson, Gladstone, the French Revolutionaries, the greatest American and English statesmen were trained, not in civics and contemporary democratic behavior, but on Plato and Thucydides, on Cicero and on Locke, Rousseau and Burke. It was lately asserted that President Truman wisely knew how to spurn the temptation of a prolonged stay in the highest office because he had learned "American" traditions through the reading of Plutarch's *Lives*. What a nation wants is not necessarily what it needs, and educators should have the courage to make it want what it needs. Leadership is not incompatible with democracy. Indeed, democracy can hardly survive without the continued ability to evolve leadership out of its own midst. The age and the countries in which the study of public opinion polls, of the techniques of propaganda, and of the behavior of men in a machine age have been emphasized have also been the age and the countries in which democracy has been dealt its worst blows. The words of warning which Walter Lippmann uttered in December 1940 are not totally unjust in their severity:

During the past forty of fifty years those who are responsible for education have progressively removed from the curriculum of studies the western culture which produced the western democratic state; the schools and colleges have, therefore, been sending out into the world men who no longer understand the creative principle of the society in which they live.

In a few other respects American education appears deficient to the foreign-born professors, who point out its deficiencies because they believe they could easily be cured, and because they are not fundamental expressions of the American temperament but slippery paths or blind alleys on which this country may have momentarily ventured.

First is the fondness for innovations. It is probably beneficent to correct and perfect a machine, to modernize it with new gadgets, to adorn it with new selling devices. But it is regrettable that our halls of learning should not be a little more impervious to tides of taste or currents of shifting opinion rushing on them from outside. Every winter, to offset their financial inability to indulge in winter sports or test the virtue of the Florida sun, college faculties embark upon their own indoor sport, overhauling the curriculum. Progress is regularly conceived by them as lying in the direction of more complexity, and deciphering college bulletins and the requirements for courses, majors, etc., has now become harder than mastering the riddles of relativity. *Quieta non movere* was also a worthy ideal. We absent-mindedly forget that many of the bypaths into which our fury for education reforming or rephrasing waylays us had probably been already explored by our predecessors and rejected as leading nowhere.

A second evil connected with the first is our desire, for publicity purposes and other reasons, to have college teachers produce intensively. There are cases when a gentle outside compulsion may indeed elicit a worth-while article or book from too modest a scholar, who might not otherwise be led to believe that his thoughts are worth printing. Having published one or several books may prove to be salutary hygiene for a professor in the same way that some countries, or some doctors, regard pregnancy as a universal panacea for some of the true creators in this world, women.

> *'Tis pleasant, sure, to see one's name in print.*
> *A book's a book, although there's nothing in't,*

mocked Byron. We have lately equated productivity with quantity, and much criticism published in learned journals hardly sprang from an irresistible inspiration. One of the wise men of our time, who has known American universities from the inside and has settled in a country which is occasionally severe to academic scholarship in the United States, well said: "If people only wrote when they had something to say, and never merely because they wanted to write a book, or because they occupied a position such that the writing of books was expected of them, the mass of criticism would not be wholly out of proportion to the small number of critical books worth reading." (T. S. Eliot, *The Use of Poetry and the Use of Criticism*)

A third and graver evil, from which foreign-born professors in America have been far from immune, is bad writing. We are too prone to assume that we have practiced new methods only if we have coined new labels to cover old or newly wrapped merchandise. A scientist hastens to invent a new symbol to designate a new phenomenon or substance. Social scientists evolve an elaborate private terminology, and zealously borrow the outer trappings of science. The contagion has extended to the so-called new critics, who bandy about epistemological jargon and, unlike Roman augurs, seem able to look at one another without laughing. Psychoanalytical jargon has invaded literary interpretation and opened a gulf between needlessly specialized writing and the general public. An American official, Paul Porter, director of the European Cooperation

Administration, had the courage to protest early in 1952 against such a disfigurement of English style perpetrated in the country which had once produced the splendid writing of the Declaration of Independence and the Gettysburg Address. He denounced "the worst writing of English today, which is surely produced in the United States Government" and the inflationary disease of five-syllable words. The disease has not been confined to Washington.

These shortcomings, which have hampered the growth and especially the qualitative refinement of the study of literature in America, may be traced to the unconscious acceptance of two ideals by academic scholars and critics: the ideals of the businessman and of the scientist. "Efficiency," "punctuality," "productivity," "co-operation," "good fellowship," "service to the community," are words rightly revered by the man of affairs. Since a business career is to most Americans the most enviable one and the one in which it is felt that the country has most conspicuously asserted its supremacy, intellectuals, writers and artists are tempted to adopt the standards and outward behavior of business life: regular office hours, availability in an office, statistical charts, carbon copies duly filed, prim and respectful secretaries whose main function is to stimulate American wives to perpetual rejuvenation and to sublimate male eroticism through chastened and secure dreams amid filing cabinets. The few hardy souls who resist such methods are wretched nonconformists who take refuge in Greenwich Village, along the California beaches, or in drinking or abnormality. The European intellectual sensibly decides to do as others do and to forsake reverie, fantasy, and caprice in his American life. But he occasionally sighs for the original work he might have accomplished in the inefficient lands where letters are not necessarily answered, appointments are irregularly kept, and telephones blissfully get out of order.

The prestige of science has been more bewitching and perhaps more disastrous. Scientists have achieved such results in the last hundred years that others have placidly assumed that only through scientific method would their discipline accede to the august rank of a science, as chemistry and biology had once done. Psychology and sociology have scored undeniable gains thereby. The gain to the interpretation of art and literature is much more doubtful. Exhaustive knowledge, accurate observation, submission to texts, relative and critical spirit, intellectual honesty are virtues usually found in scientists which literary scholars must also possess. Objectivity and impartiality are less undeniably beneficent, and it may well be, as Baudelaire contended, that "passionate partiality" endows a critic with keener insight. But when scientists ask their literary colleagues what are the precise and stable criteria on which they rest their assertions that Balzac is great and Meredith or Dreiser less great, they can only reply that stability and uniformity are in no way desirable in the opinions emitted by varied people of different ages on literary writers.

The study of literature would be even less securely based than it is at the present time if it rested on semantics, psychological measurements, esthetic tests for beauty, etc. For these are even more susceptible to change than the elusive criteria of good taste, penetration, power, intensity, and subtlety. It would be folly for literary study to ask science to provide it with models for stable values at the very age when physics, biology, psychology have been, in a span of fifty years, rocked to their foundations by tremendous upheavals. One thing is well-nigh certain: that the authors and artists of the past who are acclaimed today as great, and even some of the present time, have a strong chance to be considered as great twenty and fifty years from now. But the views held at present by medicine, genetics, physics, anthropology, and psychoanalysis are sure to be rejected twenty or fifty years hence. Our descendants will smile at most of them. "Scientific truth is an error of today," wrote J. von Uexküll in 1909, in *Umwelt und Innenwelt der Tiere*, and he was no mean biologist; it might equally be asserted that the scientific truth of today will tomorrow be regarded with pity as an outdated error.

This paper, begun in a spirit of grateful acknowledg-

ment of the immense facilities for growth encountered by
one of many European scholars in his adopted land, may
seem to have been diverted into the sanctimonious criticism
of a preacher. But it would be a disservice to the country
which has bestowed many benefits upon its refugees or
émigrés from overseas if we flattered some of its prejudices and did not warn it against setting its goals too low.
The intellectual migration from Europe has now subsided;
in Germany, Italy, France, and in most countries fortunate
enough not to have been cut off behind the Iron Curtain,
scientists and scholars are again fired with hope for the
future and are working steadily to bring about a better
future. In America, those scholars and scientists who had
migrated here have now become fully integrated into the
cultural life; their sons and daughters are American. They
may look back upon the achievements of the great country
of which they have become part and point out some lag still
remaining between the unbounded expectations the rest of
the world rests in America and the limitations to which
this country seems willing to submit too meekly.

For the intellectuals who have migrated from Europe
have a heavier duty to America than devolves upon the
average citizen of the United States. The most signal failure
of this country, which thinks it has perfected propaganda
techniques and mass media, has been its futile attempts to
make itself rightly understood by its friends and by those
upon whom it showered its benefactions. The American
man is at once superficially boastful and profoundly shy;
he will propose to the admiration of others some of the
mechanical gadgets of his civilization, but he will be em-
barrassed to talk about the soul of his country, its idealism,
its culture, its intellectual achievement. A feeling of em-
barrassment seizes him when American novels, paintings,
or musical compositions are admired abroad. Foreigners
who have settled in America and are in a position to judge
the truly great achievements of American universities, of
education, of research foundations, the unbounded promise
offered today by the quality of American youth, have a role
to play. They are best able, when they visit Europe or write

for Europeans, to stress the elements of American culture which are often underrated abroad, and the true reasons why the rest of the world may well be induced to set its hope in the country without which the world cannot save itself; and the true reasons are the intellectual and spiritual forces which are at work in this country. Better than even the Palomar telescope, electron microscopes, and the Mayo Clinic, to which any European scientific visitor will readily pay homage, are the faith, the imagination, the devotion to man and to the future which made those possible. The foreign-born student of literature, who may be credited with wielding words and a pen more readily than the scientist or the man of affairs, has a duty to perform as interpreter of America to Europe. For with all the mass media of today and the loud propaganda techniques in use, America is a strangely misinterpreted country and its true qualities are often unacknowledged.

The pioneers who first developed this continent and the emigrants who followed them in the nineteenth century were predominantly artisans, workmen, and peasants from Europe. They found unlimited possibilities when they landed in the New World, but also unlimited hardships. They had to be obsessed by the practical and, since most of them were compatriots of Robinson Crusoe, their genius lay in the realm of the practical. The culture of the country therefore took on a line from which it has hardly swerved. Changing the world through technical applications of science or through education and religion tested by their pragmatic results has continued to be preferred to contemplation of the world, to speculation on the ultimate causes of phenomena, or to the sense of beauty. The gain to this country and to mankind has proved immeasurable. It hardly behooves us, literary scholars migrated from Europe, to talk condescendingly of American achievements in the realm of the *praxis* and to affect a false superiority because we read Plato and Hegel and delight in all that is apparently useless, from metaphysics to poetry. The know-how may be an overrated and overused formula, but without it Europe would not have been saved in World War II, and today its culture might well have been engulfed by Russia.

But one thing strikes and haunts an admiring observer of this country, especially of the youth of this country: the lack of true and deep happiness in many Americans, the inordinate number of frustrations and inhibitions, of nervous defects manifested by stuttering and trembling, the frequent recourse, in the upper classes, to drinking as a means of forgetfulness or of escape, the fear of worry, of unbalance, of inadaptation in a large group of young Americans, and even of others who have ceased to be young but have not acquired serenity and inward peace. Let us grant that observers from Latin countries have a tendency to believe that they alone possess the secrets of sanity and of a happy sex life and are prone to boasting of what is left to them since other material advantages are denied them. Let us make an allowance for the sly pleasure which a foreigner tends to experience in declaring the nationals of another country universally crazy. And let us not forget that the progress of medicine in America has aimed largely at diagnosing evils which elsewhere did not receive a name and therefore remained ignored, and at pointing to the mental and psychosomatic sources of many of our troubles, as most of the germ diseases were being eradicated.

It remains nevertheless that many of us who have the future of America at heart cannot help being concerned by our observation of growing numbers of persons who seem to live on the verge or in the fear of disintegration. Breakdowns, failures of nerve, panicky terrors at themselves, psychiatric ills are all too frequent an occurrence in a land where the material level of existence has been raised higher than ever before in history and where happiness is supposed to be the goal of many. This writer for one has often been reminded, in observing his American friends and students, of John Stuart Mill's *Autobiography* and of the crisis undergone by the British philosopher whose early development had been too exclusively intellectual and had overlooked emotional forces, poetry, and beauty. The gospel of work and the philosophy of utilitarianism proved baneful to him, and analysis driven to an excess of dryness had worn away the capacity to feel. Samuel Coleridge's lines,

*Work without hope draws nectar in a sieve,*
*And hope without an object cannot live,*

he was to recite to himself after he had discovered Wordsworth and Coleridge and the love for poetry, which were to
save him from his acute depression. We profoundly believe
that the therapeutic virtue of poetry, of literature in general,
of the arts has been underestimated in American education,
and that the study of literature should also be the enjoyment of literature.

We have lost much through neglecting one of the most
beautiful words, and things, in the world, if rightly conceived: pleasure. Criticism, in the last decades, in its effort
to ape science and to evolve a vocabulary similar to that of
science, has been guilty. The teaching of literature has become more abstruse than any laboratory science. The sole
concern seems to be for epistemological values, and a self-
respecting sophomore scribbling an essay on Donne or
Proust will use the word at least three times per page.
Naïveté and naturalness are hunted out. No one is supposed to understand modern novels if he has not delved into
symbols, into Jung's archetypes and ancestral myths, into
Frazer and Jessie Weston, into Kenneth Burke and I. A.
Richards. Our debt is certainly considerable to those great
minds. But a businessman taking a daily train to his bank,
a diplomat sailing to Europe, a scientist, or an intelligent
lady no longer dares open a novel of some intellectual stand-
ing or a volume of critical essays for fear of being an in-
truder in a chapel where only an unhappy few may worship.
We have systematically narrowed literature down through
reducing it to "literature as such," and we no longer deserve the tribute paid to it by men of the past who advocated
it for what it should be: refined pleasure.*

---

* The scientist, Thomas H. Huxley, addressing the South London working men's college in 1868, reserved a large place for
literature in his address: "A Liberal Education and Where to Find
It." "For literature," he said, "is the greatest of all sources of refined pleasure, and one of the great uses of a liberal education is

If a French-born writer, whose country has long been credited with some experience in the field of criticism, may presume to proffer some advice, he would suggest that, with the immense development of literary study in universities since 1920, American scholars and critics have not yet adequately discharged their duty to writers and to the public. "Criticism stands like an interpreter between the inspired and the uninspired," said Carlyle. If the inspired are the creators themselves, they have scant reason for being grateful to critics. Except for some reviewers (whose task is one of information and who are hurried by the journalistic mores of a country in which "news" is only what has just happened or what is going to appear the next day) critics seldom take the trouble to write a thoughtful appreciation of contemporary writers. Hart Crane had been in his watery grave for a decade or two when comprehensive studies of his poetry appeared. There are very few if any which evaluate Wallace Stevens, Robinson Jeffers, or E. E. Cummings as poets. Faulkner finally gained recognition because Europe had acclaimed him in earnest and the Nobel Prize consecrated his world fame. Even such accepted giants as Dos Passos and O'Neill have had very few worth-while critical appraisals devoted to their work.

The result has been the intensification of the great cultural evil of American society: the isolation of the writer and the artist, both withdrawing into a pessimism never equaled in any literature except perhaps that of Russia, driven to bitter hostility to all that stands for "the American way of life." The talent displayed since 1910 or 1919 by the men and women writers of America is second to none. But the literature of Hemingway, of Caldwell, of Steinbeck, and of minor luminaries like Saroyan and Capote, and that

---

to enable us to enjoy that pleasure." Enjoyment has similarly disappeared from much of our criticism as it has from some of our abstract art and functional decoration, as though we were yielding to a new wave of puritanism in disguise. Of too few of the critics writing today in America could it be said, as T. S. Eliot said of W. P. Ker: "He was always aware that the end of scholarship is understanding, and that the end of understanding poetry is enjoyment, and that this enjoyment is gusto disciplined by taste."

of Mailer and of James Jones hopelessly lacks two characteristics of a truly great literature: sympathy for the country that it portrays and a powerful intellectual and psychological content. Deriding Babbitt and salesmen and commuters, and singing the praise of some amusing outlaws of *Cannery Row* or of *Tortilla Flat*, of bullfighters or huntsmen among the hills of Africa or of warriors rapturously basking in the love of Spanish or Italian ladies is entertaining for a while. But if American literature is to compete in solidity with the best that the French or the Russians have produced, it must also treat its characters with more seriousness, identify itself not only with primitives and violent outlaws but with average Americans, as Flaubert, Tolstoy, Proust did with their characters even while satirizing them. The lack of intellectual content and of a serious and constructive *Weltanschauung* has prevented a great age of American letters from ranking with the classics and claiming its share in the training of the young. Scholars and critics should have helped writers assume such a natural role.

On the other hand, we must confess that while appreciation of music and painting has grown immensely in America in the last thirty years, qualitatively and quantitatively, the appreciation of literature has not increased in a manner commensurate with the extension of literacy and with the inordinate growth in the number of people who have gone to college. There lies the chief failure of educators and scholars. The number of magazines in which some pretense of interest in literature is retained has consistently decreased since *The Dial*, *The Bookman*, the *North American Review*, and several others were decently buried. The others have steadily and niggardly reduced the space given to critical essays. The American theatre is in a woeful plight, and very few thoughtful articles ever appear in which this plight is analyzed and remedies are proposed. Over two million young people attend college at present, and only a trickle of those ever continue reading serious books after they have entered "mature" life. Financial resources flow generously to those who undertake surveys of average communities in Middletown or Elmtown, studies of Russian, Chinese, or Indonesian behavior; we will soon implement Point Four, provide funds for other countries intent on spreading their own culture inside and outside their borders. But so-called research organizations are reluctant to assist literary magazines in America, the publication of critical and scholarly volumes, in a word the diffusion of literary culture in the wealthiest but also perhaps the most incurious of great countries.

To many of the European intellectuals who have migrated to the United States and have insisted that the rest of the world is today appealing to America for more than technical know-how and material help, for an ideal and for an intellectual and imaginative crusade for a better world, such a failure on the part of American civilization to spread its literary culture without diluting its essential virtue is the one black spot on the horizon. A naturalized scholar and critic is thus led to the conviction that, while adding to the mass of extant knowledge is his own dearest pursuit, he must in this country bend more of his energy to win larger groups to the appreciation of cultural values and of other civilizations. He must become a popularizer in the good sense of the word and, as the French say, work at the democratic "diffusion" of knowledge and artistic value even harder than at the acquisition and selfish enjoyment of it. In thinking and doing thus, he is not importing "foreign" and "arty" prejudices from Europe into the New World. He is confident that he is pursuing the true cultural development of America as it was envisioned by the great men who in the eighteenth century founded this country. He is faithful to the ideal set forth by two great Americans of the last century, whose words should conclude this essay. Oliver Wendell Homes, warning us against the excessive stress on technical and specialized training in America, once wrote:

If a man is a specialist, it is most desirable that he should also be civilized . . . that he should see things in their proportion. Nay, more, that he should be passionate as well as reasonable, that he should be able not only to explain, but to feel;

that the ardors of intellectual pursuit should be relieved by the charm of art, should be succeeded by the joy of life become an end in itself.

Walt Whitman, than whom no man spoke more nobly of literature, did not mince words when, soon after 1870, he asserted in a text published in *Democratic Vistas* that "our New World democracy, however great a success in uplifting the masses out of their sloughs, in materialistic developments . . . is an almost complete failure . . . in really grand religious, moral, literary and esthetic results." He counted on literature to achieve the redemption of woman and to voice the profoundest aspirations of America to the rest of the world:

Literature, in our day and for current purposes, is not only more eligible than all the other arts put together, but has become the only general means of morally influencing the world.

# French and American Education

Any comparison between two countries offers an invitation to perilous generalizations. It can only be attempted with modest diffidence and for well-informed readers willing to add the needed nuances to statements which must necessarily appear dogmatic; for they cannot, except in tedious parentheses, take into account the exceptions which should qualify every sweeping assertion. Such a comparison should naturally be attempted with the utmost fairness, and probably ask for forgiveness through the saving grace of humor.

The importance of sound information on the way in which other countries train their youth is obvious. For education reflects the history of a nation, as well as its aspirations, and the future it is trying to build for itself. It constitutes, along with law and juridical institutions, one of the most faithful mirrors to the national psychology. A nation, even if it borrows models from abroad when it organizes or reorganizes its schools and its colleges, soon molds them according to its own needs and instills an original spirit into them. Hence the difficulty which many of us experience in trying to evaluate the educational achievement of a foreign country. Terminology is misleading; superficial analogies are deceptive; the same curricula of studies are interpreted according to radically divergent methods; the results obtained by the study of seemingly parallel subjects have little in common.

Yet there must be some underlying similarities behind apparent differences, and some solid ground for mutual understanding. Education is, along with religion, the most potent means for changing man. And changing man is to-day the momentous issue facing the modern world entering upon the second half of the twentieth century and the sixth year of the atomic era. The problems with which man is confronted today can only be solved through better education. Men of all countries must be enabled to harness mechanical forces and to offset the terrifying progress of science through a corresponding expansion of their own spiritual and moral powers. They must also succeed in increasing their mutual understanding and their co-operative endeavors to live in peace and under more social justice. They must therefore emphasize, not the factors through which they differ from each other, but those which make them members of one race and inhabitants of one world. A keener insight into the elements in their education which have made two great Western peoples different and yet complementary, and animated with respect toward each other, is a desirable goal.

Education in France can, like many French things, boast of a very long past and occasionally revolt against too overpowering a legacy. Four centuries at least of French intellects have proposed theories on education. Through a strange pattern of alternation, the French seem to go through periods of boundless hope that man and the world in which he lives can be radically improved, then through phases of skepticism in which they stress the evil inherent in human nature and the obstacles preventing man from marching toward the condition of a superman or of a god. The sixteenth century, with Rabelais and Montaigne, the eighteenth century with Diderot and Condorcet were confident that progress, through more knowledge better assimilated, could become a reality. Many of us in the twentieth century profess a similar faith sobered down by tragic disillusions. On the contrary, the seventeenth century and (insofar as one can safely generalize about a rich and contradictory age) the nineteenth, warned against premature expectations that man could be transformed through education. The Jesuits and chiefly the Jansenists, novelists like Balzac, then the Naturalists, poets and thinkers haunted by the tragic consequences of the Revolution and convinced that evil was ineradicable in man, stood for prudent pessimism.

Such a long succession of manifold views on education has left in the French some cynicism as to the educational systems which blossom forth, and often mushroom luxuriantly, in fertile America. Most educators affect an attitude of wait and see toward the "new" psychological discoveries made into the mind and behavior of children, and the tests which claim to assess their mental powers or deficiencies. An English saying would neatly sum up their position on the subject; it warns: "Never run after a bus, a woman, or an educational theory. There will be another along very soon."

Hence the legacy of past traditions is not often challenged in France in the field of education. "Plus ça change, plus c'est la même chose." The French expect less than their American colleagues from the main indoor sport practiced by faculties on United States campuses: a periodical and lengthy discussion on the reform of the curriculum. They instinctively, after they have lived through their early years of fermentation and rebellion in Parisian cafés, take refuge in traditions, assume that their predecessors were not necessarily fools or backward idiots, and take the easy course of teaching as they themselves once were taught, and their fathers before them.

Next to skepticism on educational theories and this fondness for continuity, the leading feature of French education is probably its strict organization by the State. Private universities are very few and enjoy limited prestige in France; private schools (practically all of them Roman Catholic) are more important, but they cannot confer any degrees. Their teaching staff is not comparable in quality to the *agrégés* of the State *lycées* and Universities. Yet, contrary to what many Americans might imagine, political influences play virtually no part in the French educational system. The professors enjoy full freedom of thought and of speech, and governmental interference has never, since the Third Republic came into being, constituted a problem.

The character of the French educational system, however, was greatly colored by the purpose assigned it by its founders: the Revolution and Napoleon. That purpose was to train state officials, army officers, teachers and members of the so-called liberal professions (doctors, lawyers, magistrates, etc.). Hence a striking emphasis on uniformity of training for the young men of the same social group or of the same ability all over France, irrespective of local conditions; hence also a rigid hierarchy, students being admitted to the more advanced stage of their training only after being sifted through competitive examinations. This rigidity and this uniformity, however, proved no great evil in a country geographically small as compared to the United States and has never hampered the survival of French individualism—as sturdy if not as "rugged" as the American brand.

But a more regrettable consequence has been a persistent reluctance of French youth to engage in careers other than the traditional government positions and the professions. Only at a relatively late stage did it become normal for the most successful young men graduating from school or college to contemplate a business career. While America trained her best men for business life and avowedly money-making pursuits (often transfigured by the semireligious cloak of social service), France looked down upon directing her best minds to industrial and commercial enterprise. She is now repairing some of the harm thus done, but the prejudice still lingers. French business has consequently often been deficient in imagination, initiative and energy.

To the French, the mark of a well-educated man is his ability to be sincerely interested in a variety of subjects, especially in the arts and letters, in history, philosophy. The cultured Frenchman is at once to be singled out among his compatriots through a certain refinement of speech, a valuable gift of self-expression, and because he seems to be at home in "general ideas." Matthew Arnold, after a tour of inspection of French schools once defined the ideal proposed to the French boy by the continental system of education: "to understand himself, and the world." Such an ideal is pursued through intense study of literature and the classics, through theoretical science, and a steady habit of psychological introspection. It is also pursued outside of bookish instruction. Gertrude Stein once remarked that, to be fully educated, a Frenchman also had to spend a few years in Paris, squandering away the patrimony thriftily laid aside by his family and taking one or several mistresses. This (which is also a Goethean ideal) goes by the name of sentimental education. When the Frenchman feels that he is able to talk on a variety of topics, ranging from politics to feminine psychology, from Descartes to Picasso, he returns tamely to his provincial city to occupy a post as a placid "fonctionnaire" and raise a bourgeois family.

The assumption of the French education system is, in other words, that to prepare oneself for one's probable career ("vocational education"), is a narrowing down of man's potentialities, and probably a mistaken calculation, for one seldom does in life what one has laboriously fitted oneself to do. On the contrary, leisure may well be the most precious and the most important part of one's life, especially if the expansion of mechanical devices is to increase the leisure hours allotted to modern man. And the ability to enjoy those leisure hours with some intelligence and taste, that is, with enhanced pleasure, should be one of the achievements of education. Much should be said for such a view of education for life and not merely for a career as a competent specialist locked up in one trade conscientiously mastered. Circumstances have demonstrated repeatedly, in America as elsewhere, that men trained along the traditional lines of a time-honored humanistic ideal also prove the readiest to take on new tasks when the need arises and to face unforeseen difficulties victoriously.

Finally, teachers and professors are selected with the utmost care in France, where there never was any lack of candidates for an esteemed profession. Teachers enjoy a status which affords them regular salary increases, tenure, and independence. They must, of course, have passed stiff competitive examinations which alone open for them a teaching career. Their intellectual competence is universally acknowledged, and their prestige in the communities in which they live is much greater than in countries where wealth tends to be the sole standard.

In several of these respects, the picture of education in America is to be drawn in colors contrasting sharply to those of French education.

Traditions are naturally less strong in a relatively new country and the humanistic ideal which was that of the cultured groups in America in the eighteenth century has gradually lost ground within the last hundred years, as education became more and more democratized. The consequences have been a far greater scope for innovations and a marked diversity of quality in different sections of a very wide country. It is easy to deride some of the excesses and "fads" which occasionally mar American education in some of its ill-advised reforms. Native observers have often ridiculed them. Thus personal hygiene has been made an important subject in some schools, ranking before spelling and history: it is indeed, but might be taught earlier and elsewhere and not at the expense of traditional subjects. It is reported that theoretical and practical studies on the best method of dishwashing have led to an advanced university degree; marriage problems are one of the most august subjects lectured upon on not a few campuses, without yet, it seems, bringing much improvement in the divorce situation of the country or greater domestic bliss to university graduates than to other groups. Many loudly advertised innovations proposed in some progressive schools have, in truth, shown much childishness and proved futile. Yet, and when all is said, the flexibility of American institutions is also a great advantage they enjoy over French schools hampered by routine and fearful even of reasonable innovations.

American colleges have not neglected the training of doctors, lawyers, government officials, but it is probably true that a majority of their graduates aim at a business career and the emphasis has been on training young men for industry, engineering, banking, commerce, business administration, more than for a civil service. Such an emphasis is not to be regretted; it could be fruitfully imitated by some of the older countries in Europe, now in dire need of increasing their productivity and the efficiency of their industrial management. But the formation of an able group of civil servants, of diplomats, of men competent to assume posts in the military government in Germany and Japan, in the economic agencies created since the War, in cultural and information services abroad, was not strenuously pushed until very lately. America, having to play an international role far more complex than that ever assumed by Great Britain, has too few men of wide outlook, well-informed in the foreign countries and their backgrounds, conversant with foreign languages. More general culture and less technical training (for the latter is often best acquired on the job itself) might have served the purpose.

The utilitarian prejudice has been too widespread and has blinded many American educators. While young men must obviously acquire certain skills which they may need in their chosen career, they fail to see that the practical and vocational part of their training is often doomed to remain the least useful. For one seldom stays in the career one had chosen at eighteen or twenty. Some general culture, the ability to exercise common sense or sound judgment, the discernment of men, some personal charm, are more valuable assets in life than too narrow and specialized a training.

Finally, in spite of immense progress achieved in the present century, the quality of the teaching staff is not uniformly high in all American schools. The best American universities have risen to a position of eminence which ranks them undeniably among the very finest in the world today. Many of the secondary school teachers are unequalled for competence, devotion, teaching skill, and the intellectual energy which drives them to eschew stagnation and complacency. But in several sections of the country, the teaching profession still counts too many members who adopted it because there was nothing better for them to do. Their cultural refinement and even their mastery of their subject leave much to be desired. A sentence, culled at random in *Harper's Magazine* for July 1948, is typical of the jokes which consequently assail teachers and keep them from winning the social prestige which would be desirable: "An American is never beaten. If he is too lazy to farm, too ignorant to keep books, too ornery to clerk in a store, there are always three lines he can fall back on, that require no special ability. He can teach school, govern the state, or edit a newspaper."

Underlying these differences and explaining them in part, there are obviously contrasting social conditions which have molded special answers to definite needs, and an implicit view of human nature which varies from the Old World to the New.

France is an old country, with many officials, many white-collared clerks. Her problem is to keep young men away from those overstaffed professions, and to reserve the available positions in them to carefully selected candidates. The necessary selection is practiced early: from the age of twelve or fourteen the French boy becomes accustomed to seeing only a fraction of his class (twenty, thirty per cent at most) receive grades higher than fifty out of one hundred or, as the French call it, above average. The proportion of successful candidates at the baccalaureate, that is graduating successfully from secondary schools, is forty per cent. In America, seventy or seventy-five per cent would be the corresponding average, and the parents of a school boy seldom tolerate a teacher who is a systematic low grader. "Poor dears!" they exclaim, "they work so hard!" "Why should they not deserve to pass, in this free country of ours?" Yet the selection of the best or of the fittest takes place also in America; but it occurs later, in the professional schools, or even in life itself, and it is done according to standards which take into account character, adaptabil-

ity, energy, tact, and not only the quality which every
French mother reveres almost exclusively in her child: "Il
est si intelligent!" will she declare with conviction and
pride.

It may be added without paradox that the French teacher
would feel insulted in his self-esteem if he had to give
grades of ninety, ninety-five, ninety-eight, as some generous teachers sometimes do in America. For is he not himself the standard and paragon of intellectual achievement
for his class, and therefore equivalent to one hundred? And
is it conceivable that youngsters, however gifted, could
draw perilously near to that ideal figure? A well-known
feature of the French educational system is the remoteness
from the professors which it takes for granted and for
beneficent. A university professor will consider as a matter
of course that universities exist for the sake of professors
primarily, and that students attend them to justify the professor's salary and existence. He will seldom open his door
wide for discussion with the immature students, or consent
to endless office-hours. He will expect a certain amount of
deference from the youth. To be called by his first name by
his students, or by his children, would be to the Frenchman
a familiarity at which he would shudder.

Closely allied to this remoteness is the deep-seated conviction that there is much value in discipline per se, and
that education consists above all in the acquiring of some
mental disciplines (concentration and elasticity of the mind,
the habit of steady effort, the art of clarifying one's ideas
and ordering them neatly). The French would admit reluctantly that the child or even the young man has very
much worth while to say until he reaches the "age of reason." Let him therefore until then concentrate on carefully
translating from Latin or Greek, English or German, the
thoughts of others, or build up a framework, "un cadre"
in which he will present his ideas and feelings, when he has
some which are his own, and develop a lucid and elegant
gift of style if possible. Such a discipline, far from stifling
the personality of the young man, will probably tend to
deepen it through long restraint. Besides, it inures him to

one of the most common occurrences in life, that of being bored, and teaches him how to tolerate boredom with good grace. Lessons at school and lectures in college do not attempt to entertain the child needlessly: they cultivate a certain severity, are not afraid of abstraction in thought and language.

The strange fact is that such a stern training given to young men seems to enhance their zest for enjoying life later. When the French boy is finally freed from required courses, dignified lectures, and competitive examinations, at twenty or twenty-five, he decides it is time for him to enjoy life. Indeed he does so, often until the advanced age of seventy or eighty, without an excessive zeal for work or the superstition that work is the sole pastime worthy of a busy adult. The American has been so happy in the Eden of his school and college days that the transition to life is a hard one for him. Competition then becomes nerve-racking. To spend two hours at lunch and one or two in the later afternoon at a café terrace would appear a most un-American inactivity. The graduate for whom college years were made comfortable, with passing "gentleman's" grades, secured with calculated effort, ample leisure hours allotted to games, is suddenly confronted with stark realities. He has to learn that the habit of being patiently and suavely bored, by his pompous boss, by business meetings and professional lunches, by the Sunday papers and even by his wife's chat by the fireside (or by the television set) must be acquired some time in life, since it was spared him by too considerate professors. He will insist upon a few cocktails, when he has left the reassuring activity of his office, to make the empty and tedious leisure hours palatable.

Finally, it is often repeated that sports have no place in French education and that a regrettable lack of team spirit ensues which is the bane of French politics. Whoever has traveled on French roads lately may testify to the huge number of young men and women addicted to walking, bicycling, camping, climbing, etc. Sport, as a topic for conversation, has probably displaced art, politics, even love, and now ranks second only to food and cooking in France.

Yet it remains true to say that the French do not have the religion of exercise; they practice sport for sheer enjoyment, not for its educational and moral value. Their physical endurance does not seem impaired by their spending a few afternoons a week poring over their books instead of racing about hockey fields. Besides, the relative lack of comfort of many French houses forces them to walk up and down several floors blithely every day, where Americans rush to an elevator, even to reach the very room of the gymnasium where they are going to exercise strenuously for their health. An American colleague, a disbeliever in systematic exercise, used to answer his commiserating friends who asked him how he could ever get along without exercising: "I get all the exercise I need by going to the funerals of my friends who died at forty or fifty from having taken too much exercise."

At the basis of American ideas on education, one discovers a basic creed: that the child is good and that education must not contradict or vitiate that essential goodness of human nature. In a general way, the Frenchman holds to an opposite belief, often called Jansenist, according to which evil is deeply ingrained in man, and in woman just a little more, but also more gracefully, so. Religious visitors from France to American colleges have often expressed their dismay at those young Spartans who seem to be immune from all belief in original sin. More cynical French writers on "l'amour en Amérique" (they are legion!) remark that relations between the sexes lack the Christian condiment in America, since, according to Anatole France's famous saying, "Christianity had done much for love by branding it as sin."

This optimism of American educators makes their task arduous and must direly strain the patience of American mothers. For not only is the child deemed good, but the child is right, and must be listened to. If he insists he wants a certain dish at the restaurant, then changes his mind for a second one, then for a third, one submits meekly to such whims. To do otherwise, and slap him in the face with a warning that he must have the first dish ordered for him by his mother, would be considered a cruel encroachment on the child's personality and a dangerous cultivation of inhibitions in the youngster. The fear of inhibitions and complexes in their progeny seems to haunt parents and teachers in the happy New World where Freud should have been born. Though an ironic revenge of immanent justice few adults in fact seem more often afflicted with inhibitions than the Americans; to a Frenchman, it makes them doubly interesting, and to a Frenchman of letters three times more so than his compatriots who squander their energy in extrovert talk and vehement gestures, and apparently go through life without having to pursue books entitled "Peace of Mind" or "How to Avoid Worrying." The Frenchman naïvely sipping his apéritif cannot understand the look of higher delight which beams in an American's face when he proclaims at a cocktail party: "I have to drink in order to release my inhibitions" or "my doctor orders it for my heart." But he wonders whether it was then advisable to have the same persons, as children, torment their parents and teachers because they had to enjoy full freedom from their elders so as not to become "inhibited."

One must add however that life has a regular way of contradicting all the principles followed in one's education. The Frenchman, brought up rather sadly and taught discipline, usually becomes a rebel, refusing to cooperate with his compatriots or even to acknowledge party lines, or cross a street where he is told to; his cheerfulness seems to persist stubbornly under his "Jansenist" training. The American child is often preserved from the inhibiting hypocrisy of politeness, disregards his elders when playing, shouting, roller-skating, or turning on the radio full blast for hours. When grown up, he is often the most polite and the most considerate of creatures. He is trained at school to cultivate self-expression, through child-paintings, childish poems, and later on college verse and college short stories which parents and teachers pretend to admire dutifully (alas! they may even be sincere!). Yet he is, when grown up, shy and tormented by scruples, by frustration, inferiority complexes, as compared to his French counterparts. This charming unpredictability of the results which may crown our efforts and of the baffling answer given by life to our theories is, or should be, a healthy reminder to all our builders of educational structures.

Today, the Americans and the French are better informed on each other than they ever were. Theories, examples, teachers and students are regularly exchanged between the two countries. While fundamental differences probably will persist, a valuable cooperation is also being established. The French have, during and since the war, become aware of some deficiencies in their educational system which could profitably be reformed according to American examples. Not only are they becoming more appreciative of physical education, and more in favor of trusting the youth instead of preaching it the value of severity and of discipline, but they seem to have derived four main lessons from their open-minded observation of American examples:

*1*) Make their secondary education less literary and more scientific or more empirical.

*2*) Develop technical education as the best hope to modernize their industry, and even more their agricultural methods.

*3*) Without renouncing all the benefits of an exacting but often negative critical spirit, teach French youth the value of cooperation, and show it that intelligent individualism can well coexist with team-work.

*4*) Value the qualities of freshness and vitality, present in American college youth, on a par with those of order and finish. Essays turned out by the best of American students, while unacademic and unorthodox by French standards, amateurish in their composition, unskilled in the art of transitions, are characterized by a spontaneous and ebullient vitality, fearless personal thinking, which many a French student might well envy.

In the United States on the other hand, some trends have lately been conspicuous which narrow the gulf that seemed to separate the educational views of the two countries:

*1*) A battle is being waged between the humanistic and

the scientific or technical ideals, and the second is by no means assured of victory. Many scientists, no longer convinced that the progress of science necessarily benefits mankind, seized with remorse and even with panic before the latest atomic discoveries, turn to philosophy, religion, the arts and letters, to offset the inhumanity with which modern man is threatening himself.

2) The elective system, once favored by Harvard and many eastern universities, has lost ground, and the belief has spread that education requires that the youth receive a certain amount of fundamental knowledge, so that it be made conscious of the continuity between the past and the present, and of the common store of information which educated men living together in one country should own.

3) Democracy tends to be understood in less fallacious a manner. For some time, it was foolishly interpreted as the right for every young man to elect any course he liked, integrate them as he might. It was also taken to mean a sufficient level of education for the masses, at the expense of the so-called "élite," which could afford some levelling down. America, to be sure, is not inclined to favor any class education, and the word "élite" is unsavory to her. But, as an American educator, Abraham Flexner, once remarked: "Universities must at times give the nation, not what it wants, but what it needs." True democracy can and must coexist with some leadership, that is, know how to extract from its own midst the elements best fit to serve it. In peacetime, and even more so in time of emergency, the fate of a democracy rests in the hands of a few statesmen, generals, admirals, business organizers and administrators; a great deal indeed will depend upon the training once received by the leaders of the country, and their ability to utilize the best citizens.

4) The peoples of the world have to reach a higher degree of economic, political and spiritual unity, or risk the danger of mutual annihilation. The role of America is today preponderant in all international moves. Yet the country suffers from a lack of men trained to understand the other nations from the inside, i.e. not only through statistics

of their economic life, but in their language, traditions, sensibility, national psychology. The masses of America, which ultimately determine her foreign policy, are inadequately informed on the Western nations with which their fate, for better or for worse, is bound up today. Only through more windows intelligently opened on the outside world will great nations learn how to understand, tolerate, and respect each other, and some day to alienate some part of their sovereignty in a federation, or in a series of unions culminating perhaps in a world government.

Through their long-standing friendship, their mutual trust and their community of ideals, two nations like America and France can cooperate today in exchanging the best in their educational systems, in learning different lessons from each other.

Thus they may point the way to a war-ridden world toward the end of nationalism and the growth of international understanding. Bergson wrote in his last great work that "mankind is not sufficiently aware that its future is in its own hands." Only through broader education can mankind perhaps become aware of it, and work its own salvation.

# American Literature Through French Eyes

O NE OF THE STRIKING PHENOMENA of world literature
in the last twenty years has been the emergence of
modern American literature as the more important of the
two literatures in the English language. The drama and
the poetry, but chiefly the novel, of America have risen to
a position of prestige and influence abroad seldom equalled
in history. Three out of every four translations from the
English language currently published in France—and in
Italy, Russia, South America—are from American works.
"Traduit de l'américain" has become a magical catchword
in Paris, and a quick selling device for book publishers.

This vogue of American letters abroad is all the more
remarkable as it stands in sharp contrast to the failure of
other artistic means of expression of America to establish
themselves in Europe. In spite of determined though perhaps ill-conceived attempts made since 1944, exhibitions of
American paintings organized in London and Paris have
met with a total lack of interest. American composers have
been played abroad before polite but frigid audiences. Architecture arouses greater admiration: Frank Lloyd Wright
is revered as a legendary figure; but American buildings,
in part for obvious reasons, have not been imitated to any
marked extent. As to the movies, the time is gone when

European intellectuals composed subtle essays on the profundity and the genius of Charlie Chaplin. Never has the stock of Hollywood stood so low among European (and perhaps American) audiences.

More and more, the idea of America held in Western Europe, and elsewhere among the people where literacy is widespread, is molded by American novels—and not by the movies or the travelers and soldiers whom one may have observed. This extraordinary prestige of American letters has come at an opportune moment, when several of the traditionally great literatures of Europe have seemed to be undergoing a crisis. Modern Russia has not had the first-rate novel which alone would have explained the country's revolutionary era to millions of foreign readers. When the outside world wanted to understand Russian heroism during the recent war, it turned to Tolstoy's "War and Peace." Kafka, who has been dead since 1924, and Rilke, whom death silenced in 1926, are the German literary forces most keenly felt abroad. (The influence of the Mann brothers has been slight on literature.) Little of modern Italian, Spanish, and South American letters has been able to win large audiences. France alone, with Malraux, Giono, Saint-Exupéry, the Existentialists, her war poets, has proved a great international force through the last decade. And not a little of the revived energy and appeal of French fiction has been due to its original assimilation of American influences.

As to Great Britain, the ordeal of the war strained her energies to the breaking-point without affording her the opportunity to create literature which the Resistance and the temptation to flaunt their "artistic superiority" before the invader gave the French. English literature has been so continuously rich for three hundred years or more that the present eclipse can be only temporary. But, since the passing of Lawrence, Joyce, and even Virginia Woolf, the English novel has lacked power to renew itself. E. M. Forster, acclaimed by many as the chief English novelist alive, cannot rank with the giants. Graham Greene has more forcefulness. Richard Hillary, had he lived, might have risen high. Maugham, Huxley, Waugh, Isherwood seem pale compared to the ebullient energy of their American contemporaries. The drama of England can boast of no O'Neill. Even her finest poets of the thirties, Auden, Spender, Day Lewis, MacNeice, have lately disappointed us. Time will soon tell if, as we personally believe, Eliot's "Four Quartets" has not been ridiculously overpraised. Dylan Thomas has striking originality, but reminds the French of their own Surrealists. Many British intellectuals, at a time when liberated Europe, grateful to the England of the R.A.F., expected a new message from them, were found either to have taken refuge in America or to have been seized with a new "failure of nerve" and to have resorted to Buddhism or Catholicism. England critics and readers have also been swayed by the vitality, apparently needed in Europe, which seems to radiate from American literature.

Contrary to the too diffident explanations offered by American journalists, this focussing of attention on American books is not a mere consequence of the war and a reflection of the accrued respect given the all-powerful country which owns the secret of the future. For Russian arms enjoyed immense prestige in 1942–45, and such prestige did not go automatically to their culture. We are faced with a purely literary phenomenon, which, indeed, was already noticeable five or ten years before Pearl Harbor. The wave of enthusiasm for American books began at the very time when the United States had isolated itself from Europe and when its power seemed sapped by the Great Depression. Indeed American material prosperity, and American power and complacency and nationalism, are conspicuously absent from American books read abroad and do not seem to have ever intoxicated Steinbeck, Dos Passos, O'Neill, or Robinson Jeffers.

What is more, this vogue of American writers has been in no way fostered by the renowned advertising methods of American business or by the official representatives of America in foreign lands. The French have been the past masters of efficient literary strategy. They never spare funds in exporting their bearded Academicians, their latest

Surrealist rebels or abstruse Existentialist prophets. *Life* and *Time* will readily comment upon each move of M. Sartre or his favorite café; *Town and Country* and *Harper's Bazaar* will bring the names of Camus and Anouilh to every smart lady's boudoir. Americans have had one successful traveling salesman for American culture, Waldo Frank, and they have treated him with great reserve. As to their professors of American literature, they have done their best to dampen or deride the European enthusiasm for Hart Crane, Sinclair Lewis, Faulkner, and —not unnaturally—Henry Miller. Representatives of American publishers abroad have frowned for other reasons upon the success of novels unsponsored by book clubs and feared that such novels might convey an unfavorable picture of American civilization. They have tried to divert the enthusiasm of Europeans to Henry James, to the delicate craftsmanship of Willa Cather, to volumes on American history. Their success has been scant. The author of this article has actually read and met several Frenchmen whose fondest dream is to cross the Atlantic some day to see the land of Faulkner or of Caldwell; who are haunted by the vision of California which Steinbeck or Jeffers gave them; and who enjoy the thrill of recognition when they read, on actual signs, the magical words "Main Street" or "Manhattan Transfer."

Any foreign influence is a distortion and a transfiguration. The chief interest of what is called the comparative study of literatures lies precisely in the diversity of the images of our own writers which several mirrors (translations, foreign criticism) reflect for us. The foreign observer does not necessarily gain from his perspective several thousand miles remote, nor does he necessarily lose. He does not presume to tell Americans which are their truest writers, and he is probably deaf to the finer values in their poetry; but he may apply another criterion, that of the fecundity of some works of literature which attract a motley train of admirers and inspire imitators abroad, while others, perhaps purer or more national in appeal, remain without any foreign posterity.

The French have vainly protested against the admiration which went to Alexandre Dumas, Edmond Rostand, more recently to André Maurois, Jules Romains, at the expense of much finer artists and more piercing psychologists like Stendhal and Mauriac. It took several decades for the European Continent to admit that England had greater poets than Byron. Not a few Russians are moved to indignation when foreigners celebrate Dostoevsky as "typically Russian" and endeavor, with little success, to induce us to prefer Pushkin and Gogol.

American writers have, more than any others, been the victims, or the beneficiaries, of European waves of uncritical enthusiasm: Fenimore Cooper, Mrs. Beecher Stowe, Jack London, Frank Norris, Upton Sinclair, Sinclair Lewis, and last but not least, E. A. Poe. As usual in such cases, their own compatriots have punished those writers for their excessive foreign reputation. Fenimore Cooper is studied as an artist in grave doctors' theses at the Sorbonne, and the reverence of Baudelaire, Mallarmé, Valéry, and others for Poe has had no counterpart in this country. French intellectuals are likewise reluctant to admire "Les Misérables" and "Cyrano de Bergerac" and are half-ashamed of "Alexander the Great," as D. W. Brogan recently called Alexandre Dumas, in whom he celebrated the most valuable foreign asset for France. Who knows but that the French and other Europeans may be correct in discovering profound secrets and an inexhaustible imaginative power in Faulkner or Dos Passos? They have already converted several leading American critics to their views.

The classical American literature has received a share of the present French curiosity. Whitman has been praised anew, notably by Gide and Giono. Several new translations of Melville (*Benito Cereno, Billy Budd, Moby Dick, Pierre*) have appeared since 1939. Indeed, the present cult of Melville has had no more ardent prophets than some Europeans like D. H. Lawrence, who, as early as 1923, proclaimed *Moby Dick* "an epic of the sea such as no man has equalled, and a book of exoteric symbolism of profound significance." Hawthorne, long read in Europe, has been recently retranslated. His obsession with crime and with "Freudian" repressions, as well as his pagan aspiration to joy, have made him appear as the ancestor of the present-day American novel. But in psychology and technique he brings little that is radically novel to the successors of Proust, Mauriac, and Julien Green.

Henry James is respected in France by all, read by a very few, and considered as a classic, but without living influence. Proust was content to know him by name only; E. M. Forster has been severe on him; Gide, indoctrinated by his Jamesian friend Charles du Bos, tried in vain to read him. The French, apparently, find that they have the equivalent of James in their own analytical novelists, who are legion, and find his psychology too static and devious, his pace too slow, his content too remote from common life.

Little attraction is also felt for the American writers whom one might group as traditional, or even as genteel. They include excellent craftsmen, usually of the female sex, like Ellen Glasgow and Willa Cather, even Pearl Buck, although she has enjoyed greater success, and Margaret Mitchell; the latter became a best-seller on the black market during the German occupation, but exercised no influence on the writers themselves. Some short stories of Eudora Welty and of Katherine Ann Porter have recently been rendered into French, and their skill may help revive an art which has not received brilliant treatment from French hands for forty years. J. P. Marquand and Louis Bromfield, the latter in spite of his long familiarity with the French scene, lack the power, perhaps the brutality, which the world seems to expect from American literature.

As to naturalism, which is one of the living currents in American fiction, it stems from the French school of Flaubert, Maupassant, and Zola and has therefore little novelty for the French readers of today, who have turned their back on their own realism. W. D. Howells, Stephen Crane, even Upton Sinclair, once perused for their documentary value, are now but names in Europe (except, in the case of Sinclair, for Russia). Dreiser, with all the undeniable power of his earlier works, appears melodramatic and crude. Sinclair

Lewis has long descended from the place of eminence once won with *Main Street* and *Babbitt*. Most of his later works have belonged to the most ephemeral of all types of literature: the literature on social problems. For, as even Ibsen and Shaw have experienced, nothing is deader than a play or a novel on a social problem which has been solved. Between Thomas Wolfe and Latin minds, there seems to prevail a deep-seated incompatibility: the latter find that, even in fiction, the most formless of arts, he is too unrestrained in his deluge of words and of reminiscences, and they do not discern the inner tragedy of the man underlying his long, verbose and solitary quest.

The great names of American fiction are thus in French eyes Hemingway, Steinbeck, Dos Passos, and Faulkner. Scott Fitzgerald is only now being revealed as the precursor of that group. Erskine Caldwell is occasionally added to the American quartet, with a slight note of hesitation caused by the marked inequality between his best and his least good books. These novelists are read and discussed wherever French is spoken and acclaimed by all those who in the Near East, in South America, even in Russia, are inclined to subscribe to French literary fashions. Their heroes and heroines have become familiar accessories of French life. Crossword puzzles have been devised, made up of nothing but titles and characters of American fiction. Elaborate critical disquisitions by the best critics of the day (Sartre, Claude-Edmonde Magny, Blanchot) have analyzed the secret intentions of Faulkner and Dos Passos, the philosophy of Steinbeck, the technique of Hemingway. Until a very few years ago, these novelists had not met with such thorough criticism in their own country.

Whether well-informed or naïve, misguided or penetrating, the outcome of a passing vogue or a more deeply-rooted reaction, the unprecedented success of American literature abroad is a sociological as well as an aesthetic phenomenon of striking significance.

Geographically, the region of the United States which is brought to the fore is no longer New England, once the abode of culture in the New World. It is not even New

York. The literary map of America, as pictured in the minds of millions of foreign readers, draws in sharp outlines the country of Steinbeck, the California of James Cain, the setting of "Desire Under the Elms," and the proud solitude of Carmel and Point Sur, dear to Robinson Jeffers. It also emphasizes the importance of the Middle West, from which have sprung Sherwood Anderson and Hart Crane (Ohio), Lindsay, Sandburg, Edgar Lee Masters, and MacLeish (Illinois), T. S. Eliot and Marianne Moore (both from St. Louis, Missouri).

But the most original American works have since 1930 been inspired by the South. The most active critics have been linked with the Southern periodicals: the now defunct *Southern Review*, the *Virginia Quarterly Review*, the *Sewanee Review*, and occasionally the *Southwest Review*. Allen Tate, John Crowe Ransom, and Robert Penn Warren have even dreamed of building up in the South a new economy as the basis for a better-balanced culture. James Branch Cabell, Ellen Glasgow, and Willa Cather were Virginians. Thomas Wolfe and Margaret Mitchell have popularized other parts of the South which they love. Negro writers, at least two of whom have been warmly admired in France, the novelist Richard Wright and the fine poet Langston Hughes, have added to the poetical prestige of the South. Above all, Erskine Caldwell in Georgia and William Faulkner in his Yoknapatawpha County in northern Mississippi have done for those states what Thomas Hardy did for his Wessex and Walter Scott for Scotland, Giono for Provence and Mauriac for the French Bordelais: they have annexed new provinces to literary geography, won for their native districts an epic glamor which is already attracting pilgrims there.

Such is the magic of literary creation. The South, vanquished in the Civil War, left behind in the economic struggle, the depressed area of the United States in the eyes of many Americans, has had its revenge: it has won the literary battle of America. Through the South, the immense continent seems to have gained a consciousness of tradition and a sense of history. Through the South also, it has acquired the sense of tragedy which haunts Southern novelists (Wolfe in *You Can't Go Home Again* and Faulkner in *A Rose for Emily*) like a curse; but this sense of history and of tragedy was probably necessary to the growth of American literature since its expansion beyond Concord and Boston and Baltimore. Faulkner, like Hardy in England and Mauriac in France, has tapped the richest source of fictional themes for a novelist: the excessive concentration of life in a restricted provincial environment, the jealous spying of family upon family, the bitter struggle between dispossessed traditional heirs and brutal newcomers. Above all this, he has conjured up the ghost of slavery which hovers over his novels and for which the South must still atone. The fascination of the American South has proved so great for several younger writers of France who have never crossed the Atlantic that they have unwittingly transplanted that setting into their own novels of French life; one hears Negro spirituals in the Pyrenees or drinks Jamaica rum in Burgundy to exorcise ancestral spirits; the fields are planted with cotton or with corn, and the smell of sassafras perfumes the countryside. Thus the mechanical imitation of much-admired American novels has played upon some French writers the same literary trick of which American poets had been victims in the early nineteenth century, when they conscientiously composed hymns to skylarks and odes to nightingales without ever having heard or seen those fabulous European birds!

Strangely enough, the natural scenery of America which now populates the imagination of European readers is no longer that of Mayne Reid or Fenimore Cooper, not even that of Jack London's stories. It is seldom that of New England or the Middle Western plains, for neither Robert Frost's verse nor evocations of "American beauty" attempted by Edna Ferber or LeGrand Cannon, neither Ruth Suckow's descriptions of Iowa nor Willa Cather's Nebraska scenery in *One of Ours* have succeeded in bringing those aspects of America vividly to foreign eyes. The far West and its colorful canyons, the splendors of Nevada, Arizona, and Colorado, the bays and mountains of Washington and Oregon have had thus far little or no place in American literature; the superb rivers and trees, unequalled on the Euopean Continent, have apparently beggared description or daunted the powers of writer and painter alike. As a result, the main source of local color for readers of American works is the dreary expanse of Georgia or Mississippi, humanized by deeply-rooted traditions and apparently better attuned to the tragic sensibility of literary creators.

The second feature which marks the American novels selected by the French for translation is their violence. The day now seems remote indeed when Flaubert and Zola were deemed too brutal for English-speaking readers! The compatriots of Proust and Céline apparently find their own literature too tame, for they plunge with the delight of exotic discovery into the improbable scenes of American letters. Desertion occurs in almost every war novel, from Dos Passos' remarkable *Three Soldiers* to Hemingway's *Farewell to Arms*. Rape, next to incest, might be judged, from several of these novels, to be a favorite pastime of Americans. O'Neill, Jeffers, even Faulkner seem obsessed by incest. Only homosexuality appears, again judging from literature, to find more favor with the French than with the Americans. Some recent French plays even take place in an American setting, so as to enjoy, one suspects, the advantage of a dramatic lynching scene.

But the amusement and amazement of French readers have been especially aroused by the drinking and loving habits which they find described in American fiction, heightened naturally by the intensity or by the conventionality of art. Heroes of *The Sun also Rises*, of *The Iceman Cometh*, of Dashiell Hammett and others, seem endowed with a superhuman capacity for imbibing at which the French marvel.

As to sex, the French feel vaguely humiliated by the descriptions of American fiction, which are throwing many of their own love stories into the tepid category of Sunday-school reading! Hemingway's evocations of love as the most glamorous of sports next to bull-fighting, Caldwell's *Jour-*

neyman and *God's Little Acre*, Steinbeck's *Wayward Bus* are a veritable orgy of love. Edmund Wilson's *Hecate County* has not yet found its way to France. But the greatest uproar has been caused in 1946–47 by Henry Miller. This disciple of Céline and D. H. Lawrence found himself the cynosure of literary life in 1946. Critics, reporters, moralists aligned themselves for or against him; his books were deemed so perilous to virtue that they were brought to trial, while admirers of *Tropic of Cancer* and of *Tropic of Capricorn* compared their hero to Christ flagellated by jealous or narrow-minded Pharisees! Sober commentators remarked that it had taken an American (long steeped in the most malodorous aspects of Parisian life, to be sure) to have made Céline appear more innocent than a choir-boy and Casanova an impotent weakling.

The entertainment thus derived from the debauchery of violence in American fiction does not go without some feeling of silly complacency among the inheritors of an old culture who like to think of North America as populated by young barbarians. The interest taken by Europeans in the United States has not ceased, since the "Jesuit Relations" and Rousseau, to be an aspect of their taste for primitivism. Few Frenchmen, however, are naïve enough to take the murders, the sexual prowess, and the drinking bouts of American fiction as the faithful copy of American life. Rather do they admire in that violence a healthy if brutal reaction against the monotony and standardization of conditions prevailing in America. After imagining American life as an "air-conditioned nightmare" in which cleanliness reigns supreme, efficiency crushes individuals, and conformity is the law, many of them sigh with relief when they discover that there are also the itinerant destitutes of *The Grapes of Wrath*, the nonconformists of *Tortilla Flat*, the human waifs of *Tobacco Road*, the idiot whose masterly monologue in *The Sound and the Fury* is already a locus classicus of French criticism.

Their esteem for America is in no way impaired by such a contemplation of the seamy side of things. Only Nazi Germany and Stalinist Russia have insisted upon display-

ing in their literature nothing but the clean, efficient, moral
— and lifeless — face of their country: they left the world un-
convinced. Robust and adult nations like the United States
and France know fully well that there is more to their civilization than the Champs Elysées and the Riviera hotels,
than Fifth Avenue and Miami Beach. They are not afraid
to emphasize the uncomely sights of their country in their
plays and novels. Only a few superficial observers will see
in this a proof of French corruption or American brutality.
Behind unusual aspects of the United States, the French
readers of American works seek something deeper, of
which they are in dire need: a message of vitality and a
freshness of vision which raise violence and vice to the
stature of the epic.

For the literature of Europe, however expert in technique
and subtle in psychological dissection, lacks vigor and
knows it. Kafka and Proust, Huxley and Gide, Auden and
Rilke are supremely endowed in intelligence and in sensi-
tiveness; but they lack imaginative power to recreate life,
that is, an intense grasp on the concrete. They are unequalled in self-conscious delineation of moods of frustration and of repression, in polished irony, and even in
searching exploration of the recesses of the ego. But their
readers detect signs of excessive maturity in their overrefined works and yearn for the uncouth youthfulness which
Steinbeck, Hemingway, and Caldwell seem to have in
abundance. The splendid promise of American letters, to
be sure, is seldom fulfilled: the last touches which would assure true greatness, the tranquil recollection which might
sublimate and prolong the shock of immediacy, the depth of
thought which has seldom marred good novels, are often
lacking. But Europeans who dip in *Sanctuary*, *God's Little Acre*, even *The Big Money*, are relieved to discover
characters who take hold of them and plots in which the
authors seem to have earnestly believed. We may picture
their thrill of discovery after living too long with the rare-
fied atmosphere of Proust, the effete irony of Maurois or
E. M. Forster, the unconvincing and laborious synthesis of
Jules Romains, the impalpable halo into which Virginia

Woolf dissolves her heroines, or the pretentious philosophical discourse of Thomas Mann's mouthpieces.

The ambition of the novel has been, since Balzac and Tolstoy, to take the place left vacant by the disappearance of the epic. An element of willful intensification of life has always been necessary to the epic; the power to move heroes through ordeals and battles and to relate adventures with convincingness has been one of the attributes of the epic creator. In this sense, the American novel of today, at its best, comes the nearest to the definition of the epic. Dos Passos in *U.S.A.*, Steinbeck in his admirable *In Dubious Battle*, which is a greater achievement artistically than *The Grapes of Wrath*, and Faulkner in *As I Lay Dying* rank among the epic novelists of our age.

Jean-Paul Sartre, whose prestige is second to none with the contemporary French public, said aptly in his article in the *Atlantic Monthly* for August, 1946: "What we looked for above all in the American novel was something quite different from its crudities and its violence." It was nothing less indeed than a renewal of the setting, of the subject matter, and of the technique of the traditional French novel. The present vogue of American letters is excessive; some of its manifestations are at times ludicrous and will pass away, as the waves of enthusiasm for Byron, Poe, Dostoevsky ebbed away. But they left French (and other European) literatures profoundly transformed.

The French are the unchallenged masters of the *roman d'analyse*. From *La Princesse de Clèves* to Marivaux and Laclos in the eighteenth century, then from Benjamin Constant's *Adolphe* and Stendhal to Proust and Mauriac, their vocation in fiction has been to probe searchingly into the workings of man's mind and soul, to bring to light the hidden motives of actions and the complex nuances of feelings. Proust has gone as far as seems humanly possible in that direction. Nothing was left for French novelists to do, after him, but to break away from an introspection which was becoming static and artificial. Since 1925 or 1930, French fiction, led by Malraux, Saint-Exupéry, Giono, has aimed at capturing the mysteries of man in action and not at rest, at substituting a synthetic perception of human nature for an exclusively analytical dissection. While they were thus seeking new paths away from a valuable but exhausted French tradition, they lit upon Faulkner and Dos Passos — nay, upon Dashiell Hammett, Damon Runyon, Raymond Chandler, and writers who were lesser artists than themselves, but from whom they were ready to learn. In an important interview given in January, 1945, to the English review, *Horizon*, Malraux declared: "To my mind the essential characteristic of contemporary American writing is that it is the only literature whose creators are not intellectuals. . . . They are obsessed with fundamental man. . . . The great problem of this literature is now to intellectualize itself without losing its direct approach."

Malraux converted elder writers like André Gide, who, himself more gifted for abstract analysis of man than for concrete evocation of man's behavior, had instinctively felt the need of more "raw meat" in French literature, which was addicted to dressing and softening its fare. Gide went so far as to proclaim his admiration for the superior detective stories of Dashiell Hammett (*The Thin Man, The Maltese Falcon, The Red Harvest*). The most refined of French novelists are now discovering with eagerness *Miss Lonelyhearts*, the cruel and very able story by Nathaniel West, whose untimely death at thirty-two is one of the gravest losses of modern American literature; John O'Hara's skillful rendering of the atmosphere of the twenties in *Appointment in Samara*; James Cain, Horace McCoy, Damon Runyon, and other "poets of the tabloid murder," as Edmund Wilson once called these novelists of the hard-boiled school.

This is not only contagion of literary fashion. The French have realized lately that their excessively analytical literature was too narrowly addressed to an "unhappy few": the few thousands in any country who are capable of introspection and enjoy the leisure required by such soul-searching. Millions of other potential readers, untrained in such examinations of conscience and often inarticulate, were never reached by the traditional novel of analysis.

These readers had to resort to the coarser type of murder stories. Why not do for them what E. A. Poe and the author of *Crime and Punishment* had already done: cater to their legitimate craving for sensation and the thrill of violent action, while fulfilling many of the requisites of art?

This taste for synthetic as against analytical psychology, for sensations powerfully evoked as against elaborate disquisition of hidden motives, has been apparent in France since Malraux, Giono, and Saint-Exupéry succeeded Proust and Gide in popularity (1930 or thereabout). It became more marked with the war years. The vision of brutality and swift, cruel, illogical action presented by American novels then became an all too real nightmare in the countries invaded by Germany. Any attempt at understanding rationally a baffling apocalypse or at philosophizing about events seemed ludicrous. For the men and women summarily arrested by the Gestapo, huddled together into concentration camps, for the youth exposed to the hazards of the Maquis, American books assumed a prophetic character. They proved to be the ones best attuned to a tragic era of incomprehensible violence and of brutal inhumanity of man to man.

To be sure, the French readers, as some semblance of normalcy is again enjoyed, cannot fail to be sensitive to the lack of art which characterizes much of American literature. Even at present the most gifted followers of Dos Passos (like Sartre), of Hemingway (Camus), of Faulkner (Mouloudji, Desforets, Magnane) are much more preoccupied than their models by the problem of discovering a form for their functional attempts. But such a form will be a richer one for having known a few variations from the older, and outworn, French mold. The writers of the New World have taught the French a refreshing disregard for composition, a total detachment from such rules as unity of plot, a youthful freedom from artistic restraint. Theirs was a type of writing which aimed neither at pure art nor at eternal values, which cared little for posterity or even for survival. To compatriots of Flaubert and Mallarmé, whose sin is to deify literature, the contrast was salutary.

The best among the modern French are not content with imitating their American models. Camus in *La Peste*, Sartre in *Le Sursis*, have beaten Hemingway and Dos Passos at their own game. Elsewhere they have out-Faulknered Faulkner. With more art than their masters, they have used their devices: the Faulknerian reversibility of time, the simultaneous action of Dos Passos, the "punch" of Caldwell's dialogue, the vivid narrative of Steinbeck, Hemingway's "eye on the object." The coarseness and orgy of sex and lust which entertained the French public for a time will soon be forgotten; but the lesson of concreteness, the effectiveness learned in American writing (substituted, in the canon of literary qualities, for abstractness and beauty) are likely to remain. American fiction has brought to European artists a new accumulation of materials.

A last characteristic of modern American books fitted them peculiarly to the days of wrath through which Europe has been living. Their implicit philosophy is one of pessimism. That pessimism may be a constant and deep-seated feature of the literature of America, for, with the exception of Mark Twain in his earlier years and possibly of Walt Whitman, it has characterized most of the important writers of the "young country": Emerson, Poe, Hawthorne, Melville, Emily Dickinson, Henry James, Dreiser, and all our contemporaries, including American-born Julien Green, the gloomiest of present-day French authors. The most disillusioned books about the First World War came from the writers of the country which was physically least affected by it: *The Enormous Room*, *Three Soldiers*, *What Price Glory*, *A Farewell to Arms*. The sharpest revulsion against mechanical civilization, the bitterest satire of businessmen and of ladies' clubs, of the good fellowship of Rotarians and of standardized religion have been expressed by O'Neill and Steinbeck, by the authors of *Elmer Gantry* and of *Journeyman*, even by J. B. Cabell and the Thornton Wilder of *Heaven's My Destination*.

But America need not blush at this literature of despair. Its pessimism is not the sterile mockery of cynics nor the decadent obsession to soil the beauty of the world. It is the expression of sincere idealism, of lucid faith. It asserts with eloquence that all is not well with the world, but that, by facing realities boldly, we could make life more worthy of being lived. If American literature today has scaled epic heights more courageously than any other, it has also plumbed the depths of tragedy. André Malraux, as early as 1933, prefacing the French translation of *Sanctuary*, called Faulkner's book "the intrusion of Greek tragedy into the detective novel." Few writers, since Emily Brontë and Thomas Hardy, have indeed laid a juster claim to being continuators of Sophocles than Faulkner.

The reasons for this tragic pessimism of American writing are complex: they are in part social and reflect the isolation of the artist in a society in which money values are paramount and which esteems him no more than a flute player. They are in part religious, for the fatality of original sin haunts Faulkner as it did his truest predecessor, Hawthorne. O'Neill revives the Catholic doctrine of man's guilt and Jeffers the wailing of the Jewish prophets upon the vanity of everything under the sun. The greatest American poet of the century, Hart Crane, was driven to suicide. Henry Miller, with all his obscene eroticism, is very remote from any cheerful enjoyment of life; his torrent of words hardly conceals an abyss of inner emptiness.

But this tragic obsession of American writers is to be explained chiefly by their acute perception of the gulf which divides man's power to transform the world through science and technology and his powerlessness to change himself. A similar gulf lies gaping between man's proud assertion of his freedom and his bondage to the fatalities that flesh is heir to. His official philosophy bids the American citizen to practice the pursuit of happiness, and as soon as he stops working he is oppressed by boredom and must imbibe a few cocktails so as to endure his leisure hours. He claims to live without tragedy, and he is driven to seek substitutes for tragedy in drinks, sex, or murder stories. He stares several times a day at advertisements which proclaim that women are lovely, pink-cheeked creatures, with immaculately waved hair and alluring silk stockings, intent upon welcoming husbands in the cleanest of modern homes—and no literature is more deeply obsessed than his by misunderstanding and antagonism between the sexes. Seldom has woman been hated, in fiction or drama, and love been reviled as it has been in *Desire Under the Elms*, *Tamar*, *Men Without Women*, *Miss Lonelyhearts*.

But this pessimism is virile. It is probably the deep manifestation of the influence which movies have had upon American letters. Through the shallow conventionality of its films, their sickening happy endings, their fear of the realities of life, Hollywood has driven many of the best American writers to emphasize what the screen has left unsaid: the seamy but authentic and robust aspects of modern life. In so doing, American novelists have provided the psychological life of the country with a healthy outlet. They have been led to eschew sentimentality and to reach for great subjects. Their pessimism and violence conceal a virile quality of warm humanity. Foreign observers have seen it perhaps more acutely than many Americans. The critic of a French weekly, *Action*, wrote on October 6, 1944: "The American novel is well suited to teach us the road to a healthy, powerful literature which finds, in a broad contact with the world, essential reasons for faith in itself." Others lauded plays drawn from American novels and acted with phenomenal success in Paris, *Of Mice and Men*, *As I Lay Dying*, because their humanity had helped them live through the darkest days of the war and the postwar years. J. P. Sartre, who is the influential prophet of a new French generation, paid a debt of gratitude when he declared in 1946:

The greatest literary development in France between 1929 and 1939 was the discovery of Faulkner, Dos Passos, Hemingway, Caldwell, Steinbeck. . . . To writers of my generation, the publication of "The 42nd Parallel," "Light in August," "Farewell to Arms" effected a revolution similar to the one produced fifteen years earlier in Europe by the "Ulysses" of Joyce.

# Humanistic Scholarship and National Prestige

THE PHRASE "NATIONAL PRESTIGE" is not one which scholars pronounce with special alacrity. The very name of Humanities has always implied the transcending of racial, national and linguistic barriers so as not to leave out "anything that is human." And if modesty did not always characterize the Renaissance humanists, inebriated by their newly discovered knowledge and by their superiority over the "profanum vulgus," modern scholars have developed a more sobering view of their place in a scientific and mass age.

But we are all engaged today in rebuilding enlightened and saner international relations, and scholars have an eminent role to play in the better world that we envision. Intellectuals and clerics have been occasionally guilty of betrayals in several lands; but bonds once forged by German and French students, between Italian, Polish, Czech professors momentarily enslaved and their colleagues in other countries, between Europeans and Americans of two hemispheres have almost always outlived the changing fortunes of politics and war. Friendship, mutual esteem and trust thus established among a few are one of the rare solid foundations on which our hopes rest today.

It is therefore, a source of disappointment to many

Americans to find themselves feared, occasionally hated and maligned, more often suspected and misrepresented abroad. Information and propaganda services are the target of much criticism, often unconstructive and biased. It is difficult to depict America, as Americans see it, to under-privileged foreigners without arousing their envy. It is equally hard for a democracy to forsake the sense for nu-ances and the respect for the multiple aspects of truth which it holds dear or to marshall its intellectuals behind some regimented ideas. The proper study of intelligent individ-uals brings them, not to universal toleration which would engulf all sense of values, but to the understanding even of stupidity. They suffer thereby. Gilbert Murray character-ized this dilemma of scholars and enlightened men in his little book on *Euripides and His Age:*

In every contest that goes on between Intelligence and Stu-pidity, between Enlightenment and Obscurantism, the pow-ers of the dark have this immense advantage: they never un-derstand their opponents and consequently represent them as always wrong, always wicked, whereas the intelligent party generally makes an effort to understand the stupid and to sympathize with anything that is good or fine in their attitude.

We may all feel momentarily powerless against bad faith and systematic and willful distortion of our aims. But greater harm is probably effected by potential friends whom we have failed to enlighten, by humanists abroad who are sincerely if mistakenly convinced that America is dedicated to materialistic aims and scornful of the values once nobly represented by Greco-Roman and West Euro-pean culture. Why not confess that American humanists and scholars have contributed to this inadequate esteem of their true merits? They have contributed through some Anglo-Saxon shyness or fear of all that may smack of elo-quence, through a lurking inferiority complex which many Americans half disguise through the bragging to which they are supposed to be addicted, and because they are em-barrassed by an excessively solemn and frigid atmosphere prevailing in the academies and congresses held in the Old

World. A more effective diffusion of scholarly journals abroad and a better organized representation of American humanists and scientists at conventions held in Europe seem to us two urgent tasks through which the American Council of Learned Societies may serve national prestige as well as the international interests of scholarship.

Some of our statesmen, diplomats and businessmen are at present awakening to the fact that the rest of the world, in this sixth decade of the twentieth century, expects from America, not only loans and gifts of money, not only aid and trade, not only economic assistance, missionary sermonizing and deadly weapons, but intellectual, spiritual and imaginative leadership. The president of a big company, Vergil D. Reed, proclaimed at an annual convention of advertising agencies that his country and his profession had been guilty of grossly understating America's cultural achievement. Another big advertiser, John P. Cunningham, chided his colleagues for having neglected to stress the art and culture of America. In words which professors had not in the past been accustomed to hear from businessmen, he added, as reported on the financial page of the *New York Times* on April 25, 1953:

Only yesterday we were cast in the role of world leader. The success of that leadership will depend largely upon a proper balance between material and non-material values. Frankly, it will be largely a problem of the wealthiest country in the world learning to win the respect and cooperation of the less fortunate nations who are sensitive, resentful and afraid. Ideas and not commodities, understanding and not dollars, culture and not boastful materialism, must be our means of leading.

True enough, the world at large still entertains an idea of American universities which, if it may have been valid a few generations ago, is no longer a correct one today. Even a respectable number of Nobel prizes won by Americans and the voluntary migration of many European scholars, scientists and students to the universities of this country have failed to dispel the assumptions of many Europeans and Asiatics. Those assumptions could be formulated thus:

*1*) The American mind is oriented toward the *praxis* but ignores or neglects pure science, theory (in the Platonic sense of contemplation as well as in the usual English acceptation), all that is disinterested research and speculation not immediately convertible into profitable uses.

*2*) Americans are solely concerned with the present, understood in a narrow fashion, and scornful of the past. They have evolved a new, and not altogether admirable, type of man, the one whom Ortega y Gasset defined as "a civilized man without traditions" or whom Arnold Toynbee might have characterized as "homo occidentalis mechanicus neo-barbarus." A thoughtful and influential French-Swiss critic, Albert Béguin, in a severe article published in the Catholic review *Esprit* in June 1951, charged America with being afraid of the past, hostile to memory, hence devoid of roots and of psychological stability, incapable of sympathizing with Europe.

*3*) America is consequently untouched by the beauty accumulated through the ages in other parts of the world, undismayed by the prospect of having to destroy through atomic bombing all that makes life worth living for Europeans and Asiatics. Many go one step further and vent their suspicion of an imperialist America, bent upon preparing for war and lightheartedly resigned to atomize whole provinces elsewhere and, in Tacitus' tragic phrase, "to establish a desert and call it peace." What else can be expected from a nation of mechanics, concentrating on know-how, bulldozers and gadgets but dehumanized and conditioned for television scripts?

It should be easy to retort to the first charge that Plato and Aristotle count today more readers in American colleges than in any others, that pure scientific speculation is fostered and financed in this country, that philosophical, nay, metaphysical and "phenomenological" research flourishes in this country, that Alfred North Whitehead, Henri Focillon, Ernst Cassirer, Jacques Maritain and others have found in America a congenial environment for their philosophical thinking. Their readers and followers, in "pragmatic" America, have been legion.

The critics of American civilization might likewise be re-minded of the immense role which history occupies in the curriculum of this country. Few other subjects attract a larger number of "majors." Courses in the Humanities or in the great books are fast becoming a feature of higher education. Classical civilization and an ardent and vivid ad-miration for the ancient works in translation have in many places been successfully substituted for the dwindling study of the ancient languages. If the Greco-Roman per-spective is broadened and if ethnology and anthropology have made us aware of the humanistic values contained in Asiatic cultures, in Negro and pre-Columbian art, in Islamic and Slavic books, we need not blush at our attempts to make our new humanism flexible and comprehensive. Our notion of man can no longer be that of a Mediter-ranean or even of a Renaissance humanist.

Nietzsche proposed in a famous "Consideration" that "memento vivere" be substituted for the "memento mori" which knelled through too much western history. A living humanistic scholarship may well be one which helps us live, while studying the past. Some Americans may indeed suffer from a one-track mind or be swayed by a gregarious instinct which prevents them from envisaging a possible peace while forced to prepare for war. But the compatriots of Napoleon, of Frederick the Second and Hitler often evince a short memory when systematically upbraiding the de-scendants of Washington and Jefferson.

The truth is that among the disciplines most promi-nently and most brilliantly studied in this country, are eco-nomic and social sciences, psychology, ethics, but also art history, anthropology, prehistory and medieval history, archeology, linguistics, oriental studies, history of science, literatures, literary criticism, and several others. That some of the journals published by the practitioners of those disciplines are today the most solid and the most alive to appear anywhere, and that their merits are not due to lavish financial means, but to the diligence and devotion of their editors, authors and readers. Indeed, parallel foreign re-views, assisted by their governments, often do not have to go through the financial agonies of American magazines, niggardly supported, if ever, by foundations. It is regrettable that articles, often disparaging foreign nations and hardly fair to the latent virtues of American culture, which appear in some weeklies in New York, should be immediately reproduced, magnified and misunderstood in European magazines. At the same time, foreign scholars, educators, engineers, writers clamor in vain for scientific and literary periodicals from our institutions of learning. Our information services have made the sad mistake of stressing the figures of production and the comfort of American life as presented in magazine advertising: but the rest of the world is not necessarily eager to adopt those dubious benefits of modern life. Respect for culture, attention to the pronouncements of a man of letters prominently displayed in French or Spanish newspapers, admiration for the dicta of a Herr Professor characterize, for better or for worse, the countries which are outside the Anglo-Saxon tradition. American literature has since 1930 had such an impact upon other literatures, not because it depicted violence, gloom and rebellion, but because it presented America as its cinema and its propaganda seldom did: courageous, virile, facing the tragedy of life starkly and spurning shallow and conventional optimism. Intellectuals in Europe, the Near East and South America are still the most influential group in the world; they deserve to be given the means to appraise, and probably to esteem, all that is being done by the scholars and writers of this country. No investment today would be more profitable than the diffusion, through the American Council of Learned Societies and through our foundations, of American specialized journals in the sciences and the humanities.

The rest of the world wonders today at the apparent lack of attention devoted by American officials and cultural groups to spreading abroad their better scholarly, scientific and literary publications. For various reasons, among which no doubt is the lesser influence of the so-called mass media over there, the serious reading public in Western Europe seems to be considerably larger than in this country.

England, France and Germany, each with less than a third of the population of the United States, publish at least as many books per annum as we do in this country, and relatively more books are of a serious nature. Until quite recently the lack of dollars, the unhealthy state of transatlantic trade, and consequent stringent government controls have made it extremely difficult for European publishers to print American books in European editions. It is regrettable that the damage inflicted on the cultural prestige of America by our vast export of frequently inferior films is not offset, as it might be, by the diffusion of our better published works abroad. More attention brought to this problem might at least avail to counteract the unfortunate effect of some of our exports of films and magazines.

It would seem vital to enable the United States today to make solid friends abroad and reach that very element in foreign countries whose support is most needed through devising some mechanism to publish (in translation if necessary) some of the finer books and periodicals that are at present being turned out by American publishers. There is no more effective way of combatting the European view that the genius and the achievements of the United States lie purely in the realm of the mechanical and the practical. Deeds speak louder than words: the publication abroad of a few of our better books and periodicals would be worth an incalculable amount of Voice of America broadcasts averring that we are cultured. It should be comparatively easy to link in the small financing operation involved in subsidizing translations, where needed, through using on the spot the counterpart funds accumulated by America. The U. S. Government has in the past few years provided some dollar funds for the purchase of books and periodicals, the Informational Media Guarantee, but this is almost exhausted. It should not be beyond the wit of Americans to find some way of arranging royalty payments in American money.

An eminent candidate for high office declared in the autumn of 1952 that we also needed free enterprise for the mind. Such free enterprise must clearly spread to the exchange of data, of hypotheses, of fertilizing talks on methods and results with the scientists and scholars of other countries. There again, Americans have failed thus far. Very few of them have played their part worthily at conventions of learned and scientific societies held abroad, and such meetings have offered the best opportunity to gain the intellectual prestige to which America is rightfully entitled. Some of the reasons for that serious American failure may be enumerated and perhaps corrected:

In most countries such academic or scholarly representation is usually supported by government funds. Even in countries which lately depended upon American assistance to balance their budgets, such funds were never lacking, and the top experts and scholars were often selected, without any political interference, by governmental authorities. Not so in the United States where neither the federal government nor the universities could or would attend to sending the most competent delegations to cultural or scholarly congresses of musicologists, archeologists, psychologists or criminologists. As a result, American representatives often made an indifferent impression; their embassies and consulates did not care to vie with European embassies in evincing respect to scholars from American and other countries; they rather feared that if they did so they would be branded by Congressional inquiries as leaning dangerously to the support of that dangerous and alien thing, culture. European scholars often thought America slighted them by sending only third-rate professors into their midst. Once again, the best scholarly representation could only be selected wisely by an impartial and competent nongovernmental organization supported for that purpose by the foundations.

American scholars are individualists and the chief features of American academic life, as opposed to that of Continental Europe, are probably its heterogenity and its contradictory variety. It would be preposterous for any agency to attempt to brief scholars before they go abroad or to convert them into solemn ambassadors of culture. Polonius' advice to Laertes leaving for France remains the only apt motto for all self-respecting envoys: To thine own self be true. But we would offer that, behind some suspicious diffidence and some occasional dismay at the cordial ebullience of Americans, behind some envy and some lingering conviction in the Old World that there alone has a cultural tradition persisted, many European scientists and scholars expect Americans to be themselves; that is to say, to bring to international congresses youthfulness, new ideas, thinking unfettered by hierarchies and conventionality, in a word, leadership. American intellectual leaders abroad should not play at adopting the impeccable rules of etiquette dear to some nations, the solemnity and pomp prevailing in some academic gatherings, not even at being experts on vintage or on a French sauce at one of the elaborate banquets which are the condiments of scholarly gatherings. If they do not disappoint those foreign colleagues who will be expecting from them intellectual energy, a fresh approach, some freedom from the nationalistic prejudices which have long beset other nations, a dynamic courage in breaking down age-old barriers and in converting thought into action, they will have played their part worthily.

But the chief means for representing America worthily abroad and for dispelling the current conviction of many foreigners that this country wishes to control them or to preach to them is a better knowledge of foreign languages among our intellectuals. English should and perhaps will be someday an international language eagerly spoken everywhere. But that time has not yet come and meanwhile the surest way to arouse suspicions of economic and cultural imperialism is to refuse to speak at least one other important foreign language.

Americans have taken refuge in the easy but paralyzing assumption—totally groundless, in fact—that they are not gifted for languages and are not conditioned to such a study by geography. They have been afflicted with shyness when confronted by the need to master another tongue and have cultivated inhibitions which a little courage would soon dispel. American scientists, scholars, and diplomats have thus done incalculable damage to the prestige of their country abroad, through their placid assumption that everyone else should understand English. They have spread the impression that they were bullying sensitive nations which had to be wooed. They have offset many of the beneficial results which their generosity and their kindhearted spirit of cooperation should otherwise have produced and aroused suspicion and ill-will.

Worse still, they have tended toward provincialism at a time when their "manifest destiny" launched them toward universality and a better understanding of other nations. European visitors to these shores frequently voice their surprise at the blinkers with which American men of science and scholarship seem to shut themselves off from what is produced abroad in their fields. The peril of complacent provincialism is indeed a real one in this country at the present time. Many American professors of economics, sociology, history, philosophy have to depend upon their foreign-born colleagues, recently migrated from the Old World, for information on what is accomplished and published in their field in France or Germany, or in Central and Southern European countries which are often interpreted first by France or by Germany. The first tool of the American intellectual, who will be increasingly called upon to travel and to represent his country and his domain of study abroad, is a mastery of at least one foreign language, hence the ability to be understood by others more securely because one will first have attempted to understand them.

# The Need for Language Study
## in America Today

OBSERVERS OF AMERICA have often remarked on the need for perpetual change which seems to beset American education. Some have praised it as an aspect of the soul-searching and even of the breast-beating which should characterize a religious and moral country and especially the members of the most self-critical of all professions. Others have derided it as a symptom of feverish instability and of the immature pursuit of gadgets and new recipes. The truth is that no country prizes education more dearly than does America. No country cherishes its youth more fondly, none has been more anxious to do right by it and to live up to its faith in progress through making education progressive. Some of the aims pursued may have been naïvely defined, but they were noble aims: to bring knowledge within the reach of all and make education democratic, at the risk of levelling down and of untold waste; to bring knowledge to bear upon life and to stress the practical and immediate benefits which may accrue from "a little learning"; thus to change the lot of the common man and increase the sum of happiness in the Western hemisphere.

Yet such worthy ideals have not been attained, if and when they have been, without corresponding losses. The loss to the traditional humanities has been grievous, and grievously mourned. The liberal and even the practical value of the subjects which replaced ancient languages has indeed been doubtful. The fourth and fifth decades of the present century then witnessed a concerted onslaught on the modern humanities: living languages and literatures. Attackers were undaunted by the contemplation of the shrunken world around them and by the obvious myriad links which new media of communication and the foreign entanglements thrust upon America had woven all around them. They were and are men of earnest zeal who claim that they have aligned many disinterested arguments against the study of language and that a new deal favoring other subjects is overdue.

We are convinced that they are misguided and that their sincere but hasty and perhaps unenlightened crusaders' campaign for new subjects replacing modern languages has not served American education, American democracy, and America's urgent need to understand the rest of the world better and to be better understood by it. We wish to state our reasons candidly in writing, at the request of numerous persons who have heard us do so orally.

The first duty of a teacher is to see his subject as part of a larger whole and never to lose sight of the aims of education in general, while contributing to a small province of it to the best of his ability. The aims of education as we see them may be briefly defined thus: ( 1 ) To know, assimilate and hand down in turn to our successors the best and the living in the legacy of the past. ( 2 ) To understand the present or, as Matthew Arnold once put it, defining the ideal of the French pupil in schools which he had just visited, "to understand himself and the world." ( 3 ) To prepare for the future imaginatively and with flexibility blended with essential steadiness of purpose. ( 4 ) To prepare for democratic life and for cooperation in an ever-shrinking world, it being understood that true democracy is not averse to wise and selective leadership.

Are we worthy of such a lofty program? Three trends have lately been discernible in education which may well cause some disquietude. The first led many persons to advocate a clean break with the past: the world has changed, they said, with the industrial revolutions and the machine age; let us therefore give up the old subjects—history, philosophy, the classics, modern languages—and concentrate upon the state of the world in the last few years. The second tendency rested on a false interpretation of democracy as freedom unlimited, many rights but very few duties, the discarding of grades and a taboo on the hated word "discipline." "Why not banish genders, declensions, subjunctives and other such un-American paraphernalia, unwanted in our streamlined age?" And again: "This is a free country. Let me elect any subject I like, home economics rather than French, personal hygiene instead of calculus, and in the place of English composition, I shall take a course on marriage problems and thus learn how to choose a wife." Alas! never have there been more divorces than since courses in marriage problems were established. Let us hope at least that graduates from such seminars have mastered the art of making their successive marriages more and more delightful.

A third fallacy led many people around us to say: "We live in a social age and should be prepared for our place in it. Social studies must provide the best means to such an end. It is selfish escapism to read Virgil or Goethe by the fireside, or to listen to Beethoven in solitary enjoyment. Let us learn about the 'mores' of our fellow beings, and even read gravely about their sexual behavior, thus become well-adjusted, react properly to stimuli, practice community thinking and develop into good citizens."

It would be an insult to the best in American education to waste time in refuting such ludicrous fallacies. We shall only attempt to do so insofar as they affect the study of languages and list the arguments which have been most widely and most loudly heard lately. It is natural that from time to time new subjects should come into existence or into favor and should crowd some of the time-honored and previously triumphant subjects out of a curriculum. Theology, ancient languages and rhetoric once ruled supreme.

Modern foreign languages themselves were granted an honorable place in American universities rather late. Natural sciences then loomed so large in significance that they encroached on mathematics and the older disciplines.

The trend of our age is toward the collective, toward the links binding men no longer, as in religion, in a vertical transcendence to some higher power, but horizontally, with other men in the same community or society. No sane teacher of languages bears any grudge against the social sciences as such. They have accomplished much already. They are here to stay. They will perfect their instruments as they develop further, slough off some of their youthful fascination with quantitative measurements and their naïve aping of the methods of the natural sciences. They will grant more room to the past and to the historical processes. Let us even hope that their practitioners may discover the advantages of simple, elegant, unpedantic writing. Those who call themselves humanists and who have long enjoyed the liberating and maturing influence of the study of literature should be broad-minded enough to acknowledge what is valid in the claims of the social sciences and to cooperate intelligently with the devotees of those younger disciplines. Condescension and scorn have never been worthy of those who should be living examples of the refining and broadening influence of their chosen calling. Teachers of languages and literatures have much to learn from friendly contact with their "social" colleagues. Indeed is not language itself one of the primary social phenomena, and the mirror to much that lies deepest in the soul of a people? And if there has been crude naïveté at times in the use by social scientists of literature purely as a social document, it is none the less true that literature, subtly and indirectly interpreted, has much to reveal on a given society. It has, ever since Zola and even earlier, set itself as a goal the observation and imaginative recreation of social forces.

Let us admit that we have occasionally been complacent in trusting that our field of study would automatically retain its full appeal in a mass civilization and an age which often misunderstands the true meaning of democracy as applied to education. Let us inform ourselves on the social factors in modern life on which our colleagues are placing a new emphasis. Let us buttress some of our assertions with facts, surveys, percentages, and use tests intelligently where they can be useful. Let us develop "area" courses and even resign ourselves to calling them by such a barbaric name, if the word civilization horrifies our colleagues. Above all, let us borrow from the social scientists their fresh zeal for their subject and their enthusiastic and eager ambition. More teachers of language and literature should come out of their shells or shake off their shy reserve. They should display their knowledge of problems of education, of the needs of society, of their place and that of their students in the contemporary world, claim a share in adult education and help enlighten their community. More of them should thus, through proving alert and energetic personalities, accede to the positions of school principals, commissioners of education, State Department cultural officials, deans, presidents, advisers to the Foundations. After all, great American institutions, from Harvard to Chicago and from Johns Hopkins to Yale were not inefficiently run when their presidents were men with lofty ideals and strong personalities, whose fields of specialization had been Hebrew, Greek or Latin.

In a word, there is no such thing as a traditional subject, and social anthropologists are the first to acknowledge that a break with the past entails serious consequences for a culture. It cuts off young people from their parents and grandparents, it uproots them and makes them alien to a treasure of folklore, of mythological, biblical, classical allusions which cripples them for life. But there are teachers viewing their own fields in a timid traditionalist way, paralyzed by an excessive refinement or by a critical spirit which keeps them from propagating their faith in their subject and in the values which it embodies. The word imperialism has ugly connotations. Yet all that expands and robustly displays its growing and youthful strength is imperialistic. If believers in the value of languages allow others to push their subject to the fringe of the curriculum without fighting back energetically as well as intelligently, they will soon find themselves expelled altogether.

The opposition which one is forced to establish in our time between the ancient languages and the modern foreign languages is an invidious and regrettable one. We side with those who believe that our culture and the training of many minds have grievously suffered from the almost general elimination of Greek and Latin from our course of studies. Scientists like Descartes, Newton, Lavoisier, Claude Bernard, Henri Poincaré were no less inventive and no less precocious for having been steeped in the classical languages. Statesmen and diplomats were in no way less well trained than today for having pondered over Thucydides and Sallustius. The thought of children of the last century rapturously engrossed in Virgil, as Michelet and Hugo were, or steeped in the Bible on Sunday mornings, as they were in Great Britain, may well arouse fond regrets in parents who today watch their offspring, on Sabbath day, rapt in comic strips.

Most severe of all is perhaps the loss to our democratic ideals. It was not American, British, or French history, but ancient history and oratory that long nurtured the faith of the great leaders of the West: Pericles' celebrated oration in the second book of Thucydides, Demosthenes' *Philippics*, Cicero's pleadings against the foes of the republic, even Horace's verse on "pro patria mori" and Livy's narratives, read at a receptive age, have molded the devotion to their country of many French, American, and British patriots who worked, and died in some cases, for their country. From Jefferson, Rousseau, Burke, the leaders of the French Revolution, to Gladstone, Balfour and Churchill, to Jaurès, Herriot, and Blum, great statesmen had vivified their patriotism and their democratic idealism through long familiarity with those ancient writers whom the poet Yeats called somewhere "the builders of his soul."

But the role once played by the classics can be assumed by the modern languages. In some respects indeed, that role can be filled even better. For Latin literature, as the literature which was long exclusively taught to children, suffered from a regrettable gap: there is no first-rate children's literature in Latin, if one excepts very minor works such as Aulus Gellius' *Attic Nights* or Apuleius' entertaining fantasy. Greece had the *Odyssey* and Herodotus; Spain had *Don Quixote*, Germany many fairy tales and charming blendings of "poetry and truth" by Goethe or Eichendorff; France has a treasure of medieval tales, Rabelais' giants, La Fontaine's animals, Alexander Dumas, Hugo, Daudet, Anatole France, Saint-Exupéry. If languages are to be started, as they should be, at an early age, it is essential that some reading of true quality be done then which trains children to pass from the easier and the familiar to the more abstract and the more remote.

But the practice of Greek and Latin texts used to fill another purpose in education, and their gradual disappearance has left a worse vacuum. Translating a Greek text and analyzing its verbs, its particles, its subtle syntax, construing a Latin sentence and unraveling its meaning used to teach boys to grapple with difficulty. They were then protected from the naïve illusion which deceives persons who have never learned a second language: the illusion that they naturally understand all that is written in their own tongue. Many literate persons among us and even some who are called cultured have lost the habit and the desire to make any effort when confronted with a difficult text—be it the report of a company official, the articles of some international agreement or of a contract. Reading anything but a synopsis prepared by their secretary, headlines of newspapers, or comics, seems to make their heads dizzy.

Yet reading is, and should be, an active pursuit. Joyce, Kafka, T. S. Eliot, Faulkner, Proust, require some effort on our part. Such effort will be granted willingly by him who read Thucydides or Tacitus, Pascal or Cervantes while in college. His teeth were hardened by some of the tough nuts that he had to crack, and the ensuing reward justified the effort. A person who has never attempted to decipher any language but his own naïvely assumes that he knows his own, and that Shakespeare, Meredith, Melville are his by birthright. He does not bring an active and imaginative attitude to his reading. How can he successfully tackle the perusal of his daily paper? With their cryptic headlines, their prodigality of news, often contradictory and cut up at intervals of ten or twenty pages, their distracting pictures of seductive feminine clothing and unclothing, American newspapers certainly demand from us that we exercise an acute critical spirit if we are to read between their lines and to decipher the purport of their headlines. Their readers are indeed asked to make some order out of calculated chaos. Mallarmé or Rilke are hardly less strenuous and rather more rewarding.

An eminent American scholar, Henry Grattan Doyle, has disposed once and for all of the fallacy that all good things written abroad come out in translations and make the learning of foreign languages an unnecessary bother. ("Will Translations Suffice," Language Leaflets, No. 10 (1940), the George Washington University) Alas! there is no "once and for all" in these matters and lies obstinately repeated need obstinately repeated disproving.

It is not true that all that is good is translated. In poetry it is manifestly untrue. In criticism, philosophy, history, it is hardly less untrue. In science, we have abstracts which are only incitements to go to the full text and to follow the full demonstration if the original is in French or German (or even in one of the Romance languages for which French is helpful or in a Germanic or Scandinavian language which German may help decipher). The liveliest part of scientific, social and even of literary scholarship today is to be found in periodicals. Unless a scholar, a scientist, an educator, a business man is able to leaf through foreign periodicals in one or two languages at least, he loses much; indeed he loses that precisely which marks people who are likely to go to the top in their profession, through richer information and a broader perspective than their average colleague. A man who claims to be well-informed on world problems to-day, economic, political, diplomatic, cannot substantiate such a claim unless he reads the periodical press of at least one other non-English speaking country. The best-informed American press often appears provincial to the reader who is able to supplement it with weeklies or monthlies of another country; for those see us as only others can do and enlighten us on ourselves as well as upon others. An American traveler in Europe who can only receive his news from the American newspaper published in Paris for traveling Americans can never hope to understand continental countries from the inside. Indeed he might well have stayed at home from the start, if his trip was meant at all to bring him any insight into foreign lands.

It would be easy to prove once again that translations are woefully inadequate and fail to convey the affective and the racy connotations of works in the original, the peculiar subtlety of the syntax of the foreign idiom. Nevertheless, not many educated persons will tackle the Greek or the Latin original when the translation is available; but the few whose classical training was once thorough may at least check or supplement the translation by a glance at the original and enforce their enjoyment tenfold thereby. Not many persons will master Russian, Chinese or Dutch in order to relish the untranslatable quality of those languages. But most of our graduate schools have resorted to the reasonable solution of demanding two foreign languages, usually French and German. With some knowledge, even perfunctory, of those two idioms, an intelligent person will easily have access to a body of technical writing and of literature three times more ample than the one in his native language. He will enjoy an opportunity to read translations into either French or German from other languages, and not pass for a cultural imperialist or appear as a shy cripple in international conventions where English is often not the chief language used.

Through a strange inequality of treatment, foreign languages have lately been the target of those who contend that if a subject once studied has been forgotten that study has proved vain. They apparently repudiate with horror the famous definition of culture as that which remains in us once everything has been forgotten. Their motto might well be the pragmatic line in Faust's soliloquy which condemns as a heavy burden that which one does not utilize: "Was man nicht nützt, ist eine schwere Last." They do not, however, blame themselves for not using the tools which their teachers took pains to have them acquire.

The argument that languages might well be thrown overboard because they are not used by many is a very fallacious one. By the same reasoning, do we use algebra, trigonometry, the rule of three, or even our once laboriously acquired knowledge of the multiplication tables or of the art of adding, subtracting and dividing? Do we retain a much clearer memory of English irregular verbs or of the spelling of our own language than we do of the French or Spanish grammar we once learned? Are we much more precise in our knowledge of English literature, of geology or botany, of astronomy or of physics, than we are in our enduring familiarity with the rudiments of a foreign tongue? Let us not mention, for it would be cruel, the very slight imprint which lessons of ethics, of civics and even of politeness, once dutifully absorbed, seem to have left on not a few of our mature fellow citizens. The knowledge of what was once absorbed need not remain present in our minds, which would then be painfully cluttered up with notions not immediately relevant to the hour being lived or to the problem being faced. But it may well stay, latently or subconsciously buried within ourselves, and leave us with a capacity to reacquire, when the need arises, what was once possessed. The word possessed, however, is hardly apposite, if the language was only studied perfunctorily for two brief years or if it was started too late, in persons already afflicted with inhibitions and closed to the appeal of exotic foreignness.

"Inferiority complex" seems to have become a typically American phrase, applied by Americans to themselves. The dislike for languages in many of them is nothing but a manifestation of that inferiority complex. "We as a nation are not gifted for languages" is a phrase heard daily by foreigners entertained in this country. Those who pronounce it excuse it by the geographical argument that contact with foreigners is not a frequent occurrence for those who live in the heartland of the North American continent. But the excuse is a ludicrously poor one in the present century and might well be left to the Russians, who do live imprisoned in a wide continent, meet few foreigners, and yet study and know languages. Natives of Illinois and of Kansas are liable to meet foreigners any day in their own state, in their college life, in their business trips, and few are those among the more successful ones among them who will not be called upon to travel abroad several times in their lives.

But the grievous truth is that many Americans have succeeded in convincing themselves that their minds are too sluggish, their tongues too slow, their reflexes too tardy to enable them to speak any languages but their own. Such a self-disparaging complex is, however, totally unfounded. Our conviction, based upon experience, is that far more Americans succeed in speaking excellent French than do Spaniards, Englishmen and even Italians. When languages are taught orally, efficiently, and long enough, as they are in a number of private schools in America (and in a much larger number of high schools than many Americans, too apologetic about their high school system, realize), boys and girls achieve a mastery which might well put many European teen agers to shame. It would take nothing but more confidence in themselves on the part of Americans, a little more effort on the part of pupils and teachers alike, and a firmer conviction that work is better and more natural for young people than laziness and even than play, actually to turn Americans into what they potentially are: next to the Slavs, the best linguists in the world.

But another prejudice must once and for all be demolished: the study of languages and of literatures is a difficult and a very masculine subject indeed, and not at all one which should be left to girls along with music and sewing, while "males" concentrate on engineering, accounting, marketing, compiling Kinseyan statistics. Young American men are the shyest of all creatures and label "feminine" what is both alluring but mysterious and difficult, for a foreign language requires more alertness of mind and more feeling for nuances than figures and quantitative statements and logically deduced but totally unconvincing assertions. The true courage, indeed, lies in facing those half-truths and imponderable but all-important values by which the world is in fact led and those shades of significance on which most problems hinge. "Il n'y a de vérité que dans les nuances," Benjamin Constant wisely remarked. The evasion of what they have termed "feminine" has not prevented American men from being what they are and probably should be: sensitive, emotional creatures, quick to listen to the promptings of their emotions and to respond to sympathies and dislikes, to unreasoned fears and to enthusiastic "fads."

It is moreover patently absurd to allow college boys to believe that Franklin and Jefferson and other founders of this country were effeminate because they spoke French and had read Voltaire and Rousseau; or to imply that Roosevelt and Churchill were not real "men" because they repeatedly addressed the French in the French language, made more savory by the spice of a Harrow or of a Groton accent. Indeed, the study of languages is both difficult and rewarding, like all that is worth while in this world. Forsaking it or banishing it in schools because it is not easy is profoundly un-American, and unworthy of the youth of this country, which usually does not admit to being licked without putting up a fight. The knowledge of foreign languages affords a key to the reading of Dante, Cervantes, Pascal, Goethe, Balzac, Dostoevsky: are these enervating and softening influences? There is no better ordeal by fire than such reading, no saner lesson of clear-sightedness and of intellectual courage, no safer antidote to the rosy delusions and effeminate falsifications of life offered by the movies and the slick magazines.

Indeed, it should be left to a psychiatrist to diagnose some of the motives and fears which lurk behind the aversion of many Americans to foreign languages. It is our belief that in many cases Americans are being swayed by an unconscious immigrants' complex. They remember their parents or grandparents, who had arrived here with the will to forget their "old country," yet never succeeded in speaking, feeling, behaving like native Americans. They had strived hard to cut themselves off from the traditions and the language of the country from which their ancestors had emigrated or been expelled. Their family names may have remained Polish, German, Italian, Welsh. Yet they are now the first to find it strange that Koreans, Japanese, French and Germans should not speak with an American drawl, or that Cockneys and Scots should not possess a Brooklyn accent.

We would even submit that American reluctance to generalize the study of languages is, like nationalism, racism, xenophobia, the sign of a deep-lying morbidity. An eminent Presbyterian pastor of New York, Rev. Norman Vincent Peale, in a book which was the best-seller in the nonfiction list for 1953, computed that this nation needs nineteen and a half million sleeping pills annually to lull it to sleep, an increase of one thousand per cent over fifteen years ago; that eleven million pounds of aspirin were sold in one single year, and that fifty per cent of physicians' prescriptions order sedatives to even more neurotic Americans. We suggest that they would go to sleep far more harmlessly and far more securely if only they recited to themselves the subjunctive and pluperfect forms of Spanish or French, the rules of German construction, or if they merely made the effort to read or speak another language in the evening hours before retiring.

One of our national diseases is said to be inhibition under its varied forms. The fashion has lately been to cure such inhibitions through painting or modeling. Every doctor, lawyer, dentist, manufacturer will gladly devote his Sunday to daubing and will—alas!—periodically invite his friends to admire his inhibitions translated into an exhibition. Van Gogh, Gauguin and other martyrs of painting had not so easily succeeded in triumphing over their complex through intense expressionism! Less harm would be done to canvasses, to walls and to the eyes of the onlookers if those worthy professional and business men had concentrated instead on mastering a foreign tongue. Indeed few joys are more radiantly expressed than the satisfaction which beams on the faces of youngsters, and even of grown-ups, when they have for the first time succeeded in delivering themselves of a correct sentence in a foreign language: "L'arrosoir du jardinier est sur le chapeau de ma tante" or "je crois que nous allons assister à une nouvelle crise ministérielle." Drinking, as the phrase goes, to release one's inhibitions, might well decrease by half in America if it were replaced by the strong draught of a foreign language successfully imbibed.

Education is clearly a preparation for life. But such a statement is as broad and vague as the word "life" is confusing; the qualities which will be most needed in our lives as grown-ups are indeed so diverse that they remain unpredictable. The practical-minded student, who insists on preparing himself narrowly and exclusively for his chosen profession, often turns out to be the unhappiest of men. More ironical still, he seldom turns out to be the most successful in terms of material and financial rewards. In literally thousands of grave statements, the top men in the professions of medicine, engineering, business, law, diplomacy have warned young men against narrow and premature specialization. Some educators however insist on ignoring the evidence of life and the experience of those who know.

The worship of the practical in education is a most fallacious myth. Reliable statistics have informed us that sixty-five per cent of all jobs in the country require a training of only three days on the job itself. Twenty-five per cent of all jobs require a training of four to six months. Ten per cent only necessitate a training of more than six months. Even in the latter, the men who go to the top are almost never those who prepared vocationally for their profession. They are in the majority of cases men who first acquired experience elsewhere, and thus gained the plasticity, the breadth, the imagination that a more general culture affords. The very best business brains in the country are not necessarily those of men who went through a business school. Within three years, many of our present business ideas will be laughed at, just as our present ideas on psychology, sociology and physics will become hopelessly outdated in ten or fifteen years. The medicine of 1980 will laugh condescendingly at our present drugs and techniques. While it is good to be informed on the state of knowledge in our time, it is even better to adapt oneself readily to new knowledge, to be somewhat detached from the obsession of the immediate, and thus to remain open-minded and able to face ever-changing conditions in an ever-changing world.

The most important things in life, for which education would prepare young people better if it forgot its narrow concern with being "directly useful," are in truth: (1) The ability to express oneself, orally and in writing, which is pitifully disappearing in an age when even "successful business men" talk only in grunts and have ceased to write but dictate into machinery. (2) The ability to grow after one has left school, which is not always conspicuous in alumni and alumnae. An Englishman suggested that we substitute for the conventional "How do you do?" form of greeting, and for its abbreviated American monosyllabic counterpart, a more pithy question such as "What are you reading these days?" It might indeed be quite instructive, and even more entertaining, to listen, on a bus or in the street, to the answers which such questions would elicit. (3) The ability to see ourselves with objectivity and humor and to prove tolerant enough to others, individuals, groups and nations, to understand their ways. (4) Last but not least, the capacity to enjoy leisure. For, whatever our students do later in life, let us hope they will enjoy free hours and will know how to consume them pleasantly and refreshingly, listening to music, reading good books, understanding the plays or the paintings they see. No sight is more disheartening in our world than that of grave, staid gentlemen, hard-boiled salesmen, dignified matrons so stubbornly untouched by the landscape outside or by the sight of their fellow-sufferers in boredom that, as soon as they sit in the train or in their club, they rush to the paper, disregarding news and editorials, to devour the comic strips. At home, unable to face the ordeal of two hours of serene leisure, they avidly absorb the chewing gum for the ears provided by their radio program, or else turn greedily to the chewing gum for the eyes of some television set. They even give the name of relaxing to such systematic impoverishment of their mental and spiritual life. Those who indulge in such relaxation often fall a prey to nervous breakdowns or to heart failures before they reach their fiftieth year.

The subject is one of tragic gravity. We are apparently living in the dawn of a new era. Recently discovered sources of energy will increase our mechanical facilities a hundred times and will provide us with more leisure than ever before. Are we going to devote that free time to listening to the virtues of Pepsi Cola or to devouring three detective stories a day, wondering childishly who killed whom, when both the killer and the victim never lived as creatures of flesh and blood in the first place? Should we not boldly reconsider the underlying assumptions behind much of our education, and admit that, the machine builders, the engineers, the technicians of America having done wonders in their fields, it is time to shift the emphasis to other subjects and to reestablish a badly shaken equilibrium? The humanities, democratized, revitalized, modernized, and giving to modern languages what ancient languages have lost, have an important part to play in our mechanically-minded age. Industry and commerce tell us loudly what sort of men they want. Let us raise our voices and let industry and commerce know what their real needs are.

Our society needs languages more than ever today. A glance at our daily paper informs us of the thinking of our world and of the necessity to know about other nations and to have them know us better. "We must love one another, or die," wrote the poet W. H. Auden. Let us say that we must, at the very least, understand one another or perish. We are engaged today in the process of broadening our allegiance from one nation to a group of United Nations, soon perhaps to the world. No amount of juridical explanations about the UN charter, about the need to import and thus bridge the dollar gap, or the expansion of the Point Four program, will be of much avail if we fail to develop a concrete and living interest in other nations as such: in their daily lives, in their outlooks and prejudices, in their exotic "backwardness," but also in the features by which they are similar to us, for we have long overstressed their superficial differences in our movies and in our textbooks. If language study were to succeed in ridding us of the naïve and nefarious complacency stigmatized three hundred years ago by Pascal's aphorism, "Vérité en deçà des Pyrénées, erreur au delà," it would prove the most practical, indeed the most beneficent, of all the subjects studied in our schools.

The true usefulness of language study in no way consists in our retaining a skill in the mastery of a language that we once learned. It lies in helping us escape from the temptation of provincialism and all its narrowness. Even more than history which has tended lately to be concerned with the American scene, far more than social studies which have tended to dwell upon the statistical study of Middletown or Elmstown, it is a liberating study, and education should be a liberation from what is base and narrow in ourselves, from what is too limited in our environment. The most constricting bondage to which we are all prone to be willing captives is the bondage of words. We take it for granted a little too readily that other people mean the same thing as we do (without always clarifying what we mean ourselves) when they use foreign equivalents for terms like "freedom," "democracy," "free press," "free enterprise," "peace," "socialism." But we are deceiving ourselves. UNESCO initiated in 1948 an inquiry into the meaning of the word democracy, to determine the different significance it seems to have for different peoples, even when those peoples enjoy a similar ethnical and cultural background. Such a semantic inquiry at once raises complex questions: on the relationship between political and economic democracy, on the necessity of parties in a democracy and of the danger that the multiplication of such parties may constitute, on the limits to be assigned to tolerance and freedom of speech in democracy, etc. An apparently unambiguous and familiar phrase such as that of the Gettysburg address, "government of the people, by the people, for the people," may raise several conflicts between divergent interpretations: "by the people" clearly must mean a few to whom the task of representing the many is delegated; but how few must the few be, and how must they be selected, and how are we to agree upon the interpretation of "for the people," etc.?

The scientist Thomas Huxley expressed it tersely when in 1882 he said in an address to the Liverpool Institution: "One of the safest ways of delivering yourself from the bondage of words is to know how ideas look in words to which you are not accustomed. That is one reason for the study of language." He added: "Another reason is the practical value of such knowledge. And yet another is this, that if your languages are properly chosen, from the time of learning the additional languages, you will know your own language better than you ever did."

We make no fetish of culture as such or as it used to be snobbishly conceived. But we are convinced that a democracy is sliding down a perilous slope when too many of its citizens willfully ignore what the rest of the world thinks of them and stubbornly refuse to re-examine its fundamental assumptions, to interpret them to others whose cooperation we need today in America almost as much as they need ours. Vocational education has its limited value; but it has been pushed to ridiculous extremes and it has benefited employers and industrialists far more than it has the rank and file of our citizens. A professor of philosophy and of education who worked as a laborer till the age of twenty-one and who gained his own education the hard way, Eduard C. Lindeman, remarked that industry, faced with rapid expansion, asked the public schools to accept the responsibility and to face the cost for the training of its workers, but seldom plowed back the profits thus made to help the adult education of its workmen or to assist the public school system. He concluded: "I do not believe that public school education should be primarily vocational in purpose." ("The Goal of American Education," in *Democracy's Challenge to Education*, ed. B. Amidon, New York, 1940)

German history of the last twenty years clearly shows what dangers a nation of efficient specialists may run into, if it imprisons itself into provincialism, into disregard of foreigners and uncritical acceptance of unworthy leaders blindly obeyed by the specialists in the anthill. The philosopher Bergson, long before he treated the same theme in his *Creative Evolution*, declared at the age of twenty-three in a speech delivered at the Lycée of Angers: "The inferiority of the animal lies in this: that it is a specialist. It does one thing to admiration: it can do nothing else." We owe it to the youth of this country to turn it into something more than specialists—or animals.

Indeed, an intelligent conception of democracy makes it imperative that we restore languages for all pupils in the schools at an early age, merely to be true to the American principle of equality of opportunity. The study of modern language in our schools should by no means be limited, as a class privilege, to the fifteen per cent who are likely to go to college. It should be started early, before inhibitions, self-consciousness and shyness hamper girls and boys at their puberty. It should be extended to as many people as possible. For why should children financially, geographically, or perhaps momentarily intellectually underprivileged be deprived of the opportunity of entering college some day, or of understanding the modern world in which America is incessantly in contact with foreigners, or merely of enjoying their leisure hours thanks to some literary, historical or linguistic interest?

Nothing is less truly democratic and more medieval, in the popular and less honorable sense lent to that adjective, than for school principals and school boards to decide in advance that certain boys and girls will only be trained for their probable occupation and will be chained to their status in life; that they will in advance be shut out from the eventual opportunity to go to those colleges whose graduates earn, it is said, the highest incomes. A report of the British Ministry of Education, quoted in *School and Society* (July 18, 1925), declared in a true democratic spirit: "It has been well said that the purpose of education is not so much to prepare children for their occupations as against their occupations. It must develop in them the powers and interest that will make them the masters and not the slaves of their work."

The warnings repeatedly uttered by many of the great scientists, inventors, physicians and business leaders of our time should be heeded more solemnly than the assertions of naïve educators who, having never mastered a foreign language themselves, fail to see why the opportunity denied them should be granted others. Pasteur used to say that chance has much to do in one's career and in scientific discoveries, but he added that "chance favors the well-prepared mind." Einstein was reported as declaring: "If a young man has trained his muscles and his physical endurance by gymnastics and walking, he will later be fitted for every physical work. This is also analogous to the training of the mind." (C. A. Tonsor, *Mod. Language Jrnl.*, XXII – 1938 – p. 408) The case for language study as intellectual gymnastics hardly needs arguing. But more of us, members of the teaching profession, should put to parent-teachers associations the question: "Is your child being cheated?" We should incite parents to ask their local school boards that their children be granted a chance to study languages and thus receive their rightful claim to the social and intellectual benefits which too few are at present enjoying.

If foreign language study were generalized and started earlier, as logically it should be, more boys and girls would reach college already prepared to read the works of another literature besides those written in English. In our modern world, it is only second class citizens who should be content with having only one window open upon the world: that of one single language, of one single literary tradition. Reading foreign works in the original is an accomplishment which will only be reserved to a minority. But that minority is smaller in America than in any other great country, and it has lately been reduced to the defensive. A concern with objectivity, or with the appearances of objectivity, has led many Americans to lend their credence solely to quantitative data, questionnaires, charts, curves, statistics and percentages. Such methods are deceptive in their imitation of science. They are often mere pretexts for eschewing a decision. They also delude those who compile and use them into believing that they have understood the whys and the wherefores of human motives, while in fact they have only refused to follow the bolder but more constructive process of discovery in science as in life: namely the imaginative flash which works from observation to induction and to a hypothesis which endows data with a new significance.

The value of literature is manifold indeed: if the modern world remains skeptical when we say that it affords a new appreciation of beauty, let us not blush before the word pleasure. Pleasure, in its higher form, is an essential part of happiness. But, contrary to an unfounded prejudice, literature, if it is broad enough to include the masterpieces of several cultures, may well be the most practical of all studies. History during the last fifty years in several countries has proved conclusively that statesmen who had been trained as engineers, as scientists, even as military or business men, have regularly failed when they attempted to lead men and to deal with human affairs in which irrational and unpredictable factors predominate. We have ourselves heard physicians, lawyers and politicians declare that no one should attempt to go into politics who has not mastered one art or one foreign literature.

British papers have more than once remarked since 1950 that the root of many British troubles in the Middle East and the Near East, and the root of similar mistakes now being committed by Americans, lay in the narrow quantitative approach to problems which cannot be thus solved. A little curiosity for Iranian traditions as embodied in literature or for the literary and cultural heritage of the Arabs would have gone a long way in appealing to the emotional forces which, far more than economic necessity, impel those peoples to behave sentimentally, illogically, proudly.

We would even submit that, in so far as history is made by individuals interpreting collective forces and material needs around them, it can best be understood through literature.* Dictators of the last two decades and would-be dictators or demagogic leaders of the present day are strikingly similar to characters in Balzac or Dostoevsky. The reading of novels, in which characters are synthetically and globally created through the power of imagination, would enable more men and women to interpret the minds and hearts, the obsessions and the shrewdness of many a man of business and of many a statesman. After all, for centuries, it has been the qualitative, intuitive, and emotional approach (which fiction and drama exemplify) rather than the quantitative and coldly analytical one, which has proved most effective with one half (and not the less essential one) of mankind: womankind.

The cause of languages in America today is not one that should be defended by language teachers alone. They can do much, to be sure, to establish unity of purpose and coordination of effort among the several languages; they should stress the historical and social values behind literature, give the study of French, German, Spanish a function in other fields through the light it throws on history, philosophy, sociology, etc., written in those languages and intimately bound up with those foreign literatures. Above all, teachers in the universities should make a more determined effort to break the barriers separating them from secondary and elementary school teachers, and those who train graduate students should once and for all give up their claim or pretense to be preparing only literary and philological scholars and to remain unconcerned in the teaching and in the human qualities of their students.

But the enemies of language study are not our own col-

* The words of a man who was not a literary scholar but who devoted his life to improving advanced studies in the sciences and in medicine are worth meditating: "In literature, man reveals himself and in literature man has, since the earliest times, revealed himself. If the proper study of mankind is man, the proper study of man is the literature that he has created through the centuries. No scientist, no psychoanalyst, no behaviorist had to teach the authors of Oriental texts and the Bible, Shakespeare, Molière, Dante and Goethe the proper relations between human beings." Abraham Flexner, *Funds and Foundations* (Harper's, 1952), pp. 132–33.

leagues in education or in the social sciences whom we take an innocuous pleasure in mocking occasionally and thus tend to alienate. All those who teach the youth and who believe in maintaining and in extending culture in America at the present time are or can be our allies. Every language teacher should set himself the task of converting colleagues, students, parents and friends around him. The offensive in American education, which has practically eliminated the classics, has now attacked the modern languages. If it finds a soft spot there and wins, it will at once shift the onslaught to philosophy, to European history, to sociology, to English. Indeed, premonitory signs have not been lacking. Champions of "progress" have already intimated that it is useless to learn how to write English today: executives merely indicate in terse language to their secretaries how to answer letters and draw up reports. Writing could thus be relegated to girls' colleges and secretarial schools. Unless we all unite today to resist the encroachment of the blind advocates of the immediately practical, we are in danger of hanging separately tomorrow.

For all of us, whether we dedicate ourselves to history or to French, to English or to anthropology, must agree that the dilemma for us is the following: shall we yield to those who stress the knowledge of the material means placed at the disposal of men or shall we fight for a better knowledge of man himself? Shall we, in Bergson's famous phrase, attempt to enlarge and deepen our minds and grow a soul commensurate with man's overgrown body? Favor the development of his power over matter which may ultimately destroy him or concentrate upon man as a creator? An American thinker published in England, in 1952, a book which presents the dilemma cogently: *Man Creator or Destroyer* (by George Malcolm Stratton, London, Allen and Unwin). He stressed the frightening dominion which man has gained over lifeless energies, "commanding their help in making persons from the raw stuff of human beings and in making communities from those persons." But man needs better knowledge of men, and not of the oil, coal and plutonium which are at his disposal, if he is to spare the world from annihilation.

Many a voice has lately cried that the worst American failure, since 1950, has been the failure to make this country understood, appreciated, liked abroad. That sad fact stemmed to a great extent from our own inability to understand, to appreciate and to respect the very peoples of Europe, Asia and South America to whom we were extending material help with a generosity unheard of in historical annals. We now have to admit that no amount of economic and military assistance can ever replace a genuine interest in the culture, manners, sensibilities of other nations. Such an interest must begin with some regard for their language, the mirror to all that they hold dearest to them in their past and the symbol of their will to live.

American propagandists who naïvely want to transplant abroad the benefits which they deem essential to their own comfort (64 page newspapers constituting a free but increasingly standardized press, corner drugstores, cellophane-wrapped lunches, quarterly checkup and homogenized and vitaminized candies) naturally draw the charge of economic imperialism. There is more than wit in George Bernard Shaw's advice: "Do not do unto others what you would like that they should do unto you. Their tastes may not be the same." The most generous, probably the most idealistic and the best-humored nation in the world, the United States, thus happens to be envied, eyed with suspicion, feared and even hated by many of the very people whom it tried to serve.

Wisely has one of the educational leaders in this country lately declared that an American who knows the language, understands the culture, and can predict the probable behavior of a foreign country, be it Korea or France, Iran or Germany, Russia or Argentina, is worth more to his country than several atomic physicists. The physicist might help win a war, through mass destruction, alas! The informed and intelligent interpreter of other countries might prevent the war altogether.

The phrase, once sacrosanct, about America's "manifest destiny," aroused smiles on our lips in the skeptical era which preceded World War II. But history, in its capricious bestowing of favors and responsibilities, has at present showered upon the United States its dubious favors. The mission of America has perforce to be a soteriological one. This country must save the rest of the Western world, or go down to ruin with it. It cannot succeed if it is isolated. It desperately needs the good will, the whole-hearted cooperation, and the confidence of other nations. Those nations refuse to be bullied or treated with condescension. They must be wooed, through their culture and their language. "Help save the world through the study of languages" might well be our worthy motto. Let us thus, to the best of our ability, assist man, now faced with an unavoidable dilemma, choose determinedly between the tasks of a creator or of a destroyer which the challenge of the second half of the twentieth century has laid before us.

# American Scholarship in the Field
## of Foreign Literatures

ANNUAL CONVENTIONS OF THE MODERN LANGUAGE
Association are one of the most admirable institutions in America and should fill our organizers and every
one of the participating members with deep though re-
strained pride. For alone, I believe, among the associations
which thus gather for an exchange of views and a backward
glance at the departing year, we submit with humility to
gentle preaching and even to ungentle scolding. We rejoice at being told that we write without grace and think
without originality, that our scholarship is dry, our teaching not stimulated by adequate research, that we fail to
fulfill our duty of public service. A British philosopher,
Bradley, used to say that the metaphysics of one of his
colleagues consisted in proving that this is doubtless the
best of all possible words but every particular thing in it
is a necessary evil. We are the most admirable of associations, particularly in our readiness to agree that many of
our activities are necessary evils, and not a few of our
group meetings unnecessary ones.

We are performing a noble mission in thus remaining
the last guardians of humility in the modern world. We

An address at the annual meeting of *The Modern Language Association*, December 1948

have all read about the meetings of other professional groups: psychologists who annually proclaim the thrilling progress of their efforts in measuring and developing the sex urges of guinea pigs or the homosexuality of rats; social "thinkers" who have discovered and reveal to a gaping audience that wars will disappear if only children are no longer vitiated by the gift of tin soldiers or if we learn how to bear with patience our neighbor's radio and his wife's sadistic insistence on becoming a coloratura. Businessmen's conventions seem even more thrilling: with the eloquence of figures, they tell each other glowingly of the generous services they are rendering and of the new selling devices they are contriving. Meanwhile they must be so bored at listening to each other's feats that they have to imbibe—not learned papers or words of scolding as we are content to do in our most unplatonic symposia—but more liquid and more potent beverages. One even reads that they spread terror in hotels where, having cast off all restraint as they donned a shriner's or a legionnaire's garb, they end by dancing with the furniture or tossing hostesses to the ceiling. (For unlike ourselves, they prefer to leave their wives at home.)

Our profession probably deserves some of the sermons which it meekly receives annually. It is overworked, and ever since men ceased going to church with the punctilious zeal of their Victorian forefathers, they have to seek in lay sermons the healthy relaxation which their ancestors found in holier surroundings. But one may claim for the teachers and scholars in the humanities that they are probably the least corrupt group in the country today. For, according to an honored saying, power is what corrupts, and power is most often provided by money, which is not our "Grace abounding." They are, moreover, perhaps the most critically essential group today, if it is true that changing man alone will save the world from the direst catastrophes, and education and literature are probably, after religion, the best means for changing man. Of all the careers pursued by men and women in different walks of life, none probably is so intent as we are on enabling human beings to understand, tolerate, and even aid each other, despite barriers of language and cultural divergences. I would venture to add that, in a world more and more inhabited by people seeking "peace of mind" and devouring unappetizing books entitled "Why worry?" nowhere does one meet so many eager, blissfully absent-minded, eloquently extrovert, and truly happy persons than on our college campuses. Teaching is still the best means devised by man for unburdening his mind, and occasionally for leaving it unfilled in the process. Our percentage of heart failures is almost disconcertingly low. Have we rediscovered, in a world accused of worshipping Mammon, that true success is, as David Starr Jordan once defined it, "doing the thing one likes, and being paid for it"?

Better qualified speakers will tell you of our grave responsibilities to ourselves and to the world in the present need for better international understanding. A Frenchman, coming from a nation which has traditionally preferred stressing social amenities and sociability to social duties, is not particularly qualified to discourse to Americans on their social responsibilities. He shudders at the prospect of a grave but univiting world in which the Modern Language Association will establish its cultural service stations along the highways of the country, with literary inscriptions such as this:

> *No matter where, of comfort no man speak;*
> *Relax and read the monograph series*
> *Of the scholars in modern languages;*
> *Better than all the poisons of the East*
> *They shall medicine thee to that sweet peace*
> *Which learned minds enjoy.*

On the other hand, it would be just as unbecoming of me to join in the pointed skirmish of the "old" critics against the "new" ones. The new and the old differ but little on the fundamentals, unless it be that the "new" ones refrain courteously from exercising their criticism against each other, and even from writing actual critical appreciations; they modestly stand at the threshold of the august shrine of metaphor, ambiguity, and paradox that they hope one day to erect, overawed by the all-pervading irony "of what is past, or passing, or to come" in the realm of poetry. Our age will thus have devoted itself to interminable prolegomena to a metaphysics of future criticism. We shall generously leave it to our posterity to write the criticism itself. But we owe a great debt to those "new critics"; for they have shaken some of us out of our complacency. Thanks to them, we may now acknowledge that our traditional historical scholarship has lately failed to attract brilliant recruits to our profession and to fire its own devotees with illuminating sparks. Let us remain diverse, and welcome the emulation of different methods, whenever they are practiced with talent.

My theme is an assessment of our situation in America today in the field of modern foreign languages and literatures. It may not be amiss to look backward for a brief moment. The Modern Language Association of America was founded sixty-five years ago, in 1883. The first *PMLA* (*Publications of the Modern Language Association*) were for the year 1884–85. *Modern Language Notes*, also due to our great pioneer, Marshall Elliott, followed in 1886. The first Ph.D. in the Romance Languages was recommended at our "duce, signore e maestro" among the American centers of learning, Johns Hopkins, in 1881. From Baltimore, graduates went out to found and develop departments at Harvard, Columbia, Yale, then at Chicago and Middle Western and Western universities.* In two-thirds of a century, the progress has been literally astounding. No other achievement in any other country can be even remotely compared to the American accomplishment in this field. For America began with a lag of at least thirty years on the revival of education and research advocated in England by Matthew Arnold, in France by Renan and Victory

---

* See several articles by John L. Gerig on "Doctoral Dissertations in the Romance Languages: a Survey and Bibliography," covering Johns Hopkins, Harvard, Yale and Columbia, in the *Romantic Review*, VIII (1917), 328–53; X (1919), 67–68; XI (1920), 70–75; and XII (1921), 73–79.

Duruy, and a lag of sixty years relative to Germany. Everything in the teaching of modern languages had to be created
from nothing, and the competent men had to be attracted
from afar, or slowly trained. Of course, the land of Jefferson
and Franklin had not been without cultural contacts with
Europe. In fact, when America was actually isolated, the
knowledge of some foreign languages was accepted as an
obvious requirement for those who aspired to culture; the
necessity for such an acquaintance with modern languages,
hence with the spirit and the soul of other countries, has
only been questioned since it should have been commanded
by changed circumstances, among oceans which have
shrunk and in a world attempting to be One. Poe, Longfellow, Lowell, Howells had been well-versed in Romance
literatures. But the methodical and scholarly study of those
literatures was nonexistent. The early American doctoral
theses were both thin and too ambitious, lacked both sound-
ness and finish.

Today, in contrast, the scholarly work produced, and not
necessarily published, in America is quantitatively the most
important in the world. American learned journals—from
*PMLA* to the *Modern Language Quarterly*, from *ELH*
and *American Literature* to *Italica* and the *Hispanic Review*, from two or three reviews on Germanic questions and
*Speculum* to the latest born ones: *Symposium, Romance
Philology* and *Yale French Studies*—rank everywhere
among the fullest and the most widely read and quoted.
Everywhere our work is respected for its thoroughness and
its seriousness; the faults which occasionally marred it, lack
of finish, loss of the proper perspective, fear of subjectivity
and of boldness, are now in great part disappearing, or being fought and conquered. On Spenser and Coleridge, on
Shelley and on Goethe, on Diderot and on Baudelaire, on
Petrarch and Lope de Vega, no one can deny that American
scholarly output is today not only indispensable, but unequalled in usefulness. True, we have enjoyed material facilities which compensated for our remoteness from old
manuscripts and rare texts; we have been powerfully aided
by one of the most admirable professions in America, the

librarians; we have brought foreign scholars to train our own and have welcomed those who were unhappy in their native land. Still, much credit is due to the intelligence and the zeal of American scholars and not a little to this Association for the standards it has upheld and the spirit it has fostered. Outside of France today for French letters, outside of Germany for German letters, outside of Spain for Spanish letters, the most abundant and the best work on those foreign literatures is being done in our century in the United States of America.

Such a remarkable achievement may inspire us with legitimate pride. But it must also lead us to some critical soul-searching, and to the discovery of a remedy for the shortcomings from which we still suffer. For the goal proposed to us is higher than it ever was for any country. Too many Americans are content to describe themselves as leading in technological civilization and as only the material benefactors of the world. The leadership which is expected from them, and thrust upon them, is, however, cultural and spiritual even more than technological. It requires wide information on other cultures which America must inherit, develop further, and transmit; a solid knowledge of other lands, of other ways of feeling and thinking; and more intellectual boldness in assimilating the best of the past and incorporating it into a new synthesis. The best key to such an understanding of others, when all is said, is to be provided by their language, dissected in its complexities and mastered in a living way, and in what a scientist, Thomas Huxley, called "the greatest of all sources of refined pleasure," literature.

What do we still lack that might be easily acquired, and where do our deficiencies occur? To begin with, we have not progressed with the same energy in all fields. Scholarship, with all its claims to gravity and objectivity, has remained feminine in its docile subservience to tides of fashion. We have flocked now to the Victorians, now to the Metaphysicals; we have accumulated studies on Dryden and Boswell at the expense of the Elizabethans, on Voltaire and Diderot while neglecting earlier periods; of all our sins of omission, the most regrettable is that of Italian studies. Italian literature formerly held a considerable place in the total sum of the articles and theses in the Romance field published in America; Italian letters and Italian art meant a great deal to cultured Americans, in the eighteen-nineties. We still boast of a few, a very few, eminent Italian scholars. But paradoxically enough, since this corresponds to the years when sons and grandsons of Italian immigrants have become or should have become culture-conscious and have much to contribute to America, we have let Italian lag far behind other languages and Italian scholarship be almost stifled by isolation and frustration. The part which should be played in our culture by Dante, by the finest outburst of geniuses in the modern world, the Italian Renaissance, has thus shrunk to a ridiculously inadequate one.

We have similarly fallen behind in the last twenty years in Romance philology and the study of medieval literature, of France in particular. Too few disciples have followed in the footsteps of the early generation of Johns Hopkins philologists, and more recently of Armstrong, Nitze, Ford, and others. A reaction was obviously to be expected against the old Germanic concept of European literatures taken to be unworthy subjects of study after the fifteenth century. But Germanic and Romance philology have been completely renovated since 1900 or 1910, and should again attract a new group of eager devotees. The medievalists among us should rid their subject of the conventional paraphernalia which have made it appear needlessly formidable and have severed it from the philosophy, the art, the life of the Middle Ages. The impact of many works of medieval literature should be equal, on modern minds, to that of Romanesque sculpture, of Gothic architecture, of Saint Thomas and Saint Bonaventura. We are to blame if it is not.

A second point deserves to be lamented if we are not mistaken in stressing it. There are many eminent scholars in the modern languages in America; the list of our past presidents would at once reveal the names of some of them. Yet, considering our population and our own numbers, we seem to have had since 1885 and to have at present only a very few men of towering eminence: scholars of the stature of Gaston Paris, Bédier, Lanson among the great Frenchmen of a departed generation; of the universality of Menendez y Pelayo, Baldensperger, Farinelli, of the originality of Karl Vossler, Menendez Pidal, Cazamian; of the finish and subtlety of Damaso Alonso, Grierson, Hazard. It is invidious thus to select men still active and rank them with respected dead ones; yet achievements like those of Marcel Bataillon on Erasmus and Spain, of Toynbee on history, of some German art-critics and literary critics who followed in the footsteps of Gundolf, Wölfflin, Curtius, impressive monuments like Chambers' *Elizabethan Stage* or the *Storia letteraria d'Italia* or Andler's *Nietzche* do not seem to be easily matched in America.

Why is it? Do gifted American scholars, like American novelists, like American wines, somehow fail to mature after a certain age? Are they overburdened by an excessive teaching load, too much administration, a laudable but pernicious eagerness to answer letters and to hear their own voices echoed in committees? Are we too generous in placing ourselves at the disposal of our students? Is the national disease, haste and the pursuit of efficiency, proving detrimental to the slow maturation of scholarly production? Have we frowned, with Puritan suspicion, upon leisure, whose very name meant "school" among the Greeks and has given the word scholarship, and thus become a human, all too human competitor of men in business? Have our luxurious offices, away from the din of cities, acted as less potent stimulants on our continued production than crying children and a nagging wife who often sent the European Monsieur Bergeret to his study at home, mad with rage and redoubled determination to take full advantage of the little quietude that was left to him?

Others may answer these questions. I may merely declare, as one who has seen many others at work elsewhere, that our young men are at least as gifted as those of any other land; that their undergraduate and graduate critical essays are often rich in promise and even in fulfillment. Perhaps our graduate training is not adapted to develop the best in them, and the problem should one day be examined seriously by our Association. The ferment which might be provided by emulation, in a small circle gathered around an inspiring scholar-teacher, is often absent from our seminars. Conscientiousness, scrupulousness, methodical thoroughness we have, and bibliographical zeal, and an infinite capacity for taking pains and even for enjoying boredom, which is our own brand of genius; all this we have. Do we not lack fervor? And imagination? And the contagious fire which critics such as Gundolf and Croce, literary historians like Lanson and Menendez Pidal, kindled in their circle of students?

Too often our Ph.D. is an end which seems to close the door on any further desire ever again to do or to publish research. It should on the contrary, in at least half of the cases, be only a prelude to future publications. Is the organization of the degree and of the studies leading to it sterilizing? Nothing is sacrosanct to us, and the question should not stay for an answer.

Respect for our Old Guard and reverence for the scholarly papers of the most venerable among us should not silence the younger members of our Association into awe, or perhaps into repressed but embittered impatience. Junior members, under 40 or 45, might well receive their fair share of responsibilities in our important committees and be encouraged to display initiative and boldness. Our Association never has been, and never must become, a gerontocracy.

One of our evils, too well-known to deserve very long comment here, is excessive departmentalization. It is easier to denounce it than to cure it. For departments there must be: they are the backbone of our academic organization, the channels through which we administer, the organs responsible for recruiting, selecting, and placing graduate students. They alone can provide the unity and the spirit of fervent emulation which are essential to promote the advancement of learning. But departments can be preserved without their imprisoning themselves in isolated cells. Some barriers have collapsed already and several nations are occasionally grouped into what, for lack of a better term, is called "areas" as fit subjects of studying a world endeavoring to outgrow nationalism. Literatures cannot easily be studied independently of the medium in which they are written, that is, separated from the language. But interdepartmental groups and comparative literature sections have lately been encouraged to develop in our Association and in our college curricula.

More remains to be done along the same lines. Teachers and students of modern languages are not sufficiently aware of the peril of studying literatures as detached from history, philosophy, psychology, history of art, history of music. While for the tenth time, with our students in quest of a thesis subject, we go over the sequence of Shakespeare's Sonnets, or the biographical value of the Prelude, or the architecture of the Fleurs du Mal, we overlook fresh provinces of study left untilled, such as the interrelation of literature and the arts, the picture of the scientific and philosophical world held by writers of a certain age, histories of taste or aesthetics, political thought which was often expressed with literary skill, etc. Many syntheses remain to be attempted, embracing the treatment by several allied literatures of great themes which filled the last century: the romantic spirit of revolt, the Promethean rebellion against the gods between 1800 and 1880, the concept of time in the later nineteenth-century novel, and many others. The development of three or four West European literatures has been closely parallel for a century or so, and scholars alone seem to remain unaware of it.

The lead for a broader spirit in the study of literary relations among several countries should have come from our colleagues in English or American literature. We must unfortunately confess that we have too often vainly expected from them such a leadership. They have remained in a superb isolation which smacked occasionally of complacent provinciality. Much credit will be due to the department of English which will lead the way in discarding the farce at present called "reading knowledge" of French and German and will require a true knowledge of one foreign literature appreciated for its poetical and aesthetic values, and therefore of the language heard and spoken. A graduate student in English who can decipher a page of German critical prose on Beowulf or a French quotation from Taine, but cannot feel a play by Racine or a lyric by Goethe, hardly has a claim to being called a cultured literary person even if he is allowed to win a doctor's degree.

Let us blame ourselves, teachers of foreign literatures, no less severely on another score. Professors of modern literatures have generously showed too great a deference to foreign scholars in Europe or to foreign scholars in their own midst. Professor Fife, in his presidential address at the 1944 meeting of our Association in New York, expressed himself courageously on this point in his address "Nationalism and Scholarship." Two acute observers of Germanic studies in America, Henry Hatfield and Joan Merrick, echoed and amplified his strictures in an article of the *Modern Language Review* for July 1948. America invites foreign scholars because they are foreign, and presumably more competent in some branches than many a native American, with a different outlook, and an innate feeling, as it were, for their own literature. She does not expect overhasty Americanization from those foreign guests, for that would be undue and gross flattery on their part, and might lose them some of the originality which they have been brought here to contribute. But this country also has a right to be spared constant reassertion, by those uprooted guests, of the cultural superiority of the Old World and systematic distrust of what is being attempted here, along more democratic lines and in an immense continent which lacks the benefits as well as the drawbacks of a long sense of the past. The presence of many foreign-born scholars among us should develop in this country an eclectic point of view, free from the bias of cultural nationalism and enriched by the variety of ethnic backgrounds and of intellectual methods of approach which America thus stands to gain.

But wise eclecticism does not require that American scholars strive to imitate the qualities of foreign scholars at the expense of what might be their own national (which in no way means nationalistic) approach to the literatures of other lands. French clarity and Gallic wit, Spanish verve, German profundity and metaphysical cloudiness are virtues in Frenchmen, Spaniards, Germans. But Americans need not ape them. They have or will have more and more virtues of their own which have already won respect among their European colleagues. The German scholars when they write on Dante and Calderon (Vossler) or on Balzac (Curtius) treat those writers in a German manner. So do the English when they write on Goethe or on Molière. The very remarkable school of specialists in Germanic or English studies in France is characterized by unmistakably French features. All of them write in their own language, even translate quotations from foreign prose works into their own tongue for their own public. Why should American scholars make their own critical studies appear formidable to the cultured layman by multiplying quotations from foreign works and wrapping their thoughts in "the decent obscurity of a learned language," when they should strain every nerve to win a wider audience for the results of their labors?

It is difficult to define what a specific American approach to the study of literature should be; it would be unbecoming in a foreign professor in America to attempt it. Such an elusive thing as a national style in scholarship as well as in architecture, in music as well as in criticism, can only be a spontaneous and slow growth. But many of our graduate students would hasten the day when such a spirit can become a reality if they would freely reappraise old masters like Montaigne, Cervantes, Petrarch, Schiller, Pushkin, from a point of view which would be their own; or if they would occasionally evaluate Anatole France and Kafka and T. S. Eliot with American eyes. Their tendency has been to profess an excessive deference to foreign critics who were compatriots of those writers, but were not necessarily the wiser or the less partisan for being close to them.

Let our suggestion not be misunderstood. We do not wish to imply that differences between national psychologies

are greater than their similarities: Balzac's peasants and
Flaubert's bourgeois have their exact replicas in America,
and D. H. Lawrence's or Faulkner's heroes are probably as
true, or as untrue, in France and Spain as they are in New
Mexico or Mississippi. But true universality, in culture
and criticism, is not attained through the levelling down
of valuable national characteristics. The writers most acclaimed abroad are often those who seemed the least likely
to be understood outside of their own borders, because, like
Dostoevsky or Dickens or Giono, they seemed to be the
most "national" of all. No less prominent an internationalist
in literary matters than André Gide remarked that the most
universal writer is often also the most national writer, and
the works which are most broadly human are also the most
individual ones. ("Nationalisme et Littérature"—1909—
in *Oeuvres Complètes*, VI) Although we live in an international age, we cannot reach international understanding
through intellectual monotony, but through the mutual enrichment contributed to each other by national cultures,
and the assimilation of one or two foreign cultures by those
of us who believe ourselves capable of such assimilation.

Finally, professors of foreign languages, without forsaking the scholar's prerogative to study the past and to
rise above the ephemeral struggles of the hour, owe it to
themselves to keep abreast of developments around them
and to interpret them to their communities. The influence
of contemporary books published abroad is naturally greater
than that of past masterpieces, and probably disproportionate to the place which Expressionism, Surrealism, Exis-
tentialism will some day occupy in our detached appraisal.
But the scholar cannot ignore the present-day developments
in Spanish America or in Europe if he will retain and expand his influence on the young men around him. Translations from foreign works are published liberally in America;
we should be more often consulted on which foreign works
deserve to be translated, and the choice might be made in a
less haphazard fashion by publishers, and probably prove
more successful, even commercially, than the present one
does. We should be called upon more often to review such

translated works or important foreign movements, and would doubtless do it with more competence and perhaps with more brilliance than many journalists who step in where we fear to tarnish our wings. Professors of German, French, Italian, should have provided more experts on German, French, Italian affairs, during World War II, than they did; too often they proved unable to envisage the foreign country whose culture they taught with an impartial eye and from an American (which does not mean a narrow or uninitiated, but a free) point of view. If we do not keep actively and objectively abreast of problems and moods in the country which we study and teach, we are confessing that we divorce literature from life, the books from the soil and the people in which the books grew, or that we refuse to make our accumulated and specialized knowledge accessible to a public of intelligent nonspecialists.

To fulfill such a program, we must face two more requisites squarely and successfully. On the first I may be brief, for others have eloquently formulated it. For several decades, our presidential addresses have warned us that we neglected beauty and style and were unwisely desiccating our scholarship. Such an appeal has fallen on willing spirits whose flesh apparently, or whose pen, was weak. Our remarkably active Secretary has now taken steps which should soon turn our good intentions into actual practice. Let us thus live in hope and merely repeat that we must write better, avoid pedantic jargon and cumbersome footnotes, aim at clarity, elegance, and liveliness. Even humor, grace, and a burning flame should not be absent from papers written by scholars who include many humorous and jovial older men, many women (i.e. beings endowed with grace), and not a few ardent young men. One of our tasks is to teach the youth of the country how to write, and we should first propose to them some discreet models. Too long have we meekly tolerated scathing ironies from journalists and authors, instead of proving convincingly that their sarcasms were often unfounded. A character in Hemingway's *Death in the Afternoon*, courteously wishing the death of our breed, professed that he hoped to see the finish of us all, and to "speculate how worms will try that long preserved sterility, with their quaint pamphlets gone to dust and into footnotes all their lust." Let us share that blasphemous hope if we are to rise from it reborn with a vigorous style and a keener sense for beauty when treating of things which once were beautiful and therefore have remained so. We shall then see that we, ultimately, hold in our hands the fate of writers like Hemingway, who may one day owe it to us to have their names preserved for posterity through a chapter, a page, or a line in our literary histories.

The second need in which we stand is for bolder imagination and greater faith in our accomplishment, in ourselves, in what we have to offer today to America and to the world. Science is just now suffering from a bad conscience. It can no longer take it for granted that its advancement necessarily leads to more welfare for the human race; it is obsessed by its share in bringing about what may be our indiscriminate destruction. Many are the scientists who, to offset the consequences of their own ominous work, openly pray for an increase in the study of the Humanities. They acknowledge that our own studies may lead man to more wisdom, and meanwhile afford men and women some joys while they still inhabit this unatomized earth.

Social scientists have meanwhile taken the offensive and tried to crowd out the classics, the modern languages, perhaps literature itself from the school and college curricula, in order to start more courses on the mores of the Fiji islanders, matriarchy among the tribes of Central Australia, the community spirit of Main Street and the behavior of Middletown, the necessity of being "well-adjusted" (to a none too perfect society, to be sure), and "how to be successful in married life." In many cases, the youth of this country is becoming impatient with such soulless teaching and chafes at masses of meaningless and unconnected data which are being crammed into their heads under the guise of "social studies." It is ready to return to courses in ancient and modern literatures, in philosophy, in history of culture. Difficulties do not daunt it. Young Americans are attracted by reasonable difficulties and respond ardently to obstacles which challenge the best in youth. But we have too often made the mistake of aping scientists in their dry analyses, in their statistical figuring, in their dry presentation. We have praised works of art for being produced by, or expressive of, the social conditions of an age. We should on the contrary have shown our students that literature deals with the same problems which they meet in life and in historical and social courses, but makes those problems significant, intense, radiating with life and beauty. Let us make our teaching bolder, more imaginative, solid yet broad, minute at times but at times all-embracing, filled with passion and fervor. Many a young American will then find in our teaching some of the vitality and some of the breadth of significance for which he thirsts. A dynamic and, when all is said, a great American poet pronounced in *Democratic Vistas* words which we might well remember and prove worthy of: "Literature in our day and current purposes is not only more eligible than all the other arts put together, but has become the only general means of morally influencing the world."

Some of our members may feel that such claims made for literature, and for those who teach it worthily, are merely rhetorical and that reality is otherwise when one is isolated in some small college, deprived of books and of congenial spirits, struggling against the practical obsessions of their environment. We certainly cannot impose overnight the views in which we believe. But do we not err even more gravely if we resign ourselves to mild defeatism and "laissez-faire"? Professor Howard Mumford Jones once called us—academic critics and scholars—"the uninfluentials." We shall deserve the name only if we persist in thinking of ourselves as uninfluential.

An observer trained in a foreign background insists on disputing such a pessimistic picture of American universities. "Never underestimate the power of a woman" is one of the first phrases he learns from American advertising, and he is soon brought to add: "Never underestimate the power of a professor." The universities play in this country a part probably unequalled anywhere else. On their campuses the heart of the nation beats more intensely; for the sake of the youth that lives there—training its muscles as well as its brain, "exposed," as we say, to culture, and often actually soaked in it—this youth-loving nation is ever ready to make the utmost sacrifices. Materially, the universities of America are far more powerful and secure than the Church ever was in France before the Revolution; recent inquiries reveal that they own the most varied kind of property, from book stores to a spaghetti factory in New York, a clear symbol of the tentacular eloquence of some of their teachers.

No other country holds the "experts" in such esteem. Professors, and professors of literature in particular, have achieved remarkable success during the war in realms of action far removed from their usual preoccupations. They do equally well in military government when they are given a chance. Diplomacy seldom regrets resorting to them: both the French and British Ambassadors in Washington at present are professors, and Spanish diplomats have been repeatedly drawn from their ranks. Money and politics have kept them away from similar positions in this country, but certainly not luck of ability. The most momentous revolution of the last two decades, the New Deal, was to a great extent a professors' revolution, no less profound for being peaceful. The Republican candidate for President in 1948 might have fared better in the popular vote had he surrounded himself with a professorial brain trust, facing the issues and devising the answers, while some professors of literature might have added fire and sparks to his speeches with no little profit. Several of us may say without vain boasting that they have powerfully helped launch a new book or damn a new play, and that the effect of some of our unbiased pronouncements in a public lecture has often proved greater than that of much paid advertising. Not a little of the present clamor for more vital plays on Broadway and even more of the present disfavor of Hollywood can be traced to our influence in having awakened the youth, and others who were no longer young but directly or indirectly paid some attention to professors' sarcasms and pronouncements, to the mechanical emptiness of what the stage and the screen served to the public.

We are not going to be intoxicated with the power that we can wield, but we might become more keenly conscious of it and realize that it entails responsibilities and duties. The college population in America runs at present well over two millions and is not likely to decrease. No other profession in the country enjoys an opportunity similar to ours. For the training we give those millions of young men and women may mark them for life. For a few years in their existence, those young men pursue knowledge with some disinterestedness; they champion idealistic causes, dream of a better future for mankind. A surprisingly large number of them declare they want to write. We are to blame if we fail that gifted and generous youth. We in particular, scholars in the modern literatures, shall be to blame if we do not practice a reasonable amount of propaganda for our disciplines, bearing in mind the noble meaning of a word which was originally used for the "propagation" of Christian religion. If we nourish a deep faith in what we teach and live for, we have the duty to communicate it with élan as well as with critical spirit, two virtues which can and must coexist and strengthen each other.

The Modern Language Association has achieved a great deal in its sixty-five years of existence. It is now being rejuvenated and, without forsaking any of its dignity or becoming renegade to its humanistic traditions, it can do even more. It must claim a voice in councils of educators, be consulted by the President's Committee on Education, provide colleges with deans and presidents, who have been drawn lately in disproportionate numbers from the ranks of economists and psychologists. Colleges were not run less efficiently when their deans were, for the most part, professors of Classics or of Hebrew. Indeed, the greatest of American college presidents were perhaps those who, in the last decades of the nineteenth century, created with idealism and pragmatism Johns Hopkins, Chicago, Stanford, and reno-

vated Harvard, Cornell, Yale. Modern languages have today a valid claim to being the worthiest heirs to classical
languages and literatures. Let them assert it. Let our Association join forces with parallel associations of scholars
in philosophy, in history, in classics, in history of art. Let
it use modern means of information and even practice some
lobbying without shame. It is all very well to go on telling
our own colleagues every year that our subject is important and necessary to the culture of the country; our colleagues are convinced of it. Let us live our own culture
more intensely, present it with more vigor to those who
have ears but often refuse to open them: newspaper men,
government officials, businessmen, many of whom are our
former students and have remained grateful to us for having revealed some beauty to them, and some truth, when
they sat "under us." Our Association may have to reinforce
its central office to reach those aims: perhaps, along with a
rotating President, elected annually and representing a different branch of our studies and a different part of the country as well as being a renowned scholar, we should have a
second and stable executive cooperating with our Secretary,
giving most of his time to our Association, addressing the
country occasionally through educational conferences and
committees, visiting universities, keeping in close touch
with developments in Washington, educating politicians,
if need be, and donors, approaching the Foundations on
critical needs such as that for publication funds for American scholarship—so critical a need at the present time that
the whole intellectual effort of America is jeopardized
through increased printing costs and a revision of the
policy of Foundations has become imperative.

In thus discarding some of our complacency and fear of
"vulgarity," we shall not be serving our own interests selfishly, but the culture of the country at large and the future
of America, now asked to assume a bolder intellectual
leadership in the arts and letters as well as in science and
technology. "Universities," wrote Abraham Flexner, "must
at times give the country, not what it wants, but what
it needs." Is this antidemocratic? The truly democratic-

minded man is obviously he who refuses to flatter the masses but believes in their ultimate common sense and helps democracy improve itself, and extract from its ranks the intellectual leadership which is essential to its survival. A great American and, in spite of party labels, a true democrat, Charles Evans Hughes, once said in words which we might well take as the text of many of our lay sermons: "The cure for the ills of democracy is not more democracy, but more intelligence."

# Comparative Literature in America

I<small>T WOULD HAVE SEEMED NATURAL FOR AMERICA</small> to become the paradise for Comparative Literature. For American universities have been less narrowly fettered with hidebound traditions than those of an older continent and have proved hospitable to new subjects, to the point of being accused of an exaggerated fondness for temporary vogues and whimsical fads. The ethnic origins and often the backgrounds of Americans, within the last century, have been a motley pattern contrasting with the unity and even with the educational uniformity prevailing in countries like France or Germany. Some knowledge of languages, at least nominal, is required by most respectable graduate schools and colleges. What is more, an enviable freedom from nationalist prejudices prevails in the United States. Patriotism and nationalism are not absent from this country, but they seldom assume the cultural character which marks French or Italian nationalism, Spanish pride in "Hispanidad," or the German jealous cultivation of a mysterious "Deutschtum." Americans have long been aware of the need for them to have more than one window open upon Europe and not to be content with the one literary tradition which they had inherited with the English language. In the last two or three decades, new duties developed upon this country: it fell to the lot of America to be, not only the greatest power on this planet, but the obvious link between Europe and Asia, and between the past and the future of mankind. Greco-Roman culture, as transmitted and enriched by western Europe, may have appeared less adequate than in the past, in the face of the growth of anthropology, sociology, abnormal psychology, recent physics; but that culture had first to be assimilated and carried forward before it could be supplemented.

Yet many obstacles have stood in the way of Comparative Literature in American universities, and only recently, thanks to a broader welcome in the Modern Language Association gatherings and to the faith and efficient earnestness of those who founded the "Comparative Literature Newsletters" and the specialized quarterly journal now published by the University of Oregon, has the new discipline won readier acceptance in many a center of learning. The close partitioning of departments in many universities makes innovations difficult, when each department tends to accumulate its own required courses and jealously watches its own students. Our Ph.D. has become a thorough but excessively narrow training, and the holders of that degree realize only later that their actual teaching will require more breadth and a keener awareness of two or three fields than their scholastic training has provided. Factual data are often overemphasized at the expense of breadth. A teacher of English may be supposed, after reluctantly submitting to reading tests, to be able to decipher a page by a French or German critic; but he is seldom able to read with sincere enjoyment a lyric by Goethe or Rilke, a play of Racine, or a chapter from Montaigne.

To be sure, comparative scholars may well bear part of the blame. They have occasionally been guilty of pedantry, although more often in Europe than in America; their readers have been overwhelmed and exasperated; their students have been misled by the wealth of their references, the luxuriance of their allusions and quotations, and often by the failure of their discipline to penetrate to the core of a literary work or to grasp a writer in the essentials of his creative process. The close student of one national literature naturally finds occasional confusion, superficial parallels or tenuous links, and even more unpalatable generalizations in Farinelli and Baldensperger, in Gilbert Highet's *Classical Tradition*, in Menendez y Pelayo and J. G. Robertson, Comparative Literature is strewn with pitfalls into which tyros jump all too gleefully. Several times a year, the professor must dissuade determined students from sketching one more fruitless comparison between Stendhal and Tolstoy, Proust and Joyce, Virginia Woolf and Bergson, Verga and Mérimée, Rilke and Valéry, O'Neill and Lorca. The myrtle groves of the underworld must be populated by writers of the past imploring "whatever gods may be" that they may be spared studies of sources and influences allegedly undergone by them. Two requisites should be self-imposed by practitioners of Comparative Literature: one is naturally intelligence accompanied by taste and enjoyment—"Comprendre, c'est égaler," as a wise French dictum puts it. The other is modesty; for the task is immense, and while "knowledge enormous makes a god of me" may befit Keats' Apollo and a few supermen among comparative scholars, others have symbolically perished from such "hubris."

It may not be amiss for a French scholar in America to review the several provinces of Comparative Literature and the American achievements and promises in those fields. From the start, American comparatists have been bound to their French confrères by close links. Longfellow, Howells, Lowell, Huneker, who entertained a broad view of literature in their day, looked intently at Romance countries. So did Schofield, Spingarn, Irving Babbitt. Ever since the *Revue de Littérature Comparée* and the fame of Baldensperger, then of Hazard, Van Tieghem, Carré, made Paris the most fertile center of comparative studies, American scholars have looked up to the French masters in that discipline, sent their students to them, encouraged the writing of theses in France, and envied the broad cosmopolitan spirit which prevailed there. Many of the best theoretical definitions of the aims and methods of Comparative Literature have emanated from France and their usefulness is far from outgrown.

Comparative Literature, thus called after the deceptive

precedents of comparative anatomy or comparative government, is not an ideal name; but it must be retained as being neither too pedantic nor too general, and usage has consecrated it. The spirit which prompted the creation of the new discipline was naturally the cosmopolitan current of the eighteenth century and the revived interest in national cultures and in the originality of each "spontaneous" folk creation. "Happy he who has discovered literary cosmopolitanism!" exclaimed Sébastien Mercier. The romantic movement, helped by the emigration and the Napoleonic wars, fostered the growth of the cosmopolitan spirit. Its philosophical basis was in part the substitution of relative for absolute standards of beauty and of taste and the acceptance of the organic development of each culture, stressing the autonomy of each and its ability to absorb and assimilate foreign influences. The Germans had the largest share in the framing and spreading of those views. But the French also played a role, and Mme de Staël, French in her language, had been among the first to encourage European nations to shake off the yoke of French taste. Soon after aging Goethe's famous pronouncement on "Weltliteratur," Edgar Quinet, who first used the phrase "Comparative Literature" in French, declared in 1838, when appointed to the first French professorship of Comparative Literature at Lyon: "There is a certain narrowness in the obstinate refusal to understand the spirit of foreign nations. Feeling beauty wherever it may be found is not impairing one's delicacy, but acquiring a new faculty." Later De Sanctis, while Minister of Education under Cavour, created a chair of Comparative Literature in Italy in 1861 and occupied it himself in 1871. But progress was slow and often interrupted until the end of the century. A clear realization of the purpose of Comparative Literature and some attempt to formulate its methods had to await the second decade of the present century. Even now, many problems are far from solved, hence their challenging interest.

The provinces of Comparative Literature have often been mapped out and surveyed; a great number of relatively easy subjects have been proposed to and treated by apprentices of Comparative Literature. In several respects, indeed, more conventionality seems to prevail in some comparative studies of themes, sources, and influences than in the isolated studies of one writer or of one work. This stems in part from the mistaken notion that Comparative Literature is a separate domain which the specialist must explore exclusively, thus condemning himself in many cases to touching only on the outside fringe of each national literature, leaving the core of it to scholars who concentrate on the inner evolution of one literature. In truth, while it is essential for each university to have a separate department of Comparative Literature, it would be absurd for such a department to monopolize the research into the foreign relations of each literature. For its task is to know foreign languages and to have a broader and more receptive point of view than specialists of individual literatures, and also to foster among its colleagues a comparative spirit and to bridge over the barriers which administrative necessities and the temptation of insularity tend to impose upon departments.

Such a spirit still needs to be developed among many American scholars, and the task which lies before broadminded comparatists in this country is still a challenging one. Many a recent study of American literature by Americans strikes one as ludicrously provincial in its ignorance or omission of the trends and movements which, in Germany, in France, had preceded philosophical and literary developments in America. Emerson, Poe, Howells, Henry James, Hemingway and Ezra Pound can be appraised rightly only if placed in a supranational context. The extraordinary vogue enjoyed by American literature in Europe and elsewhere since 1930 necessitates a comparative approach, for writers can no longer remain unaware of the fact that they may well be consecrated in Paris, Rome, and Stockholm earlier than in Boston and Los Angeles. Contrary to a common delusion, this cosmopolitan success does not go to writers who are themselves uprooted and international in outlook.

Comparatists do not agree among themselves, most fortunately, on the relative importance and fertility of the different domains within their empire. Each generation should always remain free to shift the emphasis from one to the other, and an imaginative scholar may at any time prove that a field that had been branded as barren may conceal untold wealth. Thus the "Stoffgeschichte" or study of themes and legends across several literatures, which has often proved to be mechanical and exterior, may receive a new lease on life from a revitalized study of symbols and myths aided by modern anthropology and psychoanalysis. Monographs on the horse, the skylark, the flea in poetry, the priest, the child or the courtesan in several recent literatures deserve some of the ridicule which they have brought upon themselves. Yet the different expressions given by succeeding generations to the theme of social and metaphysical revolt, envisaged through the symbolic figures of Prometheus, Cain, Faust, Sisyphus (lately), Antigone, Orestes, and other men and women in revolt dear to Camus and to Sartre, are well worth the comparatist's pains. The myth of Narcissus, which haunted many of the French Symbolists and their successors; the theme of metamorphosis of men into other men or into animals, brilliantly revived by Kafka, Marcel Aymé, and many a story teller of late; the obsession of many French novelists with abortion (an Existentialist device apparently) and with bastards (the latter a natural enough offspring, as Claude-Edmonde Magny remarked, in a generation of novelists whose predecessors had lavishly filled their tales with adulterous couples); the type of "l'étranger" or the alienated man would repay the research of students, if explored in depth.

The study of literary genres, long thrown out of fashion by Brunetière's excessive claims, might similarly be revived by comparative scholars. Courses on tragedy, the epic, and satire are again popular in our universities. The eclogue, the poetic drama, the fantastic tale are again being practiced in several literatures and rightly being credited with laws of their own. The mistake of Brunetière was, along with his ponderous style, to have attempted a systematic and exterior study of genres, viewed as babies slowly evolving into childhood, adolescence, and maturity, then irretrievably engulfed by old age and death. The notion of evolution, and even that of the Hegelian becoming, have caused much havoc in literary studies. Neither genres nor individual authors necessarily evolve or "become." Any life of any worth is marked by a few crises or sudden about-faces from which one emerges a different being. A writer taps different strata of his inner life according to the demands of his inspiration, then may lapse into moments of sterility like the mystics. It is probably vain to formulate laws for literary genres, since all creators are violators. But the psychological and esthetic motives which, for example, have in the last three decades reintegrated tragedy into the drama after having lent it to the novel for a long time would well be worth the attention of the critics who are struck by the parallel trends in several national literatures.

A province of Comparative Literature long favored by the French practitioners of that discipline embraces the intermediaries between two nations, two or more cultures. A respectable number of dissertations, not all of them original, treated of the travelers of one nation in Scotland, Ireland, Sicily, Bavaria, America. As traveling became easier, however, the literature of travel also became more and more superficial. The truly important subjects again would be those which, going beyond historical and biographical research, would venture into the psychology of individuals or of groups and of the imaginative and intellectual adventure afforded some travelers by their wanderings. Stendhal's vision of Italy and his original touristic literature on France, Gobineau's extraordinarily acute perception of Asia, and the twentieth-century French travelers in China and Japan have not been adequately studied. The French, who do not readily venture into distant lands, have been praised by no less a judge than Lord Curzon as the most admirable writers of travel books. Sartre, who has roamed over many lands himself, condemned the traveler in a curious passage of *Qu'est-ce la littérature* as the very image of a parasite and of the unstable stranger and perpetual witness. The attitude of each generation to travel and exoticism should be studied as a mirror to its deeper preoccupations.

The mistake of comparative scholars has often lain in being easily satisfied with specific monographs of a purely analytical character and in lacking the audacity to approach larger works of synthesis. Thus the Huguenot emigration to England or America, the Russian emigration of 1917–20, and the German-Jewish emigration of 1933–45, which have had momentous importance for intellectual, literary and artistic history, have not yet been adequately examined. Nor have the epoch-making translations from Homer, the Greek tragic poets, Virgil, Shakespeare, or Dostoevsky, which count far more in the history of culture than nine-tenths of the so-called original novels or plays. The history of the teaching of the leading foreign languages in each important country should likewise be attempted: many Frenchmen have never gone beyond the few pages of Goethe, Wordsworth or E. A. Poe which they learned by heart as schoolboys; yet the influence of those pages upon their dreams, their imagination may have been far reaching. Many Americans have lived on notions of France acquired through Daudet's "La Dernière Classe," Flaubert's *Trois Contes*, Anatole France's *Les Dieux ont soif* or more recently through Alain-Fournier or Saint Exupéry. Yet we know practically nothing about the anthologies, grammars, textbooks, methods and histories of literature used successively since 1830 or 1840 in America or in other nations.

The main bulk of Comparative Literature studies has usually consisted of research on the foreign readings of a given writer, on his sources, on the fortune and the influence of his work in another country. It seems as if everything had been accomplished in those fields and that no virgin island has been left uncharted by the source and influence hunters. Parallels have been accumulated, library archives have been ransacked to discover which books were borrowed by a writer in his youth or while he was perhaps mysteriously nurturing some of the images and ideas which he was much later to embody in his works. Lists of books

owned by authors have been searched, in the naïve faith
that we all read and remember the books which, through
purchase, bequest or imprudent loan, happen to be "owned"
by us. Overgenerous authors who, like T. S. Eliot, Gide or
Yeats himself, were unwary enough to quote from or allude
to foreign writers whom they may have read, or looked at,
have been the targets of many source studies as a penalty
for what Richard Aldington termed (apropos of Yeats)
"their misplaced intellectual loyalty."

Once again, the inadequacy of many such comparative
studies sprang from lack of boldness to go straight to the
vast but only important subjects, and from the common
fault of much criticism which takes the reader away to the
outer fringes of the work of art instead of penetrating to its
core—and its core is almost always psychological or esthetic. The really important topics of Comparative Literature have hardly been touched: Vico in France, Schopen-
hauer in England, Nietzsche in America, Rousseau and
nineteenth-century America, Hegel in France. Even the
true influence of Poe in France (felt by Mallarmé and
Valéry even more than by Baudelaire) has not been adequately analyzed. The converse, equally paradoxical (and
surprising to the writer's compatriots) impact of Flaubert
on English novelists and on American novelists and poets,
down to Ezra Pound and James Joyce, is only a little better
explored. On broader movements which spread across several countries, but often at varied times and meeting un-
equal resistance in each of them, we are not much better
informed. We hardly know, for example, how the Renaissance was perceived or conceived by the authors and artists
of Italy, Spain, France or England, and to what extent a
common characterization of the Renaissance is valid in
those countries. The recent disquisition on the baroque has,
in spite of the fanaticism of some baroque maniacs, thrown
light on the heterogeneousness of different countries during the baroque age. But much remains to be done on the
use of "metaphysical" imagery in several European poet-
ries, to which the term has now been carried over from
English usage. Preromanticism is probably the most un-

explored of all great European movements; no specific term has even been coined to designate it. A European history of symbolism must some day be undertaken. In all such cases, and many more offered by our own century (the interior monologue, the reversibility of time in the modern novel, literature as prophecy, the Spanish civil war in several literatures, the theme of fear, the political novel, etc.), American comparative studies have one advantage over European ones: while they may stress similarities between or among national literatures and show modern movements sweeping unchallenged across national frontiers, they are in a position to grant its full due to the originality of every European nation. The French, the Germans, to a lesser extent the English, have often stolen the show in comparative studies. A veteran scholar sadly lamented the scant place granted to the original literature of Spain and to other letters of "smaller" countries in our research into influences and relations. We are alluding to Farinelli's contribution to the *Mélanges Baldensperger* (Champion, 1930, I, 271–90), in which he confessed that national pride had not disappeared with the growth of comparative studies and that literatures could not be reduced easily to a common denominator at the expense of their heterogeneous singularity.

Much harm has been caused by the ambition of literary study to ape science and to conceive science as a network of causal relations. Students of countries and of relations between two or more writers would be well advised to give up in most cases the search for causes or influences, and to engage in the exploration of families of minds and of fortuitous analogies linking authors who had no awareness of one another. Parallels are dangerous if set up by an untrained novice juxtaposing two writers or artists arbitrarily. But a great scholar, like the art critic Henri Focillon who repeatedly made use of the concept of "familles d'esprits," may thus practice comparative research more intelligently and imaginatively than narrowly historical scholars who, like Browning's grammarian, seek a little thing to do, see it, and do it. Northrop Frye remarked in his *Fearful Sym-*

*metry* that Nerval, who had never read Blake, is in fact closer to him than Yeats who edited him.

The most essential task which faces the comparative scholar at the present time is to renovate and broaden his methods and to acquire a fresh conception of the essential notion of influence in literature. An influence is almost never manifested through imitation, at any rate not since the eighteenth century evolved and bequeathed to us the emphasis on personality as the basis of artistic creation. T. S. Eliot rightly declared in one of his early articles: "We do not imitate, we are changed; and our work is the work of a changed man; we have not borrowed, we have been quickened and we become bearers of a tradition." * A foreign influence is a stimulant which has the advantage of exoticism, hence of enhanced magic, and often an authorization for a young writer to accomplish what he was too timid to achieve by himself against a cramping environment or a dulled national tradition. T. S. Eliot once again may be quoted: "A very young man who is himself stirred to write . . . , is looking for masters who will elicit his consciousness of what he wants to say himself, of the poetry that is in him to write . . . The kind of poetry that I needed to teach me the use of my own voice did not exist in English at all; it was only to be found in French." ("The Poetry of W. B. Yeats," *Purpose*, 1940)

More often still, an influence in literature drives the influenced one to be more truly himself through maturing more quickly; through reacting against his own environment and the masters who may have fascinated his youth; and through avoiding what was already said, and well said, by other men in other lands. "There were many foolish things that we would say," notes Fontenelle in his *Digression*, "if they had not already been said." A history of the word and the concept of influence, paralleling the sketch once attempted by Logan Pearsall Smith to trace the

---

* "Reflections on Contemporary Poetry," *The Egoist*, July, 1919, p. 59. According to Goethe's famous reflection on Winckelmann, one learns nothing from reading Winckelmann, but one becomes better for having read him.

history of the word "originality," should be undertaken by a comparatist. It would perhaps reveal that the two notions often go hand in hand, and that the creators most widely influenced are also those who developed their originality most markedly. The bee, Henri Heine noted in his *Letters on the French Stage*, need not feel humiliated by the spider which draws the threads of its web out of its own body while the bee gathers its honey from flower to flower. The most crying need of our time, and perhaps of the country upon which is at present thrust the burden of leading the Western World, is for more imagination, so that we may conceive, sympathize with, and strengthen ways of life different from our own. Only through a broader conception and a more fervent study of Comparative Literature, resting upon a more intense study of foreign languages as the mirrors to the soul of a people, may the leading nations of the world give the lie to Rémy de Gourmont's cynical dictum that "the more nations help each other and the better they know each other, the more they hate each other."

# A Backward and a Forward Glance

*Zum Sehen geboren,*
*Zum Schauen gestellt,*

. . . . . . . . .

*Ich blick' in die Ferne,*
*Ich seh' in der Näh,*

L IKE LYNCEUS AT THE END OF THE SECOND PART OF
*Faust*, the rash speaker who offers to pierce the walls
of the past and the veils of the future should be endowed
with the hindsight and the foresight of a seer. He will confess his blindness at the outset and modestly light the dim
lantern of common sense.

When seventy-five years ago the Modern Language Association was founded, Comparative Literature was a new-
born babe in European universities. No professorship was
specifically assigned to it. Even after Brunetière, Brandes,
Menendez y Pelayo, Croce, Saintsbury, Vossler had ranged
over several ancient and modern literatures from a comparative point of view, faculties resisted the recognition of
that discipline as an autonomous one, having a province
and methods of its own. America proved even more dis-
trustful. The Modern Language Association feared the
atomization of its programs which the proliferation of
groups and sections was to entail. But the gates were

eventually stormed. Comparative Literature has now won full franchise at our conventions; it counts more professorships in the United States than in the rest of the world put together. Its journal published in Oregon, its yearbook appearing in its Carolinian chapel, its monographs at ten or twelve institutions evince its youthful, at times arrogant vigor. A sizeable proportion of the most gifted students in graduate schools are drawn to it. The prestige of the greatest comparative scholars in Europe, Farinelli, Baldensperger, Hazard, I. G. Robertson, has long since ceased to dazzle American scholars. Combatively if not always gratefully, they have lately questioned the methods and the definition of Comparative Literature once proposed by the French school and, like many intellectual products from Paris, for a time unquestionably followed by other nations. In 1958 the victory appears as a brilliant one. How will Comparative Literature in America use it? The true challenge is here and now. An immense achievement will be expected, and probably critically scrutinized, by other nations from the country whose manifest destiny it now is to lead the world intellectually as well as materially.

It would be childish of our discipline to boast of its triumph merely because it now has a variety of groups at our yearly convention, a budget of its own in several universities, the lenient ear of provosts and deans, and because the departments of English are by now resigned to an infringement of their preserves by the poaching vagrant. Our loyalty never was to Comparative Literature as a sacrosanct label, but to our universities as a whole and to the intellectual march forward of the country. Only through combining audacity and wisdom, criticism and imagination, range and depth can Comparative Literature in the next twenty-five years of our Association succeed in coming up to the expectations of those who have led it to its present proud estate.

The material means—funds, libraries, research facilities, grants for travel, secretarial assistance, fellowships for our students—we have, to a degree greater than any other country, even if not commensurate with our wishes and claims. We need ampler funds for publishing series of monographs and more particularly for two kinds of publications now grievously missed: first, collections of essays and studies to give shelter to fifty- to one hundred-page studies, too long for *Comparative Literature*, too brief for a book, but often the ideal size for publishing in revised form the best of our dissertations and the best we write later; then, a journal composed of nothing but serious book reviews, covering as many as possible of our diverse provinces, informative as well as critical, supplementing *Books Abroad*, emulating the excellent *Studi Francesi*, *The Modern Language Review* of Cambridge, *Litteris* and *Erasmus*, replacing the "recensiones" of the defunct *Revue Critique* and of many a pre-World War II German scholarly journal. But and above all we need men, a spirit of fervor burning in them, the apostolic zeal in them which would bring forth vocations and disciples, and a periodical redefinition of our goals and methods, or perhaps of the Mallarmean absence of the latter.

Great teachers of Comparative Literature have not been, and are not at present, scarce in America, either American born or (to mention only those not now actively teaching) Europeans like Guérard, Baldensperger, Spitzer, Auerbach, Vietor, Borgese who were proud of joining a faculty in the New World. For reasons which should some day be elucidated, they have not, however, trained as many disciples of distinction as might have been expected. Was their own knowledge discouragingly vast, their wealth of allusions too bewildering? Did they expect a richer classical background and a more intimate familiarity with philological science and with several languages than American students were equipped with? Is the relationship between students and teachers, behind an appearance of easy informality, less conducive to an impregnation of the students by the mind of the revered "Maître" than was the case at Marburg or Bonn, at Madrid, at Oxford and at the Ecole Normale Supérieure? Should we practice the hitherto un-American hero worship of great teachers? Or have the foreign masters been reluctant to understand the American scene fully and to continue inspiring, criticizing, stimulating their former students after they had secured their doctor's parchment? No country stresses research and production as much as America does in her faculties; no teaching staff abroad does as much to provide students with all the tools for advanced work and to spare them the hundred difficulties which men of the older generations had to solve by trial and error in their youth. Yet a disappointingly small number of our Ph.D.'s retain an urge to produce after thirty or thirty-five. Very few keep on growing and writing in the last two decades of their career. This is especially deplorable in Comparative Literature, where the bold freshness of youth, which often effects the most striking discoveries in science, has to be buttressed by a vast amount of reading in three or four languages, for which no short cut can be devised.

Is our subject itself to be blamed for the small output of important works of a comparative character? Or are our methods sterile or effete? We know that the quality of our students is high, indeed higher than that of the graduate students in English, in American studies or in languages. Many, who came to this country from war ridden lands in the early nineteen forties, brought with them a varied background in foreign tongues and acquired, not only the language, but the spirit of America and the insight into the English tradition without which there can be no comparatist. The philosophical culture of those students and their zest for discussing ideas were also greater than had traditionally been the case with Anglo-Saxon students. The philosophical approach to literature is probably the most momentous novelty introduced into criticism in the English language since 1900.

That philosophical outlook must be assigned on the credit side. It contrasted with the traditional attitude of English criticism, empirical and more fond of the description of individualities and of biographies than of imperious generalizations and of labels imported from across the Channel. Tocqueville long ago had remarked that the Americans were perilously less afraid of general ideas than the British. Their criticism has lately appeared to stand as heir to the theoretical disquisitions on literature and art which used to be favored by German scholars rather than to the urbane and Epicurean enjoyment of literature which was the privilege of Leslie Stephen, Saintsbury, W. P. Ker or Walter Raleigh, H. G. Grierson, Leslie Stephen's own daughter and Lord David Cecil. In a parallel move, we have, not without some ridiculous excess, pinnacled the effigy of Coleridge over the intense inane where supreme critics breathe the incense burnt in our temples. Conversely, we have demoted the more indigenous critics like Dryden and Hazlitt who had approached literature more naïvely but more racily.

The result has been a proliferation of works ranging over several countries, hence comparative in a loose sense, dealing with ideas held on literature rather than with literary works themselves. We are, thanks to those works, far better informed on the theory of imagination held by English romantic poets, on the obscure origins of symbolism before the Symbolists, on the unconscious in philosophy and literature, or on the latent Bergsonism which doctrinaire critics insist upon discovering in any one who wrote between 1895 and 1930. Whether we perceive the poetry of Coleridge or of Verlaine, Rilke and Valéry better for that extraneous knowledge is more doubtful. Whether the critics themselves, in the past or around us, were or are the better for holding theoretical views on literature and its essential significance is even more uncertain. A teacher (and alas! few critics can afford not to be teachers) needs a rich supply of broad ideas on which he can fall back when he has tersely declared that a work is great and is at a loss to explain why. A critic needs taste, which may, but may not, rest on an ability to perceive general relationships among diversely capricious works.

Comparative Literature has been taken to task for granting too much attention to sources, influences, to the patient but pedestrian following of an author's fortunes in a foreign land or of his readings in exotic works. This kind of study had indeed been worn thin by being turned into a string of recipes available to any tyro. It applied causality awkwardly and thought it could explain talent by its antecedents. Lately and in America in particular the trend in our studies veered sharply to another fashion: parallels were arbitrarily assigned between authors in different languages who had cast their visions of life into a similar mold or who had displayed a remotely analogous interest in the Bildungsroman or in the workings of fatality in tragedy. The peril is the same, forever threatening the comparative study of literature: a lack of respect for the unique originality of an author and for the mystery of his creative act. One of the most moving confessions made by a comparative scholar should be engraved on the walls of all our seminar rooms: Arturo Farinelli's contribution to the *Mélanges Baldensperger* (1930), in which the disillusioned Italian professor chided the national pride which lurked behind the theories of world literature and the volumes of those who specialized in pointing out influences and borrowings: "Humbly should we descend to individuals and abandon groups and huge ensembles . . . Theorizing on so-called world literature, a chimerical dream, leads to facile judgments passed on the qualities and weaknesses of nations . . . As if periods, turned into spiritual beings, molded men, while men select and determine what they believe to be periods."

Like all noble disciplines, Comparative Literature must glory in the perils that it incessantly has to skirt and not take refuge in timidity. "Better be imprudent moveables than prudent fixtures" could be its motto as culled by Gide from Keats' letters. But, like history proper, that branch of history of literature lately annexed by history of ideas, if properly practiced, should bring us fresh insight into the mistakes of others, perhaps even into our own past ones. The two reefs against which the comparative navigator must ceaselessly fear shipwreck are the curse of bigness and the curse of littleness.

Just now, and in America in particular, bigness, under the shape of philosophical speculation and the deification of literature as such, divorced from biography, history, sociology, is our temptation. It might well dampen the audacity of young workers. Fleeing dual relationships as not properly comparative and courting general literature, even in a Ph.D. thesis, demands more than average gifts. But conditions in this country impose a rather swift completion of the dissertation, and only the second book by a scholar usually proves to be worthy of him and is addressed to his peers and the public, not merely to a carping thesis committee. It is questionable whether our students would not gain from undertaking the orthodox kind of comparative study which used to be assigned by French and German professors to their meek disciples in the earlier years of this century.

Monographs on travelers from one country into a strange land may often have been anecdotic and superficial. Nevertheless, a comprehensive study of French or English travelers in Russia, of French travelers in Greece, even of Japan seen through Western eyes, would be a rich subject of study and could be turned into a profound one. Mallarmé in Germany, Rimbaud in America, Théophile Gautier and the Parnassians in Hispanic poetry are far from being worthless fields of inquiry. "Stendhal and Italy" would range far beyond the adopted Milanese's travels, plagiarisms and testaments; it might well penetrate to the core of Stendhal's psychology, with his obstinate cherishing of a vision of Italy which he secretly knew to be chimerical, the perpetual self-delusion of the analyst who contended that his whole universe was annihilated when he failed to see clearly. "Taine and Germany" is a less obvious topic than Taine and England, but perhaps a more central one. "Flaubert and the ancient world" still awaits a synthesis, as does Hegelianism in England. Kafka or Faulkner in France, if treated with both precision and breadth, might be very revealing on both the writer whose fortune would be studied and on the country which acclaimed, distorted, transfigured him. There are many fields still untilled in the vast expanse of even Western European literatures, envisaged in dual relationships. We need not yield to the vertigo of philosophical speculation or of perpetual prolegomena to a theory of literature, for fear that biographical and historical methods may be out of favor with the moderns. Fashion should hold less sway with academic minds than it does.

The weakness inherent in many comparative studies had better be acknowledged with humility. We often tend to envisage a work of art only from the outside and to explore it solely on its fringe, in the impulse which sprang from a foreign contact, in the strange or exotic experience which unleashed the creative power. The essential secrets of a work of art must still be sought in the psychology of its author and in the technical means used by him. The national history or interpretation of a literature will, in the majority of cases, remain more important than the exploration of its foreign contacts or the merging of individual writers into a lake or an international sea with currents, eddies and whirlpools. Wise comparatists shudder at those catalogues of college courses which concoct a stew or a Russian salad of tragic, epic, satirical or lyrical writers from half a dozen lands—read, inevitably, in translation. The triumph of our discipline has perhaps extended too far and wide. We have, as the professors of English have recently remarked, immeasurably extended "our usable past." English literature proper appears provincial to many who teach it and who far prefer Stendhal to Dickens, Dostoevsky to Meredith, Thomas Mann to Galsworthy, and Proust to E. M. Forster. Lionel Trilling interestingly commented on that dwindling prestige of English literature in American (and even in British) education in an article of *The Sewanee Review* (Summer 1958). But our aesthetic perceptiveness and our delight in beauty and form have suffered in the process which has catapulted us toward ideas as expressed in literature. We search for a message just as naïvely, or as all-too-humanly, as our Victorian ancestors did. But the message must not soothe our anxiety; it should rather provide us with new reasons to nurture it and to surround it with the bristling jargon which has become the modern critic's armor.

If we are justified in asserting that Comparative Literature has now reached full recognition in American academic life and runs the danger of losing the zeal which prompted it when it still was the privilege of a few seeking to convert the many, how can it gain new vigor periodically and fulfill its role in a specifically American environment?

First by eschewing nationalism which, understandably enough, reappeared in Germany after 1933, in Spain ever intent on preserving its "Hispanidad" from cultural imperialism from across the Pyrenees, in French studies of "le mirage allemand," in many a patronizing or churlish comment of British weeklies on American scholarship. Of all countries, this one has extended the most generous welcomes to foreign intellectuals and has realized that it stood to gain from their preservation of their native originality. American criticism is today so remarkably independent of influences from abroad, even so autochthonous, that it need not fear foreign imports. Our learned journals are the freest from the taint of nationalism in the world. At the same time, and happily so, American writers have preserved their own originality; they are, for the most part, too incurious of what is done abroad to bow to the prestige of Malraux, Moravia, Camus, Hesse or even that of the picaresque and amusedly angry rebels from England. Their chief obsession continues to be: What does it mean to be an American? Why and how am I one? How can I strike roots in Brooklyn, Carmel, Tennessee or New Orleans? How can I ever be big enough, torrential, Whitmanesque enough to portray this huge country?

Secondly, the specific problem facing all scholars and teachers of literature in this land is to enlarge their public, to convert a greater proportion of our millions of college graduates into readers of good books, or of books "period," after they have matured into doers convinced that only those who cannot do, read or think. We have vastly extended our usable past and assumed the heritage, not only of English literature but of two or three others, as our college curricula testify. It is the function of Comparative Literature to shake off abstruse pedantry, to rise above minutiae, and to broaden the audience interested in foreign writers and literary and artistic movements and trends of the past and of the present. Our own specialized journals are estimable but reach only a few hundreds out of twenty-five million college graduates. Foreign letters receive a woefully niggardly place in the columns of our supposedly most cultured monthlies and quarterlies.

The fault is ours in part. We have waged war against biography as a legitimate adjunct to criticism. We have thus dehumanized it. Yet can we actually enjoy and judge D. H. Lawrence, Proust, Yeats, Scott Fitzgerald, Mallarmé himself unless we know something about their lives and the circumstances in which they created? It may be weakness in us to be curious of concrete details, and the exasperation of our highbrows at the trivial and meaningless description of personalities in which *The New Yorker* or *Time* magazine indulge is understandable. But as a refined Augustan, Addison, once remarked, "A reader seldoms peruses a book with pleasure until he knows whether the writer of it was a black man or a fair man, of a mild or choleric disposition, married or a bachelor." The American reader of today is not necessarily guilty in resembling the spectator of Queen Anne's age who sharpened his interest in letters, and his taste, in haunting coffeehouses. When all is said, the enigma of talent or genius is still with us, and it invites us to inquire how a certain individual with human frailties has created a work which far transcends him.

We may well also have erred in our insistence upon a work of art as an autonomous and autotelic body of signs and symbols and in severing the links between such a work and its public. Anyone who has approached writers, who has known playwrights, who has perused the *Journals* of Gide or the desultory pieces written by such lofty minds as those of Valéry and Thomas Mann, must know that half at least of their work was prompted by outside motives: orders from publishers, from review editors, pleas from literary friends, from theatrical directors, who in their turn voiced or echoed the demands from the public. Far more essays, plays, novels, even poems than we imagine have been and are, at their inception, suggested to the creator by some outside intervention. Of course, the work then soars above the circumstances under which it arose: it be-

comes *Hamlet, Don Juan, Siegfried* or *La Jeune Parque.*
Still, in an age which thinks in terms of the collective and
when social studies display such provocative vigor, it is
paradoxical that literary criticism should thus neglect research into the public for which one writes. We have a
dozen monographs on the subject (for the theatre in particular, and for fiction); we need scores of them. Malraux is
fond of repeating that all great art maintains its validity,
not through a sovereign monologue, but through an invincible dialogue. Too little is granted in our studies to one
of the interlocutors, the collective public. Comparative
Literature might gain much from monographs on the publics (misoneist, lethargic, snobbish, hostile, provoking,
malleable) for which, or against which, literature was composed. Such studies need in no way be undertaken in a
deterministic spirit and disregard the ultimate freedom of
the creative act, the most unpredictable of all responses to a
demand or to stimuli.

Thus conceived, Comparative Literature might well enable us today to shake off the tyranny of vogues which
lately have spread over American criticism and made our
profession one of the most gregarious of all. An English
woman of remarkable common sense, Helen Gardner, in
one of her lectures collected as *The Limits of Criticism*
(Oxford University Press, 1956) wrote:

I cannot feel satisfied with a literary criticism which substitutes
for the conception of the writer as "a man speaking to men"
the conception of the writer as an imagination weaving symbolic patterns to be teased out by intellect, and in its concentration on the work by itself ends by finding significance in
what the work suggests rather than in what it says, and di-
rects our imagination towards types and figures rather than
towards their actualization.

The same author adds, with no less wisdom, that any critical method soon reaches a point where its deficiencies out-
weigh its merits. That point is reached all the sooner, indeed, as the method has held greater sway over apprentices
who have worn it thin through the dogmatic enthusiasm

of neophytes. We believe that the methods or the assumptions which were in favor in the last fifteen years have thus reached a point of no return and that the public around us awaits a new approach. The divorce between our potential audiences and our esoteric criticism has isolated us. Critics who write only for a few other critics, for those who will be subtle enough to read the same symbolic patterns in *A Winter's Tale* or the same theological message in other Shakespearean comedies as they ingeniously decipher, are doing a disservice to the diffusion of literature. A work of art is not merely an abstruse message hidden in code. By indulging our trade in the seclusion of university seminars and almost never encountering writers, we have forgotten how fallible, how pressed by time and greed and love, how eccentric and fanciful and disorderly, how tempted by plagiarism and mystification, how unlike engineers striving for symbolic structure and functional imagery inspired writers can be.

> *A perfect judge will read each work of wit*
> *With the same spirit that its author writ,*

observed Pope. We have failed to heed that advice and have dehumanized literary creation through disregarding both what a writer thought he was intending to do and the public for which he was writing. It is a sad reflection on our culture that so few critics exist away from academic centers of learning and in contact with the creators themselves.

Comparative scholars may without arrogance submit that they have, in the last two or three decades, constituted the most open and the most adventurous group of literary historians in this country, and in several others. They can continue to lead, but in our opinion they will not do so through formulating a new methodology or even by stressing problems of method. There is not one but a hundred ways of being intelligent, sensitive, penetrating, precise and solid where precision and solidity are of the essence, irrational and brilliant when only an irrational and fanciful mind can cope with a work of art which defies stern logic. The best method is to be all that, and even more.

Our task is to remain aware of our limitations as critics. Criticism is a secondary activity and should avow it. It does not have to substitute its own intellectual subtlety for the lack of it in the creator. It must not rate itself above its subject matter. A comparative scholar is even more liable than other scholars to take pride in his vast range and to drop names which dazzle the half-cultured, to warn creators haughtily that many have already attempted in other tongues and in strange climates what they are now trying to do, to tell them that they are but the reflections of a mysterious Spirit of the Age, inserted into the no less mysterious frame of reference of a certain *Zeitgeist*. Let the scholar with more humility place himself at the service of the creators. A critic's function should be to stir up interest in and discussion around a work of art, and thus to enlighten the public which will understand and stimulate the artist in its midst. We lack such discussion in twentieth-century America and we have isolated artists more than they need be. A comparative scholar's function is to contribute to the task which every thinking American must today assume: that of accepting the cultural legacy of the ancient world and of Western Europe, tomorrow perhaps of Asia, and of enriching that heritage still further through a keener awareness of American originality, transcending national prejudices. His discipline is everywhere recognized as adult and independent. But his most precious boon is the supranational spirit which convinces him that to be a man only of one country and of one age is today to be less than a man.

# Humanities and Social Studies

THE FEW SPECIFIC QUESTIONS to which this paper will be directed may be formulated thus: new challenges are today being thrown to the Humanities as traditionally conceived; what gain can be effected from some of the strictures levelled at us? Can we, as Plutarch, a Greek moralist who helped train generations of humanists, advised us, derive profit from the happy circumstance that we have enemies?

Instead of dwelling in proud isolation, we also live in a collective era in which men multiply each other's power. We are more attentive than ever before to the sweep of huge gregarious forces, more aware of their potentialities for evil, but also for good. New disciplines attempt to alter man, perhaps to save his civilization, through a wider knowledge and a greater control of social factors. Can the Humanities gain from associating with social studies, or at least from understanding them with sympathy?

A confrontation of literature (or of history, or of art history) with other disciplines is thus constantly in order. It should be undertaken with tolerance and open-mindedness, but with no undue humility or in a spirit of subserviency. The meeting ground is extensive. "More consciousness" is the goal of any intelligent person today,

which implies a keener understanding of what differs most
from him. But a sympathetic confrontation with other disciplines would, and probably should, lead humanists to define their goals and their methods anew, but also to preserve the originality of their own branch of knowledge and
the validity of their own approach. The true scientific attitude for them is not to parade as imitators of scientific
methods and achievements where those are out of place.

At no time in history have the Humanities been so much
talked about, lauded in more passionate and florid speeches,
redefined with more conviction, and also with more efful-
gent haziness, than in America today. Incoming freshmen,
departing seniors equally patient under the admonitions
showered upon them, alumni, parents, councils of educators listen to their praise. Seldom if ever is a word heard
indicting them. If humanists however "protest too much,"
it can only be due to a sense of guilt or to the consciousness
of an undefined peril which they attempt to avert with
humanistic eloquence. It may not be amiss to state the
implicit charges against the Humanities baldly and to air
grievances on both sides.

In the eyes of many, the Humanities as traditionally conceived arc too aristocratic and too exclusive: they are the
privilege of a few who used to wear their knowledge of
Latin as a badge pointing to their class superiority. A
familiarity with English poets, French novelists, German
philosophers, with art and music, is likewise taken to be the
mark of genteel refinement, available only to those who enjoy leisure and indulge Epicurean tastes. It can only arouse
invidiousness in the more practically directed individuals
whose goal is success and whose training is technical and
vocational.

Others, less harried by pressing drives in their careers,
concerned with the position of America as a world power
supporting allies in five continents and anxious for their
friendship, would submit that this country has failed to
broaden the Humanities geographically and otherwise, that
it remains obsessed by what may be termed "a Mediter-
ranean fixation." At the same time if there is any universal

validity in the Hellenic-Roman-Christian heritage which lies at the core of liberal education in the Western World, that heritage should not be cherished as an exclusive possession by the Western nations which are at present reduced to being a minority on our planet. One of the startling phenomena of our age is the spread of Western science, technique, political thought, even of separation between Church and State and of agnosticism, and of the new religion of nationalism, to the continents of Asia and Africa. But the best of Western humanism and whatever wisdom accrued to the West from its Mediterranean legacy have not spread accordingly. It is now imperative that we extend to the lands of Asia and Africa the benefit of what has been tested by time as the most precious in the Humanities and, without diluting that elixir overmuch, that we generously let many non-Western peoples drink from our once exclusive fountain. We cannot afford to leave too many "barbarians" from the outside untouched by our values and ideals, or we will soon be overrun by an invasion from the wrathful populations of underprivileged lands which would far outrange the invasions which, fifteen centuries ago, overran the Roman empire.

The danger is just as great that the humanists and traditionalists in our midst may be crushed or reduced to impotence by the "barbarians of the interior." The Humanities have barely extended their beneficent influence to a thin layer of our most democratic societies. The proportion of true humanists (and of statesmen, and even of inventive scientists) in a country of 170 million people, contrasted to the same proportion a century or two ago in a country of a few million people, is not a flattering one for us. It is reckoned that two thirds at least of those who read comics (and hardly anything else) are adults. Adult education and a meaningful utilization of leisure are the greatest needs of our democratic societies. The truest friends of labor, who with such high expectations once envisaged unions as a potential focus of cultivation of the arts and of ideas, have been disillusioned. If the Humanities constitute the fittest training for an élite, they should be made accessible to growing numbers among us and become democratized.

A final charge has lately assailed humanists: that of complacency and aloofness. It is contended that they refuse to evince any interest in the sciences which should be altering their picture of the world today; their humanism is thus cramped and lacks the courage to build a philosophy upon the sciences and upon the techniques of their day, a courage that Greek thinkers and also humanists of the times of Bacon, Descartes, Pascal, Hume had once possessed. They affect scorn for the practicality which is supposed to obsess those who "think with their hands," but seldom try to meet them half way. Their outlook upon the exterior world is thus outdated and timid. They do not display much more curiosity for the behavioral sciences or for the category of the collective, which nevertheless permeates all the walks of life around them and molds the moods of most people. Too much that is human, if not always expressed in polished language, thus remains alien to them. The partition walls which absurdly separate cognate disciplines in our universities are often of their own erecting.

Even if they will not listen to inimical arguments from those who grudge them the place their ancestors once occupied, humanists are constrained to painful acknowledgments. They no longer attract, from the colleges or from the schools, the very best young men. Those gifted and ambitious youngsters are rather seduced, not even by science, but by the managerial professions: they study law, business administration, corporation finances, economic growth. The country's interest commands that such professions be staffed by men who have been submitted to a liberal arts training and understand the motives which move individuals and nations, and have always moved them. But the persistence of a power élite conversant with humanistic values also requires that a substantial portion of the most brilliant young men elect the teaching of humanities as a vocation. The current dissatisfaction with our schools suggests that such may no longer be the case.

Our failure may be even more woeful in that we humanists do not take sufficient advantage of the captive audiences of thousands of young men and women who, at a most receptive age, sit at our feet and imbibe our words. We should be imparting to them a passion for continued reading and for the enjoyment of beauty which should outlast the ordeals of competition and the stresses of middle age. It may be understandable that the enthusiasm aroused by poetry should flag after the years of passion and that men of forty should prefer to come to terms with reality when they cannot alter it through action. As Yeats mockingly or enviously puts it,

> *For those that love the world serve it in action*
> *Grow rich, popular and full of influence;*
> *And should they paint or write, still it is action,*
> *The struggle of the fly in marmalade*

Yet it is to be lamented that, ten or fifteen years after graduation, men and women should be deprived of poetry when it is most needed in their lives.

But philosophy, political thought, even history are, by the nature of things, forced upon the young or greedily devoured by them when they are not yet fully able to understand them. Aristotle in the sixth book of his *Nicomachean Ethics* had already noted that while young men do become mathematicians easily, they are hardly fit to be students of politics, for they have little experience, and the first principles in political and social disciplines come from experience. "The young men have no convictions about the latter, but merely use the proper language." Unless college education provides the young men with more than an "exposure" to accumulated knowledge, namely with a hunger for more learning and a readiness to mature or to revise their views at middle age, it has failed to fulfill its purpose.

The sad fact is that in Western countries the nominal elimination of illiteracy and the spread of college education to all those who seem, at eighteen, to be equipped for it have not multiplied the number of those who, in middle age, can become the leaders of politics, diplomacy, education, even of business. If we are not afflicted with arrested development at thirty or thereabouts, we only remain malleable in a few lobes of our brains, while others yield to inertia if not to premature sclerosis. On university faculties as in most branches of business where progress hinges upon executives with independent ideas and where discoveries demand imagination and a challenge to conformity, we suffer from a shortage of men of considerable stature aged 40 to 55 and have to bid high for the few of them. A noxious breeze withers, in the middle thirties, the fresh promises of our young graduates. The education of many a humanist, like that of a social scientist or of a political thinker, should be undertaken anew twenty years after he has left college. If he was truly trained in the spirit and not merely in the letter of the humanities, he should then have remained plastic enough to learn again and to interpret his broadened experience of life through the lens, or the code, with which his formal studies had provided him. We cannot expect our contemporaries, with the prospect of twenty more years of active life than their great grandparents enjoyed and in a world twenty times more complex, to go on living from twenty-five to seventy-five on the lore accumulated in their years of physical growth. We should serve society far better if we insisted, in the middle of our lives, upon deepening or extending our education. The test of the validity of the humanities lies in their being lived.

Humanists are not especially addicted to self-pity or to moaning over their fate and to casting envious glances at colleagues more amply favored with material goods. They have the right to say, however, that the progress achieved in their field, and in others, would in America have been even more commensurate with the immense facilities enjoyed here if fewer impositions of a secondary nature had been made upon them. The work load of professors in America is probably heavier than in any other great country; the time allowed scholars to avail themselves of libraries, well-equipped seminar rooms, contacts with other scholars is probably the scantiest anywhere.

Dean Inge used to submit that the role of boredom in history has always been underestimated. True enough, and the biography of many a great man shows that, because he was impatiently waiting for the circumstances in which he could display his full measure, a future statesman or warrior (Bonaparte, Lyautey exemplify this) vented his "taedium vitee" in the letters of his youth. Our students may well owe more to the boredom that we inflict upon them than they realize at the time and Alfred North Whitehead may well have rightly argued that the most urgent need in American education is not for good teaching (there is much of it and it sterilizes the potentialities for research of the teachers) but for good learning.

But humanists are, or should be, humble enough to practice some breast-beating and to admit their wrongs. The relationship between the sciences, the social sciences, and the humanities is not always very cordial, very intelligent or very fruitful. It would be idle to blind ourselves to evidence. The humanists affect to sneer at the social scientists, with their specialized and often jargonic language, and to consider the scientists as deficient in spiritual values and only concerned with technicity. The scientists distrust the eloquence of teachers of literature, the vagueness of their reasoning, the vapid rhetoric under which they at times disguise their amateurishness, the poverty of their tools, their inability to marshal factual evidence. Such clashes among persons devoted to the life of the mind are not in themselves deserving of censure. Creativeness is seldom fostered by approval and by complacent applause.

Confronting our views and our methods (or the lack of them) with those of our colleagues in the sciences or in social disciplines should prove as beneficent for us as it would be for them. With all the facilities for interdisciplinary communication afforded by life on our campuses, by our "houses," "colleges" or faculty clubs, by our lip service to Integration with a capital "I" (on the definition of which our deans try as desperately, and as vainly, to agree as theologians once did on sin), we all work in regrettable isolation and fail to learn from opposing each other, if not from mutual borrowing. Listening to the doubts and prejudices which the study of literature and of philosophy arouses in the scientists and the social scientists would in no way imply that the humanists are surrendering to their rivals. Having willingly entered into the laboratories of their challengers, they would probably acquire a keener awareness of the original residue of their own discipline, of its authenticity where it is not reducible to other methods. More harm is probably done to literature and criticism by those who inscribe on their pediment "Noli me tangere" and only want to treat "literature as such" or in its purest "se" than by those who question its goal and methods from the outside. The clown's reply, in the last act of *Twelfth Night*, to the Duke who asks him how he fares, is more profound than comic: "Truly, sir, the better for my foes and the worse for my friends."

It must be confessed outright that, while humanists have for the last few decades stood on the defensive, the scientists and even more the social scientists have not concealed their arrogant conviction that they were riding the wave of the future. Their devotion to their disciplines, their fervor in promoting them, their fanatical zeal in converting neophytes, their tireless energy in publishing volume after volume on "modern sociological theory" or "the Behavioral Sciences today" should invite us to emulate them: they have arrogated to themselves the mission of saving the modern world through changing it. A century ago or even less, a similar faith swelled the hearts of the Symbolist poets in France or of Walt Whitman when, in his *Democratic Vistas*, in 1871, he proclaimed that literature had "become the only general means of morally influencing the world."

The reluctance of humanists to come to terms with the present and to deal boldly with the history, the thought, the art, the music, the books of their own time contributed to the seizure of a position of strength by the social scientists. The oft-quoted charge levelled at philosophers by Kierkegaard is not undeserved; nor is it by other humanists: "We live forward, but we understand backward." It was more comfortable to study Sophocles, Dante, Montaigne, Donne over again than to venture a judgment on the as yet unrecognized creators struggling in our midst. Of course the best in the past is constantly alive and its study enriches the present and affords us perspective and discernment. Even small details may lead to momentous conclusions when a synthetical or imaginative mind later reinterprets them. But the indictment of antiquarianism is not undeserved by us. The scornful epithet of Alexandrine is used by some to characterize our preoccupation with too minute details of a remote past. The collection of data by some of us can be a hobby, as harmless but hardly more exalted or more broadening to the mind than the collection of stamps or matchboxes.

If we do not sufficiently revitalize the past, we also give to many the impression that our concern lies primarily with the stock-taking of accumulated knowledge. It was necessary—when Renaissance humanists first rediscovered antiquity, then when the industrious scholars and editors of the Teubner or the Loeb or the Guillaume Budé classical libraries, the compilers of Pauly-Wissowa or of Daremberg and Saglio classical encyclopedias accomplished their admirable work of recension, publication and translation— that the legacy of Greece and Rome be made readily available to us. New dictionaries (of music, of architecture), new glossaries and concordances, even new bibliographies will be needed.

But too many humanistic scholars devote themselves to those tasks and eschew the more creative reinterpretation of the ancient or the modern writers and artists which requires less ant- or beaver-like patience but more imaginative boldness and greater insight. Too many departments of English consider themselves as factories turning out volume after volume of Milton's minor works, of Dr. Johnson's or his biographer's complete (and over-complete) writings, of the notebooks or diaries of every great and small American author. Exhaustive bibliographies of all articles treating of Goethe or of Gide or of Faulkner in the last decade are a worthy labor of love on the part of their authors. But they do not promote the stock of the humanities with our students or with our colleagues. They even discourage young talents through frightening them away from a fresh reinterpretation of the texts of great writers by the sad conviction that all has already been said or that they first must read every article, note and review perpetrated on the writer whom they admired. There is a time for accumulating data and there is one also for syntheses which will stimulate newcomers to the scaling of greater heights. Humanists have been paralyzed by timidity and diffidence. Historicism, as the Europeans call it, has corroded too many creative talents since it afflicted the modern world in the first years of the nineteenth century, in the same way as too much attention paid to the lessons of the past has waylaid statesmen and generals, whose insight into the mistakes of others discouraged fresh and audacious thinking and acting.

Must the humanists remain antiquarian and often Alexandrian, and stubbornly reject any accretion of prestige from the pursuit of objectivity, of scientific precision, of methods insusceptible of a general application? The complex questions involved in the application of scientific methods to history, philosophy, art history, linguistics cannot here be raised. A separate essay would be needed to deal with each of them. The remarks which follow will be limited to literature.

A century or so ago, most conspicuously with the generation of Taine, Renan (in his youth) and with their successors such as Émile Hennequin who advocated scientific criticism, the students of literature, permeated with positivistic influences, eyed the achievement of science with jealousy. They tried to formulate laws codifying the relationship of literature to society, the determination of talent or of genius by race, environment and by the spirit of the age or the momentum of tradition. A controlling force from which all other qualities stemmed was supposed to be hidden at the center of any great man. Taine's celebrated manifestos constitute the most remarkable endeavor to found criticism scientifically. They have proved frail and nothing was easier for Taine's successors than to demolish his systematic structure. Still, with all his dogmatism and the eloquent logic with which he covered up his romantic fervor, Taine remains, if not the shrewdest critic, at least the most considerable sower of ideas on literature of the French nineteenth century. Edmund Wilson has acknowledged that Taine's work "was what we call creative" and that the moral convictions of the critic who was branded in his day as an immoralist give his writing emotional power. Harry Levin, in 1948, praised Taine likewise for ridding us once for all of "the uncritical notion that books dropped like meteorites from the sky." Taine's undertaking will be imitated or emulated several times after him; it retains today its prestige with many young scholars whom the amateurish approach to literature discourages. If he understressed the aesthetic value of literary works, Taine taught us not to sever the work of art altogether from life, and that literature, in Harry Levin's phrase, is, in one of its aspects, "an institution."

History and criticism are not, as Taine had rashly asserted in April 1864, in a letter to Ernest Havet, comparable to physiology and to geology. They are, however, very close to social or, as we prefer to say today, to behavioral sciences. It would be idle to deny that several of our most distinguished works of intellectual history have, lately, been written by men who had been drawn to the social sciences, in their discontent with traditional history or with pure but overrefined and barren criticism. No influence (except that of Lanson, who himself conceded much to sociology) has been so seminal on the French school of historians and critics, between 1890 and 1920, as that of the renovator of French sociology, Emile Durkheim. Through him, the interpretation of ancient China, of ancient Egypt, of Greece and Rome, of primitive cultures, of French, English, German letters received a powerful stimulus. Social scientists have occasionally erred in America in naïvely viewing literature as a faithful mirror to the moods and "mores" portrayed in it. But the originality of the American historians of their literature since 1930 has been in their vast and social treatment of works which they seemed almost reluctant to rate as works of art comparable to those of Europe. Only with difficulty, and without converting the general public to their views, have a few academic critics raised Melville and Henry James to the pinnacle of literary greatness. However, excellent scholars have lately brought forth historical studies of original merit through the broadminded and modest attention they paid to the contemporary progress of social sciences: David Potter in *People of Plenty* (University of Chicago Press, 1954) and Henry Stuart Hughes in *Consciousness and Society* (Knopf, 1958) stand high among those builders of bridges between disciplines.

The questions which the practitioners of the behavioral sciences ask themselves and ask us have probably little validity for literary scholars at the present time. They may well, however, lead us to be less complacent about the autonomy of our own disciplines and to welcome the use of scientific methods whenever those methods prove applicable. Social scientists have sharpened their tools by collecting information in objective ways, formulating hypotheses from accumulated and as yet unexplained facts, verifying hypotheses when that can be done, avoiding unrestrained subjectivity and vagueness in terminology, and admitting their limited ability to make predictions in certain circumstances. In their fervor for emulating the more precise sciences, they have often affected a haughty rigor which ill disguised the consciousness of their inferiority to the scientists who dealt with less capricious material than individuals, societies or primitive cultures. They have developed a vocabulary which horrifies those of us who still cling to the prejudice that anything can be expressed clearly if it is thought clearly enough and that the terminology once used by Plato or by Spinoza is adequate for any thinking which goes on today. "Goal-oriented," "outward-directed," "organizational pattern," even the ubiquitous monster-verb, "to verbalize" may at some not very remote time appear to all of us as acceptable as "subjectivity" and "objectivity" against which the purists among humanists vituperated sixty years ago.

The social scientists resent our sneers at their language and at their foolhardy claims. They behave at times like unacknowledged prophets or irate superannuated maidens eager to be liked by their literary confreres and to be humanized by them, and resentful at their isolation in the traditionally liberal colleges. Where the humanists tax them with imperialist arrogance, they, in fact, often suffer from insecurity and undergo periodical crises of self-indictment. One of the most vigorous thinkers among sociologists and one of the least intimidated rapists of that coy mistress of foreign-born American writers, the American language, Pitirim A. Sorokin, also became, as he reached the age of retirement from Harvard, the severest grand inquisitor of modern sociology, in a bulky and ruthless "mea culpa": *Fads and Foibles in Modern Sociology* (Chicago: Regnery, 1956).

Literary scholars would be mendacious if they borrowed the language, the tools and the methods of science when presenting the results of their research which cannot be reduced to quantitative data. Graphs, charts, statistics, questionnaires, even psychological inquiries practiced by psychologists upon living writers, even psychoanalyses, are of real but very modest avail in the study of literary influence. Willing as we may be to welcome science in our discipline and to sharpen in our turn our very amateurish tools, we can never yield on a few essential points; it would be churlish not to admit it unambiguously and thus to deceive social scientists and ourselves. Those points are:

*1*) Much of our interest is in the past—a past which is already alive, eternally present, more timely for us than a great deal which in the present is half-dead and imitative. We can never be, like the social scientists, ahistorical.

*2*) Our concern is not primarily with similarities, recurrences of analogous phenomena, features which make one artist similar to another one in his own age and country or of another land and of another era. It is not even with influences of one writer upon another or borrowings. Indeed, literary and artistic criticism has erred whenever it laid undue stress on borrowings and influences. "Poetry," said the poet Francis Thompson, "is a rootedly immoral art, in which success excuses well-nigh everything. . . . A great poet may plagiarize to his heart's content, provided he plagiarized well." So may, and often does, a great critic, if any critic ever deserved that adjective. We deal with differences primarily. A keener insight into singularity is our goal. Our knowledge of history and of an author's background cultivates an historical taste which is essential in our studies. We learn how to appreciate historically a past era, a style, a mood and shun the narrow confines of him who is a willing prisoner of one culture and of one age.

*3*) But that historical taste, through which many an eminent art or literary historian has illuminated and explained the past for us, has little in common with another taste: that which makes it possible for us to discover, to appreciate and to appraise, to enjoy, and to interpret for others what is new, fresh, vivid, deep in the works appearing now in our midst. That personal taste, not very dissimilar at the start from the taste of a gourmet, of a wine taster, of a lover of women, of clothes, of perfumes, has not often been the privilege of those who know most about the past or who proposed the most elaborate concepts on art and letters. To know is not to feel. But to feel is not necessarily to know. And if impressionism is an inevitable adjunct of all criticism, that impressionism must not shirk the embarrassing questions of the social scientist: "Why do you feel thus?" "Can you be sure that your impression is to be lasting, shared by others, susceptible of being reasoned about, legitimized?" "Can you in all fairness set up your own impression and that of a few others who feel as you do, as a general rule?"

*4*) To distrust the subjective impressions of a cultured and presumably refined observer of art and letters and to take refuge under the "judgment" of others or of a larger group of readers would not only be shirking our duties as critics but bowing to impressions no less subjective and often less independent: for others may be swayed by publicity, hasty reviewers, tides of fashion, superficial charm. A trained and an honest critic may derive assistance from having studied the past as well as the present, literatures other than his own, the society and historical context behind the literature; in a word, he should have ascertained that he knows most of what there is to be known. But his knowledge should not be exhaustive to the point of dulling the vividness of his perception or antiquarian to the point of instilling into him the distrust of novelty. Goethe, when he failed in his assiduous attempt at composing an epic on the Achilleid, confessed sadly that "only faulty knowledge is creative." American critics, even more than their British cousins such as Dr. Johnson, Hazlitt and Pater, in whom the proximity to the wine tasters across the Channel maintained some sensuous delight in art, too often resemble missionaries in search of souls to be saved or engineers seeking solidity, structure, and the "resolution of tensions" in a work of art. Lord David Cecil, who likes to mock his Puritanical colleagues of the New World, wrote in *The Fine Art of Reading* (London and New York, 1957) "Art is not like mathematics or philosophy. It is a subjective, sensual and highly personal activity in which facts and ideas are the servants of fancy and feeling; and the artist's first aim is not truth but delight. . . . It follows that the primary object of a student of literature is to be delighted; his duty is to enjoy himself." That Epicurean message, meant at arousing the ire of grave graduate students who read only to evaluate and seldom to enjoy, is a timely one. In a world which prizes its anxiety too highly and wallows in its tragic sense of life and of men, the now disregarded French advice of cultivating pleasure and turning it into happiness may be more than flippant cynicism.

5) Whether it be a weakness or a strength of their studies, humanists are forced to formulate value-judgments at every stop of their pursuits. Let them do so with all the honesty and the conscientiousness, with all the precautions dictated by diffidence of fleeting impressions that they can muster. Let them define their vocabulary whenever they can, and not just words like "classical," "romantic," "modern," but words of praise or blame which they bandy about with glibness: "great," "poor," "personal," "sincere," "intense," "profound," "moving." We may well have to confess that, ultimately, we never know why a work is "great" and that a novel may be "good" and lasting, while having very few, or even none, of the features which we usually list as elements worthy of praise: structure, tension, sym-

metry of parts, perfection of form, justness or depth of underlying ideas, psychological insight. Literature is closer to life in this respect than other sciences or disciplines, for we likewise fail to pin a name upon the virtues or faults which make a man more alive, more powerful, more creative than others.

When all is said and while pursuing their quest for precision, for intellectual rigor and submission to facts and to texts, literary scholars must proclaim with no undue shame that they do not judge according to fixed standards; for standards, usually established from past practice, would have the corrosive effect of closing our taste to the new, the unprecedented, the irrational, the chaotic in which the seeds for new greatness are perhaps germinating. Art, like life, is often irrational in its essence, and criticism should be irrational also if it is not to divorce itself perilously from creation. Impulse and emotion may be viewed as destructive in engineering, in chemistry, in the behavioral sciences. Only the quantitatively measurable may be deemed acceptable there. But even scientists do not inhabit a rigidly mechanical world. They are as emotionally directed as other human beings whenever they deal with politics, affections, education. The value of literary and artistic studies lies in averting the prejudice that emotions, impulses, value-judgments can be shunned in the life of the spirit. Even stern T. S. Eliot avowed in *Poetry and Poets* "we do not fully understand a poem unless we enjoy it."

Once the humanists, typified here by the students of literature, have made it clear that the very nature of their subject precludes surrendering their originality to social scientists, they are, or should be, all the readier to cooperate with sociologists in exploring the border provinces of their domain. Much remains to be done in attempting a sociology of literature or a social history of art. *The Sociology of Literary Taste* by Levin L. Schucking, translated from the German in 1945; Robert Escarpit's lively sketch of a *Sociologie de la littérature* (1957); Arnold Hauser's *Social History of Art* (reprinted in 1957 in four volumes) or the fragmentary views of a widely cultured pianist, Arthur Loesser, in *Men, Women and Pianos, a Social History* (1954) are only approximations to the systematic studies on the interrelations of arts and social disciplines which should be undertaken. The most intelligent program for such interdisciplinary studies was sketched as early as 1904 by a French scholar, Gustave Lanson, who cannot be suspected of ever having betrayed literary history, in a remarkable article on literary history and sociology first printed that year in the *Revue de Métaphysique et de Morale*. That program has not yet been fulfilled.

Literary study deals with individuals in the more original aspects of their individualities and with works which are singled out by posterity as differing from the mass of mediocre books published daily. Yet we view those writers and their books as representative of their culture and of their age at the same time as we call them "great" because they transcended their age. Do they indeed express, consciously or unwillingly, the group in which they appeared? Are they the mouthpieces, or as Victor Hugo phrased it, the sonorous echoes of their culture, or the anticipators of a social and intellectual state of things as yet unborn but which their work helps create?

Answers to such questions require painstaking inquiries on a great many cases, the classification of those cases into categories, the careful attention to the distinctions to be traced between isolated and relatively independent creators (poets, painters) and those who depend upon the observation of a social group for their material (novelists of manners, realistic novelists); between those who can afford to wait for their public and gradually to mold it (poets) and those who cannot survive without being understood, appreciated, assisted by collaborators and interpreters (composers of operas and symphonies, architects, dramatists). Not social scientists necessarily, but rather literary historians who have willingly learned from the techniques of behavioral disciplines should be the men to undertake the patient research necessitated by such questions.

Similarly, much loose talk has gone on and goes on around the *Zeitgeist*, or spirit of the age, which we con-

ceive anthropomorphically as a force animating all the practitioners of the different literary or artistic genres at the
same time. We imagine that there was one common spirit
permeating the writers or artists whom we now call
baroque, or the English poets living around 1815–30
(gladly forgetting Jane Austen, the Utilitarians, the many
unromantics of those same years, the rifts among the so-
called romantics, the mutual hostility of successive generations, etc.). We do not wonder why, if there ever was such
a thing as a Symbolist atmosphere in France around La-
forgue, Verlaine, Villiers, Mallarmé, Debussy, Odilon
Redon, Gauguin, it was breathed by such a small band of
unrecognized men and failed to affect fiction, philosophy,
the drama, most of the painters, the musical enthusiasts of
Wagner, of Offenbach and of Charpentier. In our opinion,
few assumptions are more frail than that which, long after
the event, assigns a common social context and a similar
*Zeitgeist* to the several creators of a certain age and of a
given country. A few pioneers, usually ignored by their contemporaries who banish them as abnormal, obscure, de-
lirious, asocial, unrepresentative eccentrics (Shelley or
Manet or Baudelaire or Gide or Proust of Joyce or Lawrence), are, long after they have reached success or the
refuge of the grave, exalted by historians as the mirrors
to their age. The question of the representativeness of creators and of their relations to their own era is an infinitely
complex one, on the elucidation of which literary scholars
familiar with sociological research should launch concerted efforts.

Again, in several branches of literature and of the arts,
masterpieces can only be created after a language has been
gradually formulated and a technique has been evolved:
atonal music, Greek or French tragedy, Elizabethan drama,
psychological novel, romantic poetry. *Hamlet* is hardly conceivable in 1580 or *le Cid* in 1620 or Monet's "Impression" in 1830. Several abortive but useful attempts had to
precede those works, and in not a few cases public discussion on the doctrine underlying them or on the technique perfected around them had to take place before they

could emerge. Most great artists inherit a form or a technique and use it in an original way which either reorients the tradition which they had inherited or derives strikingly novel results from it. There is a collective element even in the most individual of masterpieces, in Rimbaud's *Illuminations* or Alban Berg's *Wozzeck*. Gustave Lanson rightly acknowledged it: "The most important problems of literary history are sociological problems and most of our research rests on a sociological basis or reaches a sociological conclusion. What do we want to do? To explain the works. And can we explain them otherwise than through resolving individual facts into social facts, through replacing works and men into social series?"

Lastly, the complex relationships between art or literature and the public for which or amid which works are created constitute an immense and almost untilled field for research. A very few books exist, such as the now antiquated thesis by Alexander Beljame, translated with a fifty year lag and published in London in 1948 as *Men of Letters and the English Public in the 18th Century*, or that of Mrs. Queenie Leavis on *Fiction and the Reading Public* (1932), and Erich Auerbach's small volume on *Das französische Publikum des XVII Jahrhunderts* (1933). No student of literature could ever contend that the most unpredictable and the freest of activities, imaginative creation, can be accounted for in a deterministic fashion by outside demand. But at the source of the stimulant which first unleashed the creative energy of a writer, there often lies an impulse provided by a review editor, a publisher, organizers of lecture series, some dim perception on the author's part of a latent need in his audience which he wants to satisfy, perhaps to deflect, even to contradict. There lurks more truth than many of us suspect in Goethe's oft-quoted assertion that great works are often dictated by circumstance. Even the most detached from worldly links among poets, Mallarmé, composed his stately "Toast funèbre" at the request of friends of Théophile Gautier, just then deceased (1872). Valéry composed essays or poems with punctilious coquettishness in order to fulfill a request from

a publisher. These and also Gide, as his *Journals* repeatedly show, were prompted by a demand from a strategist of
literature who was sensing and voicing, or anticipating, the
collective needs of a limited public.

The use of the singular, "a public," is misleading. There
are at any given time several publics coexisting, and the
bold creator is he who divines the as yet unformulated aspirations of the ascending generation and crystallizes them,
thus antagonizing the tenants of established taste. A good
deal has been loosely asserted, in the last hundred years,
on literature as a way of knowledge and on literature as
prophecy. A systematic yet not over rigid examination of
those claims and of the many cases when men of letters
(Balzac, Baudelaire, Rimbaud, Apollinaire, Proust, to
mention French writers alone) seem indeed to have antici-
pated, perhaps to have molded, what was to come would
be in order. In all such cases, the prophet whose literature
or art, as Oscar Wilde's famous saying has it, was imitated
by life should be studied in relation with the group around
him. The multifarious means through which his impact
upon a narrow, then a gradually growing audience was
felt should be analyzed.

It is shocking that, after two centuries of attention to
literary mechanisms and of repetitious assertion of the so-
called dependence of literature upon society, we still know
so very little about the mechanism of that collective fact,
success, and, with success, which can be measured, of a
more imponderable phenomenon, influence. There should
exist a social and, as it were, secondary history of ideas and
of literature which, paying relatively scant attention to the
intrinsic qualities of the works, would be concerned with
their fecundity and their prolongation of themselves in their
age and country, or in later eras and foreign lands. We affect to smile complacently at the fame of Delille and of
Béranger, even on a much higher level, at that of Byron,
Alexandre Dumas the elder, Poe, outside their native lands,
at the wide influence of Théophile Gautier on English,
American and Hispanic poets, of secondary German thinkers on Spain, of Sinclair Lewis on Blasco-Ibañez. Yet the

collaboration of history, of sociological techniques, of literary perceptiveness should help courageous research men to inquire into those collective groups of events. Intellectual history, which has lately tempted many historians away from the recording of facts, has too exclusively turned into a history of thinkers and of men of letters, more or less loosely related to each other and to a hypothetical spirit or mood of the age, which they supposedly expressed and created at one and the same time. The true province of intellectual history, however, is the more complex research into the varied mechanisms through which ideas of Bergson, Durkheim, Pareto, Max Weber, Nietzsche, Croce (to take a few names prominent in Stuart Hughes' excellent monograph on *Consciousness and Society*), filtered through to teachers, journalists, intermediaries of all kinds, and eventually became dynamic ideas exercising an impact upon society and often upon politics and changing the West-European world. The degeneracy of "pure" ideas into beliefs, creeds, myths, superstitions (*Ideas y Creencias* is the apt title of one of Ortega y Gasset's most pregnant essays) should be the theme of many sociological-literary monographs today. The abundance of the materials is overwhelming, as in all that pertains to modern history; qualitative criteria have to be added to the collecting and the weighing of the data available. But there are enough men of good will and of talent among humanists who everlastingly rewrite the same volumes on Leopardi, Melville, Joyce and Camus, and who in so doing bring scant credit to the pioneering spirit of their profession. If it be true that our century is one of wars of ideas or of myths, i.e. high-powered emotional concepts applied like levers to life, humanists to whom nothing human is alien should cooperate with specialists of behavioral sciences in projecting a little more light into seas of darkness. Many great ideas lay dormant in Hegel, Marx, Gobineau, Husserl, and before them in the forerunners of the American and of the French revolutions, until collective beings and masses became fired by those concepts, crudely distorted them but also instilled life into them.

Such studies, building bridges between the social sciences and the humanities, are in no way unworthy of humanists and would not detract from their individual enjoyment of the beauty and of the depth of great works of art and of literature. It would be idle to contend that, after two or three centuries of sharpening our critical faculties and elaborating aesthetic ideas, we can still approach a work of art as the contemporaries of Shakespeare or of Calderon approached their plays, or the amateurs who first looked at the Sistine Chapel or at pictures by Vermeer and Hogarth. Imaginative creators can no longer ignore the existence of mass media around them. They have, since the Romantic era, wailed their living and feeling in a desert in which the so-called élite from the middle classes failed to encourage them or to understand whatever was revolutionary in their message, be they Berlioz or Hugo Wolf, Delacroix or Cézanne, Keats or Baudelaire. They may well indeed pin their hopes on a broadened public, less sophisticated, less obsessed by its cult of tradition, less fearful of innovations. Proletarian art, even in the lands most attached to social realism, has thus far disappointed us. Too often, it debased itself through attempting to effect crude propaganda and to palm off the meretricious and the tawdry upon a public which deserved a better fare.

America, however, prides itself of being less conscious of class distinction than European societies. The attempt to democratize education has gone farther here than in Western Europe. The number of the young men and women who go through college, and later through our graduate schools, is higher here than in most other lands. They are probably more malleable, more receptive to the teaching imparted to them than are European audiences, less deflected from the pursuit of science and knowledge by ardent political passions and feuds than in Europe, Asia or Latin America, more impelled by feelings of fraternity and of solidarity with the rest of the world and more earnest in their touching determination to improve the fate of their fellow-beings elsewhere. Yet the number of Americans who are vitally concerned with understanding their own age through literature and the arts, those splendid factors of broadening of sensibility, of deepening of the mind, of stimulating of the imagination, is not growing at a pace commensurate with the increase of population or the plentifulness of educational facilities offered. A very great American literature, a painting and a sculpture second to none at the present time in vitality and energy, a rich critical movement affect a woefully small portion of the American public. Humanists have erred, and failed in part, in talking and writing to and for their ilk, proud of their own subtlety and, like the medieval scholastics, content to encircle knowledge within the walls of their seminar rooms and to disdain the possibilities for the life of the spirit off of academic campuses. The very best among the American literary scholars, historians of culture, art critics, musicologists are at least the equals of the best in any other country. But they do not fire their students with enough enthusiasm and generosity so as to lure more of them to preferring the pursuits of the mind and the excitement of research to other careers. They have not succeeded, or tried strenuously enough, to expand the American public which might appreciate and encourage still more imaginative creation. Less scholasticism, less complacent satisfaction with the narrow perspectives of university life, less unjustified fear of the social disciplines with which the humanities may fruitfully ally themselves in the pursuit of a well-defined common goal would serve the country, and the humanists themselves, best in the years to come.

# Facing the New Decade

YOUR PRESIDENT FOR 1960, as he prepares to vanish into oblivion after his one address in sovereign capacity, first wishes to express his gratitude to those who selected him, and his apologies for the pretentious title announced. In this country, from the beginning and throughout her entire history, action has prevailed. Yet the nation has never showed much aversion for words. Politicians, preachers, college presidents, generals, men of affairs spreading relaxation through warmed up after dinner anecdotes, members of those faculty committees to whom, in these days of trial and error and perseverance in error, the Almighty seems to have relinquished the running of the world, all indulge their propensity for eloquence. Those whom Homer might have called the shepherds of people, in Moscow and Havana and equatorial Africa, strike back at our garrulous nation with massive retaliation.

Torrents of words may flow in the sumptuous hotels where our Association once a year congregates late in December (just before the inebriating vigil through which we shall pray for a virgin year to wash out our unfulfilled

Presidential address to *The Modern Language Association*, December 1960 promises and our harrowing regrets over unwritten articles). But scholars and teachers are happy to leave boastfulness to other professions. An American ambassador to the Court of St. James, John Hay, once told an audience, in the antediluvian nineteen-nineties, that "the national American flower ought to be the violet, the emblem of modesty and self-effacement." Let us behave like violets and, after having exhaled our fragrant satisfaction at the state of our affairs and even at that of our treasury, may we not try and listen to the demands which the world outside is soon likely to make upon us?

The state of our nation of scholar-teachers stands in need of yearly re-examination. When delivering his famous "House Divided" speech at Springfield, Illinois, in 1858, a great American uttered words which are still timely in 1960. "If we could first know where we are and whither we are tending, we could then better judge what to do and how to do it." What good speeches of gentle admonition or of stern upbraiding do in America to those who meekly listen to them is a problem for our friends the social scientists to explore. Some good at any rate seems to be selfishly achieved by him who delivers himself of such lay sermons and imagines for a moment that he is helping reform the world. A dissertation on the influence of presidential addresses on the intellects and on the morale of the MLA will surely be written some day. Meanwhile, let us repeat with some pride that self-criticism remains the life blood of our profession and that, if our conventions at times do not altogether eschew the slight boredom which is the necessary accompaniment to all good instruction, at least they perpetrate no evil on the public. Adam Smith mockingly remarked in *The Wealth of Nations* that "people of the same trade seldom meet together, even for merriment and diversion, but the conversation ends in a conspiracy against the public, or in some contrivance to raise prices." The only price which is likely to be raised here is that of the yearly subscription to our invaluable quarterly journal, and our sole conspiracy is against our own purses and for the enrichment of our minds.

The year 1960 marks the twentieth anniversary of what

was perhaps the gloomiest year in our century, the gloomiest in the history of the modern world. Four neutral lands ruthlessly invaded, Finland mutilated, France collapsing, two dictators sharing the spoils in the East while poised for a showdown, Britain undaunted but anguished, this great country uncertain and unwilling to read the threat written on its very walls. The events which filled the subsequent two decades need not be recalled here. The rebuilding has been as remarkable as the collapse was fast and total, and, almost equally important, economic and political improvement has been matched by intellectual progress. No other score of years ever witnessed such strides in American scholarship in modern literatures. We write more and perhaps better studies than ever before. University presses vie with each other for our manuscripts; new learned journals appear every year, clamoring for new omnivorous readers, or for those of us who are lucky enough to be blessed with insomnia. We undertake gigantic collective editions of the most prolific of English polygraphists. Foundations no longer refuse to finance our foreign language programs; they generously buy us research time, fly us to remote lands as quiet, or unquiet and happily disquieting Americans, but never ugly ones. It is no exaggeration to say that millions of eyes throughout the world are now fixed on American scholarship, American education, and American culture.

Such a state of affairs imposes new duties upon us. It ill behooves a man of foreign birth, untrained in Anglo-Saxon understatement, speaking the American language gracelessly, to proffer advice to colleagues, many of whom he admires unstintingly. But he shares with Americans a passion for general ideas, or for generalities "period," and with his age a vocation for commitment: a scholar's commitment to his profession, to his community, to the country at large and to the ascending generations. If that means introducing politics into our holy precincts, let us not be ashamed of it. For what are politics ultimately but the art of living together in society and of helping to organize such a society?

We, literary and philological devotees, are in no way en-

vious of the historians or of the affluent society of economists who have the ears of our leaders and whose brains are
ever ready to be picked. Still, we have our part to play in
the nation as a whole and far more prestige and power than
we imagine, if we only dare wield it. Since we cannot admit
more than a fraction of those who knock at our college
gates, we are today invested with authority we never possessed before—the authority to demand meaningful curricula and thorough teaching of essentials in our high
schools.

"If people become inattentive to the public affairs,"
warned Jefferson, "you and I and Congress and assemblies
. . . shall all become wolves." We do not intend to
change into wolves, not even in sheep's or in asses' skins.
But one of our functions is to train the youth, and we can ill
afford to ignore the rumbling of a world in turmoil. Nor
dare we refuse to recognize the rebellion of the young
against the image of herself which America, paying scant
attention to intellectual factors, has projected in Korea,
Japan, Vietnam and Turkey, in Cuba, Venezuela, Africa,
and Western Europe. Fifteen years appear to be the span of
time needed to repair the ravages of a great war, after
which a new and rising generation clamors for an audacious
forward move: as happened in 1830 and in 1933, the year
1960 may well have ushered in an era of crisis and of revaluation in many a realm.

The word "communication," however inelegant and im-
precise, denotes one of the striking features of our age.
There are no more islands, no more silent and secluded
vales preserved from the sad, if hardly still, music of humanity; the youngest among us may live to see the day
when they will be catapulted to another planet to initiate
science-fiction's "bems" (bug-eyed monsters) to Shakespeare, Pascal and Melville. We believe in the benefits of
a literary education and in humanistic values; we are devoted heart and soul to the beauty of arts and letters, even
if at times, as Wilde naughtily put it, our way of liking art
rationally takes on the appearance of solid dislike. We go
on delivering speeches on the humanities and their benefits,

voicing our fears for a cult which we see declining but do little to revive. The truth is that, unless we succeed in spreading our passion for literature and our enjoyment of humanistic values to wide groups of scientists, technicians, men of affairs, workmen (as we modestly call them, pretending that theirs is a more real work than ours) in an age which is of necessity a technological one, we may as well resign ourselves to the slow death of the humanism that we have known and worshipped. It will be largely our fault if we fail to convert those whom we might complacently call the barbarians outside our Hellenic microcosm, and also those inside it, to the values which we cherish.

The potential audience for literature and for much that pertains to it has grown a hundred or a thousand fold or more. Over half of the high school graduates in the United States go to college and are presumed to be exposed, as the euphemism puts it, to courses in English composition and even in foreign languages. It has been prophesied that there will be as many as six hundred million Americans sixty years from now and they will all be subjected to mass media. (A hundred thousand might then be readers of *PMLA*, and half that number might be congregating at our conventions, absorbing five thousand papers and fifteen thousand drinks daily.) Should we not attempt with more determination to win a vast proportion of that increasing public to the enjoyment and trained reading of literature, through mass media if need be, and also through a clearer and more pleasing way of writing about it? When a magazine today doubles the number of its subscribers from twenty to forty thousand, a weekly or a newspaper from two to four hundred thousand, must it automatically lower its sights and debase its standards to reach these new readers, or endeavor to raise them gently to the level of their fewer predecessors?

We have lately preferred moaning over the general debasement of standards, implicitly proclaimed the failure of education in a democracy and resorted to the comfortable device of blaming press magnates and manipulators of the screen, of television and of newspapers. If they are to blame, so are we. For most of those who run the Luce stables and the Chicago newspapers and Madison Avenue advertising firms and even Hollywood studios sat at our feet at some time or other. Many graduated, perhaps as English majors, from the Ivy League nurseries. They listened to us while we expatiated on Chaucer and Fielding and Dante and Henry James, and sought the golden bough through the arid plains and groves of the Waste Land. Why have we failed to give them the inspiration to read more and better books, to write better, to share with others the privileges which they once enjoyed under our guidance? These alumni, once our captive and responsive audience, should, and probably would, enjoy rereading the classics, discovering new works of quality, even keeping up with some of our critical elucidations and incidentally purchasing our books, if only we helped them by meeting them half way.

Our age has heard good music, music which has reached millions, and, through the sale of records, we have literally retrieved from oblivion centuries of past music for the many to enjoy. Our age has proudly pointed to the museum as the successor to the cathedral. A scintillating volume on the role of the imaginary museum in fostering a new humanism lately dazzled thousands of readers. More people are reading Homer, Herodotus, Greek tragic poets, even Dante and Strindberg, than at any time in the past. The Pelican has become a venerated bird in the United Kingdom, which, in its ornithological voraciousness, also prides itself on being a Penguin Island.

Meanwhile, as Lionel Trilling lately warned us, the share of English literature in our usable past as a means of education of the young has been steadily shrinking. We have more profound critics of all degrees of newness, discovering mysteries in the simplest poems, measuring tensions, framing the fearful symmetry of their elaborate categories with tiger-like relentlessness, producing admirable if melancholy anatomies of their victims. Great and thoughtful men who, in earlier ages, would have worn the mantle of a Jonathan Edwards or the red garb of a Cardinal, have earnestly denounced the affective fallacies by which naïve readers used to convey their exultation or their boredom in the presence of a work of art. In the halls where great teachers of literature once touchingly fired their disciples with the communication of an ecstasy or even with moral indignation, we now instruct our students to shun the gravest of all sins: venturing value-judgments.

Those of us who acknowledge in all humility that they are incapable of scaling those icy peaks and breathing there the serene objectivity praised by Lucretius, Goethe and other priests of "templa serena" might well wonder whether we have not unduly erected forbidding walls around our sanctuary. Are we any closer to scientific precision or to scientific objectivity when we refrain from feeling? Let me not be misunderstood: feeling is not knowing, and the two processes should first be separated before they become reunited again. Organic and structural values do count in art; even logic can be beautiful, provided it be, as Rémy de Gourmont asked, perceived as a pleasure. But all our attempts at teaching schoolboys and college students how to read literature would be of small avail if, after elaborate disquisitions, we did not send these young people back to the work of art with keener insight and—let us not banish that unpuritan word—intenser enjoyment.

The very profundity of our critics, who are often far more cultured and intelligent than the authors and artists they elucidate, tends to frighten away many timid potential readers: the uninitiated dimly sense that there should also be room in art for the unlimited, the unfinished, nay, for disorder, and for contradictions which remain unresolved; for chaotic forces and unconscious promptings and unruly passion and the expansion of the animal impulses of man. There are limits to a rational approach to beauty and to the fetishism of unity and organicity which almost make our critics exclaim with Henry James, when life in its raw irrationality faces them: "Stupid life again at its clumsy work!"

Literature, for its true lovers, is more alive than life itself; even a novel or a play which is ultimately not destined to survive can rock us to our affective foundations as reality perceived by us would fail to do. The Germans were lately moved to more indignation and pity by *The Diary of Anne Frank* than they were when extermination camps smoked under the Third Reich. We, teachers and critics, underrate the power of our subject and the effectiveness of our communication of that electrifying or destructive force to our audiences.

There are some among us in this society of spirits whose vocation is for theorizing about literature and for questioning and revising all our assumptions and our methods of criticism. They bring to less abstract minds invaluable assistance and, in their philosophical ambition, they display much modesty: for they usually dally in the antechamber of criticism and refrain from passing judgment on individual works or from approaching the productions of new writers. Others are historians of letters, and their research is indispensable to any fair appreciation of the past, and to any inquiry into the way in which the present is inserted in the past and modifies the past in its turn. Finally there are those who insist upon being primarily critics, who are convinced that the most difficult and the most pressing of tasks is the evaluation of new works and that criticism inevitably remains a secondary activity, the handmaiden of works of art or creative works of thought; hence that the contact between criticism and contemporary literature must not be severed. We have argued the point at length elsewhere. May I only repeat that, more than ever today, the American study of modern literatures would abdicate if it failed to understand, to interpret, to assist modern writers, here and abroad, and to win devotees to literature by utilizing the eager curiosity of young people for works by their contemporaries.

Writers and artists may be self-centered, arrogant, vulgar, morbid, and exasperating. Still we have more to learn from them than from our genteel and learned colleagues. A wise man, Montaigne, warned us long ago that "les sages ont plus à apprendre des fols que les fols des sages." We have, through the appointment of a new class of honorary fellows prudently selected among eminent living writers, evinced our eagerness not to impede a marriage of diverse but equally true minds.

Would I even dare submit that, if we proposed more value judgments and committed ourselves to the present more generously, we might even help rescue contemporary literature in America from its present passion for depravity and its weakness for grime and slime? Obviously no one would advocate Victorian standards or a return to Mrs. Grundy's prudish cant. Equally obviously, Sunday school morality and girl scout idealism are not to be mistaken for the higher morality with which literature is instinct. But, from an objective point of view, should we not warn our students and readers that the truth does not always lie in wallowing in abjection, in endless and mournful portrayals of decadence, in dismal abnormality and in so much sexless writing about sex?

A few stale formulas have held undue fascination for us, such as the famous dictum that "a poem should not mean, but be." An English critic and poet, John Holloway, retorted the other day in *The Fugue:* "Poems dare not merely be. They mean. They yield. They yield." Bonamy Dobrée in Britain, Alfred Kazin and Richard Brustein in this country have lately raised their voices in protest against the fallacy of emptying literature of all moral content. Our novel and our drama should indeed recapture the role of fiction and drama in other ages when they offered us, in Russia, France, and England, perhaps the sharpest of all social criticisms. Literature and criticism might aim at filling the pre-eminent role in our culture history once played at the time of Carlyle and Prescott and Michelet. Philosophers have become excessively fond of disserting about language and meaning, and they write more and more for their own ilk in learned journals. Plato and Descartes and Spinoza, happily for their contemporaries, had no learned journals in which to bury their message. But literature can give flesh and blood, and an audience, to philosophy and even to ethics—and it need not, indeed cannot, do this in the form that has recently been called the nonfiction novel.

We teach our students in critical seminars all about Longinus and Dr. Johnson and other sages; but we apparently fail to convince those of them who subsequently write fiction, plays and criticism of the undying value of "the sublime" and of the aptness of some of Johnson's statements, such as: "The only end of writing is to enable the reader better to enjoy life, or better to endure it." Paul Valéry, surely hardly a sentimentalist befogged with illusions, rightly warned us in one of his aphorisms that "l'homme n'est pas si simple qu'il suffice de le rabaisser pour le comprendre."

In more practical terms, what might we accomplish during the seventh decade of the century, when this octogenarian association becomes a respectable dowager? First, realize that, through the coming of age of generations more numerous than we once were, in every country of the world and particularly in this one, we are living today in a young man's world. The manner in which that youth is clamoring to be heeded is not always a traditionally genteel and respectful one. But we, the older groups, may be guilty of having too often looked backward instead of forward and not having proposed enough challenging tasks to the youth, not having discerned how much frustrated idealism lurked behind their hurried cynicism. The most creative age in science, in the arts, and probably in scholarship and criticism extends from twenty-five to forty-five, due allowance being made for numerous exceptions. We should, in the universities, teach so well, love literature so passionately, that we fire young people with zeal, lead them to question our values and propose new ones; we should not reduce criticism to a series of recipes, but turn literary seminars into places where new ideas run riot.

At our own MLA meetings, could we not avoid the appearance of a "slave market" which we have too lazily assumed, finding even that odious phrase humorous, and answer the expectation of the young men out of graduate schools who are entering the most generous of all professions? Could we not give the young an opportunity to listen to truly important papers in which renowned scholars would offer the most substantial result of their thinking to the young, and invite the young to contradict or to question them? Would we not multiply meetings of regional or sub-branches of our large Association where papers and debates of quality could be heard, and the seeking of jobs or of teachers would be less mercantile or less obtrusive? We have allowed sections and groups to proliferate with ridiculous ease, and are now afraid of the vested interests of candidates for chairmanship, secretaryship, nominating committees, bibliography committees, each seeking to have his name on the program. A drastic reform is imperative, with groups agreeing to meet every second or third year, but to offer their members a more substantial fare and to stimulate future research, not just to listen to specialized reports in a crowded room where women come and go, talking . . . perhaps of Michelangelo as the crowded and smoke-filled room arouses visions of the Last Judgment.

If ours is a young man's world, it is also a woman's world. Some of us who are fortunate to have women among our graduate students and as young colleagues are extraordinarily impressed by the high level of their work. Indeed, we often wonder if criticism will not make substantial strides forward, blending the cognitive and the affective values, taste and a rational approach, the logic of the intellect and that of the heart, only when women take over a large share of it, as they are now out-numbering men as teachers of English and of languages in many schools.

This country witnessed a bold feminist movement several decades ago. The second sex then conquered all the rights and courageously accepted corresponding duties. College presidents in women's colleges were in many cases women. In anthropology, archeology, psychology several American women have been outstanding. This has also been true in journalism. Why not to the same extent today in philology, medieval studies, literary history, criticism? Are men to blame, wary of these potential rivals, preferring to utilize women's generosity and their capacity for devoted attachment by keeping them as secretaries and obedient confidants of their profound male cogitations? Have women put so much energy in once winning equality and security that they are now content to enjoy these rights, and to look upon maternity and housekeeping (now easier than ever before) as their sole vocation? Men in any case have the duty to make room for them, to incite them to express themselves more boldly, to elect them to more positions of power in this Association and in others, to ask them for the healthy challenge with our duller brains need to receive from their keener perceptiveness in matters of art and literature.

Lastly, and through resorting more confidently to the enthusiasm of the young, to the devinatory gifts of our female companions in the profession of criticism and teaching which requires both enthusiasm and some divination, let us combine our thoroughness and independence as scholars with our other function of guiding the public taste. Why should it be impossible to write both for *PMLA* and for literary monthlies and weeklies? It is easy to rail at some of the book reviews being published in our magazines for the general public, but it is more essential to write better ones, to encourage the founding of new literary journals and not just of scholarly ones where we aim only at each other, and to evince the first quality of a scholar, intellectual honesty, by expressing ourselves without jargon. A man who bears our breed little affection, but whom we have long presented to our students as a classic (a classic who can lapse into slumber far oftener than Homer), Ernest Hemingway, bluntly declared in words which even we may find apposite: "If a man writes clearly enough, any one can see if he fakes."

We have showed too much inclination to sink into defeatism and to believe that we were doomed to remain uninfluentials while American literature pursued its course as a vigorous but untutored and often vulgar adolescent, immature in its delineation of passion, scornful of the Emersonian "inner check," eyeing only shock values and royalties and sales to Hollywood. The American public which we have trained in colleges for the last thirty or forty years deserves better than that. It feels the twinges of a bad conscience when it delights in *Forever Amber* and *Peyton Place* and Mickey Spillane, and it does not esteem us particularly when we, scholars, pretend to rejoice in Ellery Queen or to acclaim *The Catcher in the Rye* and *The Old Man and the Sea* as classics for our schools. We underestimate our power as enlighteners of the public taste, and wrongly believe that the present is too bewildering for our timid prudence and that, faced with living literature and culture, we can only take refuge in the academic greyness of yes and no or in a provisional suspension of judgment which we prolong into permanent abdication. Our profession could well do with more audacity as it enters a world in revolutionary turmoil.

It could also combine its enjoyment of beauty and of solitary research with more generous communication of its privileges to others. Albert Camus, an honorary member of our Association whose tragic death was universally deplored as this year 1960 opened, pronounced words in his Nobel Prize speech which it may be fitting to apply to ourselves: "I cannot live as a person without my art. And yet I have never set that art above everything else. It is essential to me . . . because it excludes no one. . . . To me, art is not a solitary delight. It is a means of stirring the greatest number of men by providing them with a privileged image of our common joys and woes."

# Higher Education in the United States

THE TEMPTATION TO GENERALIZE about a foreign country is great and the best way to embrace a varied, often contradictory experience is probably indeed to generalize upon it and to conclude, from a motley array of disconnected facts, to a few underlying principles. Of all countries whose educational system might be thus appraised, however, America is without doubt the one to which the skeptic's formula, "ab uno disce omnes" is least applicable. There may be intellectual monotony in this country and at times a regrettable conformism of the minds, against which all educators inveigh these days; but there is certainly no standardization of institutions, no pattern offering an appearance of harmonious uniformity. Heterogeneousness prevails, often to a bewildering degree for the person accustomed to the rigid framework of educational organization in several lands of Western Europe.

The word "philosophy" is not well-suited to a description of American education, for it might imply that the educational institutions, the methods, the goals rest upon a clearly preconceived and well-defined body of theoretical thinking. A few countries, after a thorough upheaval, may have undertaken to build a new system of institutions, breaking with traditions and formulating broad rules which newly created organisms should fit. Such was not the case in the United States. A number of thinkers who applied themselves to questions of education, such as John Dewey, others who perfected the technique of tests or studied the gradual growth of children in the tradition of Rousseau's *Emile* but with an eager zest to establish laws, have exercised a far-reaching influence over American education. But empiricism crept into reforms thus effected; other forces acted in contradiction; tides of taste, or of fashion, even fads succeeded each other; the local forces in each region, at times in the school system of each city, the conflicting demands of city and of country, of the East, of the South, and of the Western frontier resisted or modified whatever current of ideas reached them from outside.

Whatever philosophy underlies American higher education in particular had better be construed empirically and formulated without any rigidity. The higher educational system of a country like France could be described analytically, with categories and diagrams and carried over wholesale, as indeed it often has been, in other countries, new ones or old ones bent upon overhauling their tottering institutions. Not so with the American or the British educational, or governmental, or parliamentary institutions. No towering pyramidal structure stands here which might be reconstructed elsewhere. Like American free enterprise or the American so-called two-party system, it cannot be deduced from principles, but it works somehow, with a minimum of muddling through.

But some essential remarks must be added: Americans may pass for a boastful people, prone to deliver sermons and admonitions to the rest of the world and replete with self-assurance as to their achievement and their wisdom in eschewing the entanglements of the Old World or the adolescent revolutionary impulsions of Asia and South America. But such complacent arrogance, if it ever existed, has been dealt hard blows in the last few decades. In no realm perhaps are Americans so assailed with doubts as in that of education. Parents nod their heads envying the schools of Britain, France, Germany, nay, of Russia; school principals hold schools of Europe up to us as paragons of greater intellectual achievement; college presidents look up nostalgically at the venerable halls of Oxford and Cambridge, at Heidelberg and at the Sorbonne, at institutions where alumni do not have to be cajoled into becoming donors and where the customer is not necessarily right, especially when the customer is a sophomore. Faculties in America are houses divided against themselves, even more than elsewhere; they change their minds and their votes easily, they experiment, they try reforms which they forget having already tried ten years earlier and found wanting. Students are often afflicted with a vague inferiority complex where European education is concerned. From Woodrow Wilson when he assumed the presidency of Princeton University to John Maynard Hutchins at Chicago, from journalists like Walter Lippmann to historians like Arthur Bestor and George Kennan, the critics of American education have been and are legion. They are more vocal, and they are more soberly headed by the public at large, than in any other country.

The launching of the Sputnik in the fall of 1957 shook American opinion violently. For the first time, this country had to concede that its technological supremacy was being challenged; that, within thirty years or so, a country which was supposed to have hardly emerged from a backward state, with a majority of illiterates, had overtaken the proudest scientific power. An agonizing reappraisal of the teaching of science, of the intellectual content of American education has since taken place. Senators have delivered themselves of grave scoldings to educators and to educationists. The scientist and the intellectual, who had never played golf with the President, never had to meet a payroll, never mastered the art of salesmanship, were on the way to being hailed as the new heroes of new frontiers, those of space and of the future.

This crisis of conscience is the most conspicuous feature of American higher education today and it vividly exemplifies its capacity for humility, but also for reform. That flexibility of institutions which do not rest upon a rigid or a static philosophy is the most admirable characteristic of American teaching and research to be proposed to foreign observers of this country. There was a time, half a century ago, when every conquest of science was counted as a definitive one, decreasing the ever dwindling share of the unknown in the universe, when medicine could view its own achievements as final and physics thought it had pierced the ultimate secrets of the structure of matter. At that time also, Americans could consider that they had reached a plateau of stable prosperity, a land of promise in which, with a minimum of technological education, everyone could enjoy the fruits of science and of peace, and possess happiness without even having to pursue it. The child had to be taught "to fit in" in a prosperous society and the aim of much secondary education was defined as life-adjustment. The gifted pupils were somewhat troublesome in such an almost Byzantine order and they received no especial attention; if anything, they were held back for fear that they might become ill-adapted.

That touching dream has been shattered by the Depression, the tragedy of World War II, the atomic age and what a theologian, Rheinhold Niebuhr, has called "the irony of American history," the necessity for democratic, well-meaning rulers to commit evil in order to avert an evil perhaps more ominous; by the events in China, in Hungary and elsewhere. Nowhere at the present time does a sense of anguish, perhaps even guilt, certainly of courageous if tragic responsibility, permeate the youth as much as in this country. A foreign observer, Simone de Beauvoir, did not err when she declared that the chief hope of America today lies in the uneasy hearts of its young people.

The butt of most of the strictures levelled at education in America is the American high school. Even though this paper is primarily concerned with higher teaching and research, a few minutes may be spent on secondary education; for higher teaching is naturally conditioned by it and must fill the gaps left by previous training, remedy unsatisfactory working habits, do over again what was done faultily. A few considerations may be dryly enumerated here on the character of secondary education in this country, with more imperious generalization than wisdom should permit:

*1*) Unlike many European systems of secondary education, America's was not intended to train state officials, army officers, teachers, members of the liberal professions and, generally speaking an élite destined to form the backbone of the country's administrative hierarchy. From the start, its goal was to prepare men for life, and life, in a land of boundless opportunities, diffident of all federal administrative encroachment over local groups, meant chiefly business enterprises. Success was first of all measured in terms of money-making ability, at times transfigured by the semireligious cloak of social service. Hence the stress on vocational education and on subjects deemed to be practical, and a lesser concern than in less democratic countries for general culture.

*2*) This country had to confront a situation which no Western European land had encountered: the need to assimilate, through education, on an immense continent with few traditions and a scattered population, a large number of children whose parents had come from all over Europe, from Ireland to Greece and from Norway to Poland to Sicily. In several urban communities, those children of immigrants, often stemming from the least literate elements in the Old World, constituted a majority of the pupils; they were alien to the English languages, to the civic and religious traditions of the new country. Teachers had to be found to teach them. Since traditional colleges and universities evinced little inclination to train such teachers in the numbers required, teachers' colleges were set up; requirements were hastily proposed, which stressed the techniques of teaching and a few recipes on child psychology rather than a thorough knowledge of the subject. There remain to this day glaring weaknesses in American schools; but it must be remembered that no other country, until Russia undertook an even more drastic effort, had to face the similar situation of training everyone for democracy within a very few years. It may be that, as John M. Hutchins has often asserted, since everyone had to be educated and we were not in a position to give everyone a good education, we ended by giving a bad education to everybody. But, viewed in the political and social context of the years 1880–1930, the noble experiment of a summary education for life was necessary, and its credit side outweighs its debits.

3) The quality of the teachers in the rural schools, in many an urban community, was not high. The very best secondary school teachers in the top private schools of America, in many a public school, are equal to the best anywhere; and their load is heavier than at Harrow or Winchester, than in a Paris lycée or in a Gymnasium in Vienna. But their classes are large, their hours are long, their leisure time is decreased by the supervision of nonscholastic activities, their social prestige is incomparably less glittering than in Europe. Bergson, Durkheim, Sartre in France, Carducci in Italy, Antonio Machado in Spain and countless others taught school and thought, wrote, while they did it. That would be difficult in America. A grave flaw in the American system is the almost total impossibility of passing from a high school (or even a private school faculty) to a university faculty. The relationships between college professors and high school teachers in this land of equality, are in effect marked by more aloofness, more diffidence and less cooperation than in most European countries. This is all the more deplorable as, for the notion of education for life-adjustment, the goal of education in the high school for adjustment to college should now be substituted. Nearly half of the secondary school students at present aim at a college education. Colleges often appear to be hardly cognizant of the fact. They have not utilized the desire of American youth to enter college, hence to satisfy the requirements set by the colleges, as the powerful lever which it is to act upon the methods and the contents of high-school education.

4) America basked for several decades in the conviction that she was destined to remain a new country, with

unlimited opportunities for the youth, the constant opening of a new frontier for candidates to a success story, and more positions to be filled than there were able men to fill them. That contrasted with the old countries, where very selective competitive examinations were to keep young men away from overstaffed liberal professions. Such a selection would have appeared like a derogation to the principle of equality. It was the duty of teachers to lavish more attention on the retarded child, so as to correct nature's unequality, to avoid fostering emulation or envy of the more gifted ones, to reward effort more than achievement and the safe, solid merits of "plodders" at least as much as brilliance. To be sure, a sifting did occur later in life, in the law schools, medical schools, engineering institutes; those who had been coddled too long by kindly teachers sometimes broke down mentally or otherwise when the ordeal of life revealed their inadequacy. But one clung to the American myth of equality of gifts and of distrust of a favored class of zealous and brilliant intellectuals, suspect of being uncooperative. To this day, the concept of intellectuals is repugnant to many Americans, as if it implied that they would let a group of theoretical thinkers or a brain trust do their thinking for them.

5) Implicit in the subconscious substratum of elementary and secondary education in America is the notion, strange in a land in which Puritans once denounced the pitfalls of the devil gaping in front of every child and adult, that human nature in its essence is not corrupt, that the child is fundamentally good, and that education, in the Rousseau manner, must not contradict or warp the essential rectitude of human nature. The result has been that many parents leave children alone as much as possible, that is, let them be among those of their own age and seek their entertainments, before a screen, among themselves, without the intrusive presence of parents. Children educated in boarding schools enjoyed the privilege of having their education prolonged through most hours of the day, and extended to games, character-building and habits of work. Those who attended high school or day school received

very little supplementary education from their parents and are seldom advised to read or to reflect; the failure of families to play their part in their children's education is probably a more real flaw in this country than the dubious quality of much teaching in the schools. The climate of intellectual eagerness and of scientific or artistic curiosity which might then be created around the youth frequently does not exist.

Nevertheless the faith in a college education, along with some superficial aspects (desire to make friends, to establish relations, to "make the team," to escape from the elders and to associate with young persons of the other sex on an idyllic campus vaguely reminiscent of the Garden of Eden) is perhaps the strongest motive in this country today. It is bound up with the myth of success which long swayed the youth of America; but it is even more closely linked with a semireligious desire for self-improvement and for saving the world through technology and social science.

If we now turn to a consideration of American higher education, by which we mean undergraduate teaching at its best and graduate teaching and research, we find that self-criticism, which is and should be the life blood of anything pertaining to education and to science, is equally unsparing; but fairness demands that we place such criticism, at times ironical and condescending, at other times devastating and even masochistic, in its true perspective. Higher education today in America, as a whole, is second to none; research in the sciences, in the social disciplines, but also in literary history and criticism, in philosophy, in art history stands today, for its quantitative output and for its average quality, at the top of any country.

Some of the reasons for a truly striking achievement need only be recalled briefly: unequalled material resources, part of which (never adequate, yet substantial) has been devoted to research and advanced education; the healthy rivalry of centers of learning scattered over the country, vying with each other to attract money and brains, to create a spirit favorable to research; the mobility characteristic of

the American people, their distrust of routine, of conserva-
tism, of academics, their reluctance to turn universities
into self-reproductive institutions. To those and other factors must be added the shrewd and generous impulse which
has invited those scholars and scientists who were threatened in Europe to make their homes in America.

A considerable portion of the task of higher education
consists in the communication of knowledge: the word
knowledge is to be understood in its broad sense, for teachers impart to their students, not so much what they know
as what they are. They fire them with the urge to learn
more, to live their lore by applying it to life, to become their
own selves. The most impeccable of experimenters among
French physiologists, Claude Bernard, rightly observed in
a letter: "That alone is learned well which is learned with
passion, with furore." The American way of communi-
cating knowledge and zeal for it is through lectures and
seminars. The lectures are less formal, less rhetorical than
in Europe: the untranslatable adjective "casual" denotes
the quality (at times a studied one) most prized by American audiences. The seminars are an excellent institution,
for they limit the number of students attending a class to a
score at the maximum, they afford an opportunity to ask
and to answer questions, they invite the teacher to rethink
his ideas, to watch thought being formed and formulated in
students treated as friends; if he is skilled at maieutics,
he can play the patient Socrates to would-be Platos. Seminars are probably a wasteful manner of training the young;
they reduce the teacher to student ratio to the point where a
great man reaches only a favored few through his spoken
word; but they do not drown the gifted student, as happens
in Europe, in a sea of passive robots who can only take notes
and prepare to render up to the master, on examination
day, what was his—with some inevitable degradation in the
process.

The European student returning to his own country
after a year's stay in America is likely to find his own confrères subservient to hierarchies, overrespectful of "chers
maîtres," too intimidated by hidebound traditions to ques-

tion their professors with freedom or with impudence. It is true that the American system allows any youngster to say almost anything, occasionally obstructing the class or arguing sophistries for the sake of argument. It is also true that such unlimited freedom is not always used to the full, indeed that, where the right to criticize anybody, including one's teacher, is lavishly conceded, many people will practice "escape" from that freedom. Thus a certain timidity appears to hamper young scholars in America. There are not enough dissenters among them. Too few dare go against the tide and venture the kind of paradoxes which might become the truths of tomorrow. Europeans are more fond of intellectual polemics, and controversies of scholars and scientists turn more readily to acrimony in the Old World. Obstinacy in proving to one's adversary that he is a mistaken fool can enhance the debater's confidence in his own superiority; it can also turn into dogmatic arrogance. When not based on a lack of conviction, much should be said for the gentle spirit of toleration, often linked with a valuable modesty, which prevails in intellectual controversies in America.

This is not the place to debate in detail the merits and the demerits of the programs of graduate studies in this country. American institutions have been engaged, since World War II, in a revaluation of their advanced degrees and of the studies leading thereto. The debates have been inconclusive. With the individualism, verging on anarchy, which characterizes American higher education, each institution has undertaken to improve its own program. The chief points at issue are these:

*1*) better selection of graduate students, so as to avoid encouraging or admitting those whose costly training might have to be interrupted; clearly publicized warning as to requirements of desiderata, such as language reading tests;

*2*) more attention granted to the training of the future teachers' teaching ability, through practice, advice given by experienced teachers, if need be, some insight into the methods and psychology of instruction of the subject of specialization (for example, in foreign languages, some familiarity with audio-visual aids);

3) flexibility, so that some future doctors may achieve in three years what requires four or five years for others;

4) variety of interests to be fostered in future teachers, so that they enrich themselves through the opportunities in graduate school to associate with young scholars from other disciplines.

5) American educators should some day undertake a drastic re-estimation of the terminal degree of graduate education, the sacrosanct Ph.D. Ritually, deans of graduate schools devote their annual report to a few perfunctory lines on the subject, concluding that the Ph.D. dissertation must remain with us and its completion be accelerated, but acknowledging that the ambitious formula defining it as a substantial contribution to knowledge is more honored in the breach than in the observance. It can be a remarkably able work, worthy of immediate publication in a few cases, and sadly unoriginal in others. Like old German dissertations, Ph.D. theses when published in obedience to some rulings, merely skim the cream of a fine subject and spoil it, or add needlessly to the bibliography of the question to be sought out and discarded by future scholars.

The social background of our graduate students has radically changed over the last hundred years: relatively few are persons of independent means belonging to the leisure class and in a position to travel from one university to another, to haunt libraries and laboratories for half a dozen years before securing their degree. Fewer still are wholeheartedly dedicated to a youth of prolonged celibacy and to a monachal, penurious existence until they secure the coveted doctorate. The pressure hurrying them on is not only economic; it is social, for they are needed by their country to serve as soldiers, as technicians or to staff the schools and colleges struggling with a teacher shortage. Most dissertations written at twenty-five are hasty and immature. In probably eighty-five per cent of cases, they are never followed by a second and maturer work, which should constitute the real contribution of the scholar to knowledge. If anything, they sterilize the apprentice who had to make an excessive effort too early in his career, realizes later the inadequacy of what he wrote, and is intimidated forever after.

It might be more candid to admit that at twenty-four or five there are very few perceptive critics, original philosophers, archeologists with flair and audacity, historians of unusual range who should be encouraged to develop into teacher-scholars, and eventually into graduate-school teachers. We should lose little if we gave up the requirement of a formal thesis and replaced it with a more thorough preparation for teaching itself and with a few essays on varied aspects or periods of their field.

Happily, the Ph.D. in America is seldom the one criterion of merit. Recommendations by the candidate's masters, other publications by him, interviews in which he can express his qualities of mind and of character also receive attention. On the whole, the advanced degree has proved to be a guarantee of solidity, of thoroughness, of intellectual achievement, if not necessarily of brilliance. In the last thirty years, the level attained has constantly risen, and the goal is being set ever higher.

The immensity of the country, its heterogeneousness and its traditions of private universities and of state universities umbrageously jealous of their independence from anyone but their state, preclude America from ever developing anything like an "agrégation" or a "Staatsexamen" which has served other countries satisfactorily. Such an examination can insure a uniformly high level of intellectual distinction among the teachers of the same subject. But, set aside early in life as the most gifted, those selected teachers sometimes cease to grow, slumber on their cushion of laurels, fail to add, to their intellectual gifts once tested, the devotion of their work, the cooperation with others, the eagerness to pursue research which would be desirable.

Still, with a little more uniformity, secured through a friendly agreement among the twenty-five leading graduate schools in the country, we might establish a new and less pretentious but truer Ph.D. in English, history, philosophy, classics or modern languages to serve the needs of higher education in America. Revision of the curricula and of the standards might be undertaken every five years. The employers of those graduates (chairmen of departments, deans, presidents of small colleges and even of large ones) should have a voice in the matter, more so than they have today. Steps would be taken to provide the leaves of absence, the fellowships and the other encouragements needed by those among the young teachers thus graduated who want to pursue research and writing. Those men would work for a later and higher doctorate, with a thesis which should be published and to which not only honor but some increments would be attached. The holders of that higher doctorate would have the privilege of fewer hours of teaching, of a favored salary scale such as is already the practice in schools of law and of medicine. They would normally constitute most of the staff of graduate schools in this country.

The separation between graduate and undergraduate teachers may at first appear regrettable to some of us. But it is hypocritical not to acknowledge that it already exists. The country can no longer cling to the fiction that a productive research man who trains several Ph.D.'s a year can also administer, lecture for another three or six hours a week to undergraduates, read their papers and correct their English as well as their substance (if the word may be used without irony). Requiring all that, plus the research man's availability to youngsters during office hours and his attendance at sundry academic functions, prandial or oratorical, borders on inhumanity and evinces lack of respect for the intellectual whom older (and younger) countries honor more worthily.

The word research is sacrosanct in America. It can serve as a cover for much hypocrisy, be undertaken merely for purposes of obtaining publicity and a promotion. Every institution likes to see the names of its professors in print and rewards them for "production" as it is called, and a production which can only be weighed by bulk. A substantial number of works are done by their authors with persistence rather than from inspiration and do not bear the mark of an inner compulsion. The obvious need today in American scholarship is to show more scholarly achievement of outstanding quality. The very greatest historians, philosophers, art historians, medievalists, Romance scholars of the last three decades are Europeans or Europeans who migrated to America. The very gifted men either are not adequately stimulated into becoming great or do not enter our profession.

Be that as it may, American research in all branches of knowledge has, in the last three decades, won the respect of the world. Its preeminence is in part due to the ample means placed at its disposal: close to 20% of a total sum of two billion spent on higher education, public and private, is alloted to organized research, as against 5% (of a smaller total) twenty years ago. Such funds are provided, directly or indirectly, by federal agencies, by foundations or by industry. That research is conspicuously free from control. The spirit of free inquiry is in no way curbed. Yet, insidiously but not perfidiously, research in the sciences and in the social sciences can be inspired by the sources which provide the funds. Attention is directed toward some problems while others are temporarily neglected. Team work is often overemphasized. The "curse of bigness" hangs over donating institutions: it is easier for foundations to allot one million dollars to one team than a hundred times ten thousand dollars to as many individuals or projects. Hence the temptation to inflate some projects and to apply for sizable, or colossal, grants.

Big projects imply the mushrooming of committees, subcommittees, executive assistants, deputy executive assistants, deputy vice-presidents and all the paraphernalia of organizational society as mockingly denoted by Parkinson's law. A good deal of the time which professors should devote to their research is taken up by serving on committees, as if, beyond a certain age, their colleagues feared that scientists might have few novel ideas and scholars had better not write. Executives in a quandary act like the statesman whose difficulties are pathetically described in the second part of T. S. Eliot's *Coriolan:*

> *Cry cry what shall I cry?*
> *The first thing to do is to form the committees:*
> *The consultative councils, the standing committees,*
> *select committees and sub-committees.*

A solution might appear to lie in the development of a separate class of organizers of research and of administrators of universities, on the assumption that those combats with the unknown, or with demons, are too important to be left to professors. Therein however lies another peril: politics is to be run very differently from business and education is a human, all too human affair. Lecturers are sometimes prima donnas; researchers are temperamental dreamers who chafe at an excess of efficiency around them, cannot work at regular hours and profit most from dreaming or observing with the nonchalant freedom of imagination. An excess of organization of advanced research can be detrimental to the boldness and freedom of inquiring minds. "Ever let the Fancy roam!" Keats' line can be meaningful also for scientists and for scholars.

Many scientific visitors from South America and Europe have commented upon their American experiences and their reflections have usually concurred on this: that the most impressive assets of research in this country are not the material means or the efficiency in organizing, but the confident trust of people in one another and the spirit of cooperation. There prevails a greater faith in one's fellow beings in this vast continent, including one's fellow scientists. Envy, cantankerousness, jealousy of the young, secrecy practiced to one's research assistants and secretaries are less often to be encountered than they are in older lands.

Some nationalism has lately sprung up among musical composers and artists, who have attempted to play down the arts of Europe in order to proclaim the vitality of their own creations; it has not carried much conviction with it. In general, American science and scholarship have become sufficiently self-assured to afford to be generously open to what comes from abroad. Americans realize how much they owe to the variety of their ethnic origins and open their facilities, provide their research and fellowship funds to persons of other nationalities. They have done so in exemplary fashion in the Fulbright program of Exchange of Persons. They have benefited Europe in doing so, and, for the first time in world history, they have treated their own wealth, in Carnegie's words, as a sacred trust to be used in the interest of other peoples. They have also benefited themselves. The truest friendships among nations are those which have been formed by the gifted individuals of those nations when, in their receptive youth, eager to observe what was foreign to them, fraternally open to what was different, they made a prolonged stay in another country, saw people at work, learned to appreciate their achievement and returned home broadened by their experience. To be the man only of one country, of one culture and of one age is to be less than a complete man.

# A Bid for Contemplation

GENTLEMEN OF THE CLASS OF 1958:
Education is commonly defined as a process, a painstaking yet a pleasurable process, of initiation into life. It consists in fact of a series of initiations which will successively open up for you the worlds of learning, of sports, of extracurricular activities, of military adventure, of love and marriage, and of a professional or business career. Each of those phases of your development is traditionally ushered in by a speech of solemn advice, to which the docile candidates to manhood listen with dutiful respect. "Favete linguis," "favor me with the silence of your tongues," was the bidding of the master of ceremonies in ancient mysteries.

You will not be reduced to silence while at Yale and you will soon discover that education, as we practice it here, is a Socratic give and take, with ample opportunities for discussion, and self-expression, even with seminar courses in which you will sow robust young seeds in the wearied brains of your professors. Today, however, while you are still fresh, coy and awe stricken, a member of the Yale faculty has been delegated to address you in this august

An address to the freshman class at Yale, fall 1954

hall and he is not a little embarrassed at the task proposed
to him. The part of a stern moralist and of a dispenser of
advice on what my colleagues in philosophy called "the
good life" (which a Frenchman hopes can also be a cheerful
life) is an intimidating one. Educators who have to assume
it occasionally can only bear in mind the sobering maxim of
La Rochefoucauld, according to which "old men like to
give good precepts, to console themselves for being no
longer able to provide bad examples."

Advice will be lavishly showered upon you as you enter upon this momentous phase of your education; four
years at Yale which will in all likelihood be the most fruitful as well as the happiest in your lives. Counselors will
help you unravel your problems, untie your complexes if
you are fortunate enough to have some already, and extract
the deeper significance of a Yale education. Deans and associate deans will gently redress your erratic steps, reward
your zeal with a generous inclusion on their coveted dean's
list, protect your frailty against the two chief temptations
of a student's life: oversleeping in the morning and over-
indulgence in pernicious weekends. You will one day appreciate to the full the beneficence of our cut limitations
and thus learn the value of reconciling freedom and authority. As one of the sovereign pontiffs of our age (T. S. Eliot)
put it, "freedom is only true freedom when it appears
against the background of an artificial limitation." Through
upperclassmen or the more sophisticated ones among you,
you will also learn all you need to know about the respec-
tive qualities of movie and beer houses in New Haven, and
even about the comparative merits of the young ladies in
the belt of satellite girls' colleges (separated from you by
no iron curtain) surrounding our male university and to
which conscientious Yale crusaders believe they must, "con
amore," carry the torch of their *Lux et Veritas*.

My ambition today is not to duplicate such kind of precise information or to offer to you pills of concentrated wisdom which you might chew over your first Yale weekend.
More than ever before, in these years of grace and alas! of
disgrace, an educator feels impelled to link education with

the world around him, and to propose a few reflections of general import to the youth which will have to face formidable difficulties. If education consists in part in transmitting to the young the very best in the legacy of the past, it also demands that we prepare for the future intelligently and imaginatively, and therefore assess the present with unflinching clear-sightedness.

The generation which is coming of age in this decade has to face the breakdown of several great dynamic ideas, or myths (which does not mean fables but powerful ideas charged with emotional force by which our predecessors lived). I would briefly define those great ideas or assumptions upon which the fabric of our Western World used to rest, as:

*1*)   The belief in an absolute, that is in stable and universal religious and ethical values, which began to be seriously undermined in the eighteenth century. Most of us nowadays are no longer convinced that we possess the Truth and that we should impart it to other nations, whose duty it would be to bow to our missionaries or emissaries. We are by no means skeptics rejoicing in a Heraclitean world of change and addicted to ironical negation. But we cannot claim to live securely in a world battled by insecurity. We search for standards, but we are aware that searching for them is probably healthier and more comforting than finding them once for all. Old shrines have to be destroyed, or at least deserted, in order that new shrines may be erected. Not many if any of your Yale teachers will confidently assure you that they have all the answers to the world's enigmas, and to yours, and proclaim to incoming freshmen, in the noble words of Keats in *Hyperion:* "Receive the Truth, and let it be your balm."

*2*)   The myth or idea of Progress, which, from the eighteenth through the first few decades of the twentieth century, bid fair to replace the crumbling faith in an absolute, has lately been dealt deathly blows. It implied an unbounded faith in mankind and in the undeveloped potentialities of man, aiming to rise above his own self and to emerge triumphant, almost godlike, in the twilight of the gods. Science and technology, continuously growing, were bound to increase human happiness and to improve that perfectible creature, man, and man-made institutions. From France and Britain, the faith in progress emigrated to America, where it became naturalized and almost an established religion. We lived by it, except for occasional dissenters, until World War II. Then we had to witness a regression of civilization, the slaughter of millions of Jews in scientifically organized extermination camps, the ruthlessness of Communist tyranny, the advent of the atomic era. The unquestioning confidence which made our ancestors believe that, as science developed and material welfare increased, man's happiness was correspondingly enhanced, is no longer with us. The nightmare of a brutal collapse of our civilization, indeed of our planet, now obsesses us.

*3*) The myth of success was another of the implicit articles of faith upon which Western society was built. Victorian England, post-Napoleonic France as depicted in the novels of Stendhal and Balzac, in which every young man, looking back at the meteoric career of the Emperor, whispered "Pourquoi pas moi?", had cherished material success, the respectability and the complacency which it brought in its train. It became the creed of the ascending middle class.

America then took over the cult of success as the reward of hard work, rugged individualism, mass production and know-how. Many still pay lip service to it. Yet, the depression of 1929, then the events of 1940–41 which shook the country out of its serenity forever, the drafting of over ten million young men, the maze of foreign entanglements through which we now have to thread our way, killed the fond belief that America would remain immune from the ills of the Old World and seek success undisturbed.

A young man entering Yale in 1954 no longer entertains the conviction that, if he does well in college, receives decent gentlemen's grades and forms the proper connections, he will be content with becoming a bank president, joining the country club and owning two Cadillacs, and will recite

to himself and others that "the best is yet to come." Literature has pictured for him the death of a salesman disillusioned by the inner emptiness of success, the sad plight
of the falsely successful businessman reaching the point of
no return. Even popular magazines and the radio, and the
very air which we breathe daily have forced us to accept
tragedy as omnipresent. This country, at mid-century and
basking in the highest material prosperity ever reached, is
in fact permeated with the tragic sense of life. One of our
religious writers has called it "the irony of American history": the tragic irony of having to manufacture H bombs
in order to avert war, knowing all the while that armament
races have regularly ended in war; of having to prepare for,
indeed to perpetrate, evil for the sake of what we believe or
hope may be a higher good.

We thus have lost some of our moorings at the very time
when the problems we faced had become more momentous
than ever before. Fear, and the fear of fear itself, which
had been familiar fixtures of life in older war-ridden continents, have now invaded the New World and afflicted
the youth of this country. Something would be amiss with
us if it were otherwise. Like Hamlet, the generations of
young Americans now on the threshold of bright college
years may be tempted to lament the rotten or the broken
world in which they have been thrust and to regret that
ever they were born to set it right. The catastrophes with
which nuclear energy threaten us differ from the evils of
past centuries (the eruption of Vesuvius, the Black Plague,
the Lisbon earthquake) in this, that they are of our own
making. Our own elected executives and statesmen had, in
our very name, to take the decision to drop atomic bombs
on Japan, to manufacture hydrogen bombs, to risk incalculable chain reactions. Those decisions, in the opinion of
many of us, were let us not say right, but justified and
probably unavoidable. The fact remains that, for the first
time in history, man in democratic countries has ceased
to be proud of himself. He, and the science which he has
developed, suffer from a bad conscience.

Why remind young men, who have enough pressing

problems of their own, of the gloomy picture offered by the world into which they are, through four or more years of steady learning, preparing to enter fully equipped? Because all is not lost. Nothing in fact is lost, provided the young generations rise to meet the challenge thrown to them by history.

Much vain talk has been squandered on the issues which confront us today. Some have chosen to declaim against science, to vituperate against "soulless" scientists, and to suggest some panacea of their own. The lot of atomic physicists is not an enviable one. True it is that science should not become the exclusive arbiter of our consciences, and that a scientific education, obviously necessary for a large part of the youth in the country which has to lead the world scientifically, should be supplemented with a strong background in the arts and in the humanities. But we are not going to turn our backs against science, still less to hold it responsible for the evil use to which we have put it.

Others have preferred to mourn the chain of events which has brought us to our present plight. They scold us for having fully deserved God's wrath: they delight, emulating the sombre eloquence of a Jonathan Edwards, in depicting the new Apocalypse and the infernal abysses gaping before us. Or else, brilliant "fugitives" from the agrarian South, lay preachers invested with all the authority of sons of the Tennessee Valley, they deride the Jeffersonian and Rousseaustic faith in the goodness and perfectibility of man. They recall to us our wretched state of sinners and ransack literature to prove to us that awareness of evil alone makes a man worthy of interest and woman presumably a little more so. With St. Paul they discover anew "a law that, when we would do good, evil is present in us." But do we not need today more faith in our ability to do good and all the optimism we can muster?

Others still have taken pride in the sense of tragedy which they assume to be the privilege of their generation. They sedulously cultivate their anguish and find in it a convenient pretext to excuse their own inadequacies: procrastination; scattering and waste of their energies, a common fault of juniors who are too confident of having world enough and time; conceit, a common fault of blasé seniors; excessive readiness to forget all that was poured into the sieve of their intellects, a fault of some alumni. They reason that, the world being sadly out of joint, the literature and art of their time can only reflect disintegration and their own work express disorder and frustration. No more dangerous fallacy could be proposed to young men. On the contrary, it is in troubled times and days of anxiety that the best minds should strive for serene contemplation, for lucid and orderly thinking, for beauty, harmony and wisdom. A university is the proper setting for such an attempt. There we are reminded of Socrates and Plato who evolved methods of thought while the Peloponnesian war raged, of St. Augustine, Descartes and Goethe, whose age, no less than ours, was one of transition, of strife and cataclysm, yet who set about rebuilding.

None of your teachers is the happy contriver of a recipe which he can pass on to you, to enable you to solve the problems which you will have to face. He may, however, make bold to offer a few counsels to those who are now entering upon the advanced stage of their education.

Times are tragically grave. But do not let yourself be overwhelmed by them. The myth of the sorcerer's apprentice has been resorted to far too often by prophets of gloom. The worst evil that could befall us would be for us to undergo a failure of nerve such as brought about the disintegration of Greece two or three centuries before Christ. You are not going to abdicate passively, and your teachers stand ready to help you acquire the intellectual and moral equipment that you need.

Do not forsake humor and the healthy capacity to laugh at yourselves, to laugh at the ironies of fate, to smile at the high seriousness of Kierkegaard, Dostoevsky, Kafka, Faulkner, of Freud and his unrepressed progeny, of Marxists and Existentialists. Do not be seduced exclusively by the siren songs of the Tragic Muse, dear to young men; let the comic spirit smile in you and lighten your burden.

Accumulate knowledge while you are here, and especially knowledge of the past, which will provide you with lessons, will enrich your memories with stores of associations and acquaint you with the cultural heritage which it will be your lot to preserve. Removing yourselves for a while from the immediacy of the present is no selfish escape. It means acquiring the proper perspective in which to view and interpret the present. It may also mean learning how to repeat the performance of the greatest among our predecessors: the Greeks, the men of the twelfth and thirteenth centuries, those of the Renaissance, the Founders of the American Republic, the heroes of the French Revolution who, faced with obstacles similar to ours, boldly jumped ahead and out of the threat of chaos brought forth a new synthesis.

A great university is a collective and molding force, with its ideals, its traditions, its banner and its totems and its rites, a valuable "esprit de corps" of which Yale is justly proud. But in a university also, a spirit of conformity, of social snobbery, of intellectual monotony may grow. You might be attracted overmuch by the desire to "adjust yourselves," to group together, act, think in a herdlike way, become afraid of being yourselves. Be on your guard against such an alienation of the most precious thing in the world, your personality. Remain, or rather become, yourselves amid large lecture courses, spacious dining halls, bulky assignments, lengthy sermons, long, or repeated, drinks. Distrust quantity in all its forms, including the arrogance which may seize young men belonging to the first university in the country and apt to look upon themselves as the embodiment of the best in Yale. A southern poet, Sidney Lanier, once mocked Walt Whitman's inspired rhetoric by summing it up thus: "Because the Mississippi is long therefore every American is God." Here we modestly rank ourselves third, after God and country. Yet do not assume that, because the Yale Bowl is colossal and the Sterling Library immense and the Harkness Tower majestic and the Yale Faculty second to none, therefore every Yale man is destined to greatness. Yale will be what you make it some day.

Above all, consider these four years as crucial ones for you, and for the world. Whatever field of specialization you elect (and the field matters less than the spirit in which you cultivate it), do not fail to learn a few essentials while at Yale: how to work, that is to say, a method for organizing your time, your energy, your ideas and your manner of expressing them; how to save time by never being content with superficiality, but going in depth into anything you attempt; how to concentrate, losing sight of the distracting unessentials around you, training your memory, your attention, your power of analysis to rush to your assistance when needed. Do not divorce your academic culture from living problems as you might be tempted to do when your young minds delight in the discovery of their own subtlety. Do not let yourselves, you band of happy few, become divorced from the unhappy many who have not had the good fortune to enter Yale. Do not forsake the clear language of common men for metaphysical or legal jargon. Do not indulge in the hairsplitting and the sophistry of what T. S. Eliot once called "minds refined beyond the point of civilization." For your learning and your profundity would be of little avail, unless you shared them with others and reached out to them.

Trust the Yale Faculty. It is eager to cooperate with you without restraining your independence. We, of the older generations, do not feel too proud of the world that we are bequeathing to you. We shudder at the magnitude of the burden which will be yours, in 1960 or 1970. For the very survival of this earth, of the civilization of which America has become the leader and the trustee, may well hinge upon decisions taken by you and others like you ten or fifteen years from now. The issue before you will be whether man will choose to be a destroyer or a creator. The same nuclear energy which may unleash untold catastrophes may also spell unbounded benefits for mankind. If we may be horrified at the latest development of science, we may well be seized with wonder and with hope at the genius of man assuming full control of his fate. I for one am full of hope. A very great deal is expected, all over the world, from the coming generation of Americans, and far more than material and technical assistance. Great civilizations have always faced, and responded to, similar challenges. Arnold Toynbee may well be right in this, if not in his mood of gloom. Let your class, through the training of character, of intelligence, of imagination which we shall try to provide for you, stand ready to meet the formidable yet stimulating challenge which awaits America and its leaders in the decades to come.

# From Knowledge to Wisdom

I DEEM IT A GREAT HONOR to have been asked once again to address an audience in a school which bears an illustrious name and has proved consistently worthy of it and of its lofty ideals. Its graduates rank among the ablest students enrolled in the most demanding colleges and universities in the country. Its alumni are not content with providing examples of successful men after which the young students hope to mold themselves. They retain an active and devoted interest in the nursery of keen minds and of fine characters where they once were trained, and they are anxious for the school to continue to improve itself so as to meet the ever more difficult exigencies of leadership which are likely to confront the ascending generations of Americans. The presence of many of them tonight is an encouragement and a challenge to the guest speaker. He will pay you back, as speakers are wont to do, with gentle scolding and austere admonitions.

Complacence is supposed to be a characteristic of many Americans. It is perhaps true that, in several realms, the fundamental conviction of Americans is that the customer is always right, that the present is uniformly rosy and that not to smile at it, or not to grin, is a sin. But a far different

An address at the Taft School, April 1955

mood has always prevailed in the field of education. Every year classes of honor students, of Phi Beta Kappa and other selected groups, even of average students pulling through, if not over, scholastic hurdles with "gentlemen's grades" and damned with faint praise by Deans as "healthy good citizens," graduate from our schools and colleges. Ritually, as if to prepare for what we call an active career in which many speeches will have to be delivered over melting ice cream and tepid coffee, and many more listened to with subtly disguised boredom, those young men and future leaders are treated to lay sermons by educators. What good it does the young men has never yet, I believe, been statistically explored. The good it does the lay preachers is beyond dispute. We, teachers and preachers, are all chronically pregnant with ideas, advice, anecdotes, jokes, and quotations, of which we have to deliver ourselves as ana-aesthetically as possible. We are reformers at heart. But since we long ago gave up trying to reform our wives, our secretaries, our friends and, of course, ourselves, we find it wholesome to cast our eyes and wag our tongues elsewhere in the hope of reforming other teachers' students and education in general.

Education seems to take it good-humoredly. Indeed therein lies one of the most puzzling paradoxes about this country. On the one hand, education is for all of us a religion; we look upon it as upon one of the very few potent means we may have of changing man and of bringing about some progress in an otherwise discouraging world. We consent to enormous sacrifices in order to educate our children. We take pride in our colleges, where we erect towers and libraries and sport palaces to shelter our youth for four years in a blissful oasis. Yet, at the same time, a dim realization that our schools are not all that they should be lurks in the minds of many of us. Americans often voice their discontent about their school system, their anger at the waste they detect in the last year of high school; they even suffer from an inferiority complex about it and envy foreigners who appear to have mastered mathematics, history and languages better and to have acquired a more mature intellectual discipline in their West European education.

Criticism of American education by American educators is indeed one of our oldest traditions. It is also one of our healthiest ones. For it is not sickly delight in humiliating ourselves or abject autocriticism in the Russian manner, but the reminder that criticism is the lifeblood of all creation, that perfection is not easily, if ever, reached in the complex two-way process called education. It is to the credit of a long series of American educational leaders that they have mercilessly scathed the inadequacies of our colleges and raised ever higher the ideal toward which we should strive. As early as 1902, Woodrow Wilson, elected President of Princeton University declared: "You know that the pupils in the colleges in the last several decades have not been educated. You know that, with all our teaching, we train nobody. You know that, with all our instructing, we educate nobody."

Five decades later, President R. M. Hutchins of the University of Chicago, who had donned the mantle of a prophet of gloom once worn by Wilson, used sharper language. He wrote, in *The Conflict in Education in a Democratic Society:* "It may be useful to raise the question whether America has become rich and powerful because of her educational system or in spite of it."

The remedies advocated by Mr. Hutchins have not met with the approval of many of us, who have found them reactionary and unfit for a democratic society in an age of science. But we have found food for thought in his criticism of existing conditions. Not all is to be accepted as valid in another onslaught on American schools, *Educational Wastelands*, by Professor A. E. Bestor, of the University of Illinois. Yet his main proposition can hardly be disregarded: "that schools exist to teach something, and that this something is the power to think." A conference of educators, the Association for Higher Education, convened in Chicago in the early days of March 1955. It made the headlines in several New York newspapers, which quoted extensively from the grave charges proffered against higher education by all the speakers. I shall summarize some of those charges here, not in an acrimonious spirit of idle recrimination, not as a foreigner judging American intellectuality with condescension, but as an educator whose own career and ideals are identified with American education. The distinguished young men who are being honored today in this school deserve more than perfunctory or conventional compliments. They will some day be leaders, and they will want to be aware of the imperfections which their elders have perceived and denounced in the most important of all American enterprises: the training of the youth.

Two of the finest achievements of American civilization have been the development of efficiency and productivity which, through rationalizing and saving human labor, made possible the astonishing success of business in this country; and the expansion of confidence in our fellow beings, the eagerness to join them in organizing community life and in practice as well as in theory, a living faith in the noblest idea yet evolved by mankind: fraternity. But all things in this world are always threatened by an insidious ambivalence which can turn them to evil as well as to good. Both business efficiency and the readiness to merge in a community, when they entered the realm of education, have entailed harmful consequences.

First, as asserted one of the participants in the above-mentioned Chicago conference, Dr. Henry David, executive secretary of the National Manpower Council at Columbia University, too many colleges, impressed by the successful operation of assembly plants, of department stores and supermarkets, have become defensive about their intellectual functions and responsibilities. They have fallen back upon the much easier problems of organization and administration, and they operate as educational service stations. Presidents have aimed at running teaching institutions smoothly, with the twofold ideal of not incurring a deficit and of not having trouble makers on their faculty — happily, an unattainable goal. Many teachers have also been contaminated by the pursuit of administrative efficiency; they have gone in for large-scale organization, aping big business executives. They thus tended to forget that teaching well is more difficult and more valuable than administering, and that research and writing, far more difficult than running an office well, are essential to great teaching. And the hardest challenge should always be the goal of intellectuals worthy of the name. A British prelate recently suggested that we abolish all typewriters. Life indeed might well thus recover some serenity, and much of our useless routine might be abolished if not only typewriters and dictating machines but other instruments of torture like telephones commanded less fetishism among scholars and educators.

Second, the ability of Americans to forsake the stressing of their ideological differences and to merge them into the concerted pursuit of one common goal may well fill with envy a Frenchman, whose countrymen suffer from a congenital reluctance to agree to disagree. It is a magnificent asset in political life. Even in economic life it has proved a boon, except when perfidiously utilized by shameless publicity, intent upon standardizing the needs of individuals and upon conditioning them all to the same stock demands and responses.

Things are otherwise, however, where the life of the mind is concerned. Several American scientists have lately voiced their concern over the relative lack of originality which they detected in their countrymen, working as teams in which the superior individual, the paradoxical but inventive research man, was too often neutralized and paralyzed. Our schools and colleges likewise favor the person who is "popular," likely to be elected to societies, clubs and boards through co-optation by others of his ilk, but who shuns intellectual independence. The famous phrase "well-adjusted" has indeed wrought much harm. For must a student be adjusted to the very temporary and artifical conditions of his narrow group, or to the deeper and permanent values which ancient cultures have transmitted to his own, or even to a vast and changing world in which other continents can no longer remain ignored?

For young Americans of the second half of this century a grave peril lies in uniformity and unimaginative intellectual monotony. Tocqueville had prophesied with his usual acuity that the crucial test for American democracy would be in the development of the superior individual. More recently, Ambassador George F. Kennan, in a speech delivered at Notre Dame on May 15, 1953, deplored "the powerful strain of our American cast of mind that has little use for the artist or the writer." He added:

What is it that causes us to huddle together, herdlike, in tastes and enthusiasms that represent only the common denominator of popular acquiescence rather than to show ourselves receptive to the tremendous flights of creative imagination of which the individual mind has shown itself capable? Is it that we are forgetful of the true source of our moral strength, afraid of ourselves, afraid to look into the chaos of our own breasts, afraid of the bright, penetrating light of the great teachers?

Mr. Kennan, who had not forgotten the horrors of Nazi Germany and was familiar with Russia, warned us how easily such uniformity of thought and habit can be put to evil use and lead to the domination of our spiritual and political lives by demagogues, advocates of intolerance and of suspicion. Historians will doubtless some day shudder retrospectively at the gravity of the blows which were dealt American ideals in 1952–54. National common sense prevailed, but some consequences of that moral crisis linger with us: distrust of the intellectuals, herdlike grouping around orthodoxy, and a rift between the scientists, upon whom any progress in national defence today must depend, and politicians.

The task of educators is to draw the lessons from recent developments. What are they? First of all, that the development of education in the early decades of this century, which tended toward uniformization and levelling down, must be reversed. A democracy needs superior individuals. A dictatorship fosters acquiescence and submission and thus stifles any minority group which could endanger one-man rule; it provides for no alternative leadership when the dictator falls or dies. The strength of a democratic regime is that it can count on a supply of competent leaders from several social strata and parties.

Promising and potentially superior individuals can often be detected early in their school and college days. They should not be set apart or induced to grow conceited or arrogant over their mental ability. The truest sign of belonging to any élite and of being born to lead is never to boast about it and perhaps not to be aware of it. The gifted student should be impressed with the notion that he has more duties than the average one, and fewer rights. Instead of gently coasting along in college because he can count on good grades, he should be faced with ever new obstacles to overcome. Happily our educators have, in the last few years, begun to pay more attention to the gifted student.

Such a student will usually be recognized through the questioning quality of his mind, through an impatient and rebellious nature, fretting at passivity. He will not easily be shackled by orthodoxy—he will not easily be content with assignments, mechanical tests, large impersonal lecture-courses. He will prove "a little difficult," as all that is interesting does, a wife, a child, a horse, a machine. He will be severe on bad or mediocre teaching; but he should also be a good learner. An eminent educator, Dean Harold W. Stoke of the University of Washington, lately deplored the exclusive emphasis on good teaching in our educational pronouncements and theories. Such an emphasis, separating good teaching too sharply from the whole educational process, said Dean Stoke, leads many to forget that good learning on the student's part is a necessary counterpart of good teaching:

The burden of expectation for educational accomplishment has somehow subtly been shifted in the American school system . . . Actually we do so much of his [the student's] work that we give him little opportunity to learn . . . it should be a part of our art not to teach what we like to teach, but to enable him to learn what he ought to learn. [*Journal of the Proceedings of the Association of Graduate Schools*, 1954]

The leaders whom the country needs more direly than ever, as it faces ever more formidable issues in our shrinking world and in our era of nuclear fission, will have to meet simultaneously two requirements which educational theorists have too readily presented as incompatible: they must be trained as specialists and also as humanists. All education in its advanced stages always was and must needs be vocational: doctors, chemists, engineers, clergymen, professors have to know their subject well. Their thinking must feed on precise knowledge, their acting must have weighed all the factors involved down to the minutest details. It is nevertheless true that vocational training has been developed to a ludicrous excess in our educational system and has been started at too early a stage. It has produced on the one hand specialists "who know everything about practically nothing," teaching schoolboys and students "who get to know nothing about almost everything." Those were the words used by Dr. John F. Gummere, Headmaster of the William Penn Charter School of Philadelphia, at the recent Chicago conference. It has on the other hand narrowed down many semieducated people to the level of the ideal specialists, the animals. Animals, bees, ants, beavers, do one thing to perfection, but nothing else, and cannot face up to a new situation and invent an original solution.

Humanists have hurt their case by conceiving humanities in too traditional a way, when they should have been revitalized with fresh zest, broadened so as to encompass a much wider world than the Mediterranean area which was their cradle, and democratized instead of being too often presented as a genteel aristocratic training reserved for a sheltered leisure class. The whole concept of our leisure class must be thought out anew, in a context far different from that of Thorstein Veblen. Not bankers, industrialists, men in the professions, but mechanics, foremen and the new fabulous and envied heroes of our age, plumbers, constitute the new leisure group. And how to put our growing leisure to satisfying and enriching use is one of the vital questions in our democracy today.

The answer is in continuing, or doing over again, our education after the college years. An informed citizen in

1955 or in 1975 will need to know ten times more (in geography, history, anthropology, psychology, sociology, economics, languages, literature and, of course, in the exact sciences) than this ancestor did in 1875 or 1900. Yet the time allotted to our education has, if anything, decreased as education became more costly and as impatience, our modern malady, seized parents and students alike. As a result, many of us, ten or twenty years out of college, woefully fail to come up to Matthew Arnold's definition of the educated man as one who is able "to understand the world, and himself." Hence the sight of middle-aged persons of both sexes who appear like waifs stranded in a changing world or like fossils, unable to comprehend new conditions, still less to cope with them.

When we talk of adult education, we smugly imagine it as reserved for those who never had the opportunity to go to college. We have summer schools, but we like to think that they are reserved for schoolteachers, for a few single ladies in search of spiritual romance, and a few cranks who believe in studying after they have left school. The so-called normal men, who graduated from respectable schools and colleges, seldom read a serious book. They buy their wives subscriptions to the Book of the Month, as a handy feminine present requiring from the giver no undue imaginative exertion; they glance at *Time* and *Business Week*, and offset the reading of the severe Stock Market columns in their daily paper with the relaxation afforded by the illustrated pages tragically called "comics."

Yet history unfolds around them at an accelerated pace, and Americans are thrown in the very midst of the maelstrom. Very few take advantage of the most revealing mirror to the concerns of our age, literature. They dismiss modern works as obscure, or as unhealthy. Their vision of the world remains conditioned by a few half-obliterated notions absorbed years ago at school. Yet, every quarter of a century or so, our outlook upon the world, which is dependent upon physics, astronomy, psychology, etc., should undergo a radical change. If we reread Sophocles, Shakespeare, Balzac, Dostoevsky, Proust at fifty or sixty, we would realize how differently, and how little we understood them at twenty. There are even subjects like political science and economics, which it is no use studying too early, before we have any concrete experience of the subject matter.

We educators have to confess our failure if we do not persuade the youth that education is a lifelong process and that, as Sir Richard Livingstone warned Englishmen in the darkest hour of their history (in *The Future of Education*, 1941), to cease education at fourteen (we should add, at twenty) is as unnatural as to die at that age. "The one is physical death, the other intellectual death." New facts have to be learned every ten years, old ones have to be interpreted anew. Our worst enemy is hardening of our mental arteries. Doctors have lately aroused us to the pathetic problem of sixteen million Americans over sixty-five (there will be twenty million in 1975, ten times more than in 1900, indeed seventeen per cent of all voters) who encounter great difficulty in "easing into retirement" and do not know what to do with themselves when they are no longer needed.

We are to blame if we have not imparted to those people, and to many others in their forties and fifties, the intellectual curiosity, the spiritual eagerness, the zest in discovery of new provinces of knowledge, the enjoyment in living fully which ought to be the prime objective of education. We are even more to blame if, as is reported, one American out of seventeen is slated for the psychiatrist's couch. He may have stored up factual knowledge. But there is another word, not necessarily synonymous with knowledge, indeed often opposed to it, which our education should have stressed; it designates a thing which many of our college graduates, many of our leaders, many of our executives, many of our cocktail party addicts lack. That is wisdom.

An English poet of the eighteenth century, who could well prize wisdom since he had suffered from a deranged mind, William Cowper, wrote in *The Task* (VI, 88–91, 97–98):

> *Knowledge and wisdom, far from being one,*
> *Have oft times no connection. Knowledge dwells*
> *In heads replete with thoughts of other men;*
> *Wisdom in minds attentive to their own. . . .*
> *Knowledge is proud that he has learned so much,*
> *Wisdom is humble that he knows no more.*

The generation of bright young men who are being honored today will, two or three decades from now, have to make momentous decisions involving war or peace, the survival or the destruction of the civilized world. My own contact with American youth has inspired me with confidence. They have courage, self-reliance, rectitude; their intellectual gifts are second to none; if properly advised, they learn eagerly and they store up valuable knowledge in their school years; they are endowed with more valiant faith and more respect for greatness than the young men of 1920–35 who recognized themselves too complacently in *Sweeney Agonistes* and other hollow men and who thought themselves interesting when they paraded their anguish everywhere and hailed themselves, as in the terms of W. H. Auden's title, as living in "The Age of Anxiety." But there is one wish which I often formulate when observing them and the difficult but challenging world which we are bequeathing to them. Let them be persuaded that their true education will only really begin after they have left college, and that its goal should be to marry with the audacity and impetuousness of the young the wisdom which the world will expect from the country destined to lead history in years to come.